Belonging and Inclusion in Identity Safe Schools

We dedicate this book to those who came before and to future generations working to disrupt inequity, create opportunity, and build a world where all young people feel valued and seen simply for who they are.

Belonging and Inclusion in Identity Safe Schools

A Guide for Educational Leaders

Becki Cohn-Vargas

Alexandrea Creer Kahn

Amy Epstein

Kathe Gogolewski

Foreword by Shayna Sullivan

FOR INFORMATION:

Corwin
A SAGE Company
2455 Teller Road
Thousand Oaks, California 91320
(800) 233-9936
www.corwin.com

SAGE Publications Ltd.
1 Oliver's Yard
55 City Road
London, EC1Y 1SP
United Kingdom

SAGE Publications India Pvt. Ltd.
B 1/I 1 Mohan Cooperative Industrial Area
Mathura Road, New Delhi 110 044
India

SAGE Publications Asia-Pacific Pte. Ltd.
18 Cross Street #10-10/11/12
China Square Central
Singapore 048423

Printed in the United States of America

Library of Congress Control Number: 2021907648

President: Mike Soules
Associate Vice President and
    Editorial Director: Monica Eckman
Program Director and Publisher: Dan Alpert
Content Development Editor: Lucas Schleicher
Associate Content Development Editor: Mia Rodriguez
Production Editor: Gagan Mahindra
Copy Editor: Terri Lee Paulsen
Typesetter: Hurix Digital
Proofreader: Barbara Coster
Indexer: Integra
Cover Designer: Candice Harman
Marketing Manager: Sharon Pendergast

This book is printed on acid-free paper.

SUSTAINABLE FORESTRY INITIATIVE
Certified Chain of Custody
Promoting Sustainable Forestry
www.sfiprogram.org
SFI-01268

21 22 23 24 25 10 9 8 7 6 5 4 3 2 1

Table of Contents

Visit the companion website https://resources.corwin.com/
BelongingandInclusionISS for downloadable resources.

About the Authors

Becki Cohn-Vargas, EdD, is the coauthor, with Dorothy Steele, of *Identity Safe Classrooms, Grades K–5: Places to Belong and Learn*. In 2020, she coauthored *Identity Safe Classrooms, Grades 6–12: Pathways to Belonging and Learning*. She designs curriculum, publishes articles, coaches schools, and produces films for Teaching Tolerance, Edutopia, Not In Our Town, and other organizations. She presents internationally at conferences and provides professional development in schools and districts.

Dr. Cohn-Vargas began her 35-year career in early childhood education in Sonoma County, California. She lived abroad for five years where she did earthquake relief at a hospital in the Guatemalan Highlands and produced educational films for the Nicaraguan Ministry of Education. She returned to California and worked as a teacher and principal in Oakland, curriculum director in Palo Alto, and as superintendent of a small district in San Jose. She also served as an adjunct professor at the University of San Diego, Mills College, and Cal State University, East Bay. In each setting, she focused on educational equity and effective strategies for diverse populations. Dr. Cohn-Vargas and her husband live in the San Francisco Bay Area and have three adult children and one grandchild.

Alexandrea Creer Kahn, MAEd, after earning her BA at UC Berkeley and MA in Education from Stanford University, started her career in education, working to support elementary school teachers and leaders to engage in the school improvement process. Over the course of her career focusing on educational equity, Alex has worked in several roles in K–12 and higher ed including teacher, school coach, principal, and district leader, as well as lecturer for Stanford University. Recently, Alex coauthored the book *Identity Safe Classrooms, Grades 6–12: Pathways to Belonging and Learning*. Alex currently oversees the clinical practicum program for Alder Graduate School of Education as the Senior Director of Academic Programs. Alex's areas of expertise include school leadership, school transformation, teacher education, coaching, professional learning, and curriculum and instruction. A Bay Area native, Alex enjoys spending her time with her husband and two sons, writing, and spending time outdoors.

Amy Epstein, MSW, is the founding partner of Data for the People, working to transform data into valued and accessible information centered in the knowledge and priorities of those closest to a context, problem, or goal. She has worked as an administrator and consultant with many school districts, schools, foundations, and other nonprofit organizations to advance equity in education, particularly in the areas of evidence-based inquiry and dialogue, coordinated services/tiered support systems, data systems and processes, and assessment. Amy was a coauthor in 2020 of *Identity Safe Classrooms, Grades 6–12: Pathways to Belonging and Learning*. Amy lives in San Francisco, CA, with her wife, Liat. She is anchored and made joyous by drumming, singing, meditating, and spending time outdoors.

Kathe Gogolewski, MAEd, taught science as well as first, third, and fourth grades in Bay Area elementary schools, serving culturally rich and racially diverse students from all backgrounds. During her tenure, she worked as both a master and mentor teacher, working with new teachers and new teacher candidates in both classroom management and curriculum. She provided teachers with a framework for creating nurturing classrooms that welcomed students of all identities and backgrounds. She taught at California State University in the teacher credential program and has presented at workshops and conferences across the United States. Since moving to San Diego, Kathe supports and volunteers for various nonprofits, including Embracing the World, serving populations in need across the globe; San Diego Rapid Response Network, creating safe spaces for refugees and people seeking asylum; and Casa de Amparo, providing care for children before their placement into foster care. She has worked as a volunteer science and language arts teacher in the Vista, Carlsbad, and San Diego Unified School Districts. She has published a children's book, *Tato*, and a number of children's short stories, all with themes that support and foster compassion toward oneself and others. A transplant from the Bay Area, she lives now in San Diego, with her husband, Ray. They have four children and seven grandchildren.

Acknowledgments

We have been honored to write this book together. We could not have done so without the inspiration and support of the courageous people in our lives and in the world who stand up to racism, hate, and intolerance. We are grateful to you. Writing a book during this moment in history has been intense—the pandemic, the murder of George Floyd by police officers and subsequent protests, the election of President Joe Biden and Vice President Kamala Harris, and the January 6, 2021, uprising at the U.S. Capitol by domestic terrorists, racists, and Nazis—events which all served to increase the poignancy of this work.

We are indescribably indebted to Dorothy M. Steele, who led the original research on identity safety, making this and the previous books possible. She still is sorely missed since her death in 2017. We continue to be inspired by her husband, Claude Steele, for his work on stereotype threat. We appreciate his willingness to share his research and wisdom with us.

In addition, we would like to highlight the people who contributed to this book, starting with members of the "Small and Mighty" group from a San Diego school district. This dynamic group of Black parents, Roxanne McCray Gordon, Amon Gordon, Chas Rogers, and Dhalia Balmir, together with Joe Erpelding, the principal, not only worked to educate their school community but also took time to meet with us to share insights.

We are extremely grateful to Louise Bay Waters, an inspirational leader who wrote many vignettes for our book, bringing to life her experiences as superintendent and principal over many years. Her honest reflections added depth and authenticity to our descriptions of the challenging role of leading a diverse school. Her feedback allowed us to improve our organization and clarity.

We thank Shayna Sullivan for her beautiful words in the foreword, insightful research around racial identity development within schools, and commitment to teacher education. We also wish to thank the many educators who contributed their stories: Bailey Brown, Kelly Palma, Don Cox, Jennifer Corn, and Matt

Colley, whose vignettes highlight aspects of identity safety, leadership, and practice. Their words brought forth a wide array of creative strategies that paint a picture of the many paths for bringing identity safe schools to life.

We are exceptionally grateful to leaders who inspired and supported our efforts in a variety of ways. We studied their books and appreciated their sage advice: Carol Dweck has always been very supportive of our efforts, and we continue to learn from her. Elena Aguilar's books on coaching and educator resilience guided us on ways to reach, validate, and inspire educators. Zaretta Hammond's culturally responsive teaching strategies have linked equity, instruction, and literacy for us, and highlighted the importance of student–teacher relationships. Pedro Noguera, with his decades of work on equitable schooling and deep learning, has shown us what effective schools can accomplish. We appreciate the support of Eddie Moore, founder of the White Privilege Institute, who has called out white supremacy for many years and who has provided pathways for White teachers to look at themselves and better serve Black students.

It has once again been a pleasure to work with the Corwin Team. We greatly appreciate Dan Alpert, our amazing editor, who has always believed in our work on identity safety. He edited the first two books, and now this one, as well. The team of Mia Rodriguez, Lucas Schleicher, and the production team, including Gagan Mahindra and Terri Lee Paulsen, have all shown patience while offering great advice and standing with us throughout the process. We are proud to be published by Corwin Press, who has increasingly been leading the publication of books for educators, particularly ones that call for equity and social justice.

Finally, we wish to express our gratitude to Amanda Gorman for her inspirational poem, "The Hill We Climb," read at the 2021 Presidential Inauguration. She calls on us to "rise, rebuild, reconcile, recover," and to be brave enough to see the light, inspiring people across our nation to be hopeful and work for a more just and equitable society.

To Kenny, my best friend, love, and confidant—thank you for your love, unwavering belief in and support of me at all stages and facets of our lives together. You are truly a special being and an inspiration. To my sons, Theo and Harris, my babies, you are the embodiment of my joy, my hopes, and my dreams. Thank you for making me a better human and reminding me daily of my purpose. Like many, being a full-time working mom with small children, working, writing, and caretaking during a pandemic remains a challenging endeavor. I am deeply appreciative to those in our circle who helped our family stay sane and healthy during this precarious time. To my mother, Dana, words will never be enough to express the love and gratitude I have for you. You taught me how to be kind, work hard, and advocate for others. To my sister Dominique, thank you for your tireless support. Nicole, Mariah, and the rest of my siblings, thank you for being there throughout challenging times. There are too many to list, but I want to share deep appreciation for the many mentors and guides who created the conditions and space for me to grow and learn. Thank you, Becki, for this incredible opportunity to learn together and collaborate; Cedric Brown, for your early belief in me; Shayna Sullivan, for your friendship and just sheer amazingness; Amy Epstein and Louise Waters, for the guidance and beautiful partnership; and Elena Aguilar, for your masterful coaching. To Amy McGeorge, Lisa Pitters, and colleagues past and present, thank you for your faith and partnership in creating transformative experiences for students and families.

Alexandria Creer Kahn

I am grateful to my husband, Rito, who brought me drinks and snacks as I hammered away at my keyboard day after day writing this book. He put together my new desk and even built a carpeted footrest for all our Zoom book-writing planning meetings. Each of my children also inspired me during this time—Luna, who worked as a nurse during this challenging moment; Priscilla, who remained upbeat in spite of the many challenges with her new business; and Melania, who I have watched blossom into a mother. All three have kept me hopeful and steadfast while listening to my woes along the way. I am grateful to my parents, who are no longer with us, but who gave me the commitment to live a life dedicated to serving others, and Tikkun Olam, a Jewish concept defined as repairing and healing the world. I also appreciate my sisters, Ruth and Barbara, who have been at my virtual side along the way. Finally, I would be remiss without thanking my three coauthors— Amy and Alex, who embraced identity safety and brought it to life in their practice as educators while educating me along the way, and Kathe, my longtime friend who has given so much of herself to me over the last 30 years, who challenges me to explain my thinking and speak from the heart when I get lost in intellectual musings or leaps of logic.

Finally, I want to thank my grandson, Anteo, who turned 1 in March 2021. He grew up virtually before my eyes, watching him on FaceTime during the production of this book. His unending smiles have cheered and encouraged me as he learned to roll over, to crawl, and now to stand, trying to balance himself. I am sure he will be walking by the time this book comes out. It is for him and all the children growing up today that I write this book.

Becki Cohn-Vargas

I am forever grateful to my wife, Liat Barnea, and the joy, humor, adventure, balance, learning, and nourishment she brings to my life. My deepest thanks to my parents, Evelyn and Barry Epstein, for their steadfast love and support. Thank you to Louise Waters and Alex Creer Kahn for their friendship and for all I learned from and with them during many years of collaboration. Through Alex I met Becki, to whom I am deeply grateful for the Identity Safety framework, for her partnership as an educator, and for her presence as a human being. I am grateful to all the teachers among us and to my teachers Jan Willis, Tanjore Ranganathan, Margo Okazawa-Rey, Effie Poy Yew Chow, and Carolyn Brandy. To friends and colleagues, thank you for the love, beauty, sustenance, laughter, tears, and growing we share. Together we make the road by walking.

Amy Epstein

My career in working with the principles of identity safety began under the mentorship of my dear friend, Becki Cohn-Vargas, who has been drawing me into her work supporting students of all identities and backgrounds for decades. I have watched her perseverance and dedication throughout the years in this work, sometimes in spite of great odds. Her latest project, this book, has kept me plucking at the computer keys for countless hours, happily extolling the unmatched benefits of identity safe classrooms and schools. I am deeply grateful. My gratitude extends also to my dear husband, Ray, who has patiently supported my time on this project in so many ways, even generously serving up a delicious salad every day for lunch. Behind a project of this nature, too, lies a well of inspiration for which I have no shortage of examples. The deep resilience of children I have met in classrooms who have endured assaults against their identity, their cultures, religions, or race have provided me with everything I need to know about why this work is important. The amazing courage of the immigrants I have met and their astounding stories of survival have shown me why this matters. The uncomplaining children waiting apprehensively for a foster family to step up and claim them—this also tells me why this work must continue . . . for as long as it takes, until equity, belonging, and inclusion is a given for them all.

My love and gratitude, too, go to my family: my daughter, Rose McGuire, always ready to listen, share her insights, and make me laugh; her husband, Chris; and my family through my husband—his adult children, and all seven of our grandchildren! And to Lakshmi Sukumar, who led our study group for the book *Self-Unfoldment*, by Swami Chinmayananda; I am humbled and grateful for her wisdom and guidance while sharing her deep knowledge of the *Bhagavad Gita*. My eternal gratitude and love, also, for my guru, Mata Amritanandamayi—there are no words. Jai Ma!

Kathe Gogolewski

Foreword

I was introduced to the term *identity safety* approximately 10 years ago while in conversation with one of my son's elementary school teachers. In this particular parent–teacher conference, we discussed possible teachers for my son's upcoming academic year and the criteria by which students were grouped in classes and matched with teachers. Among criteria shared, the teacher described a practice of placing similarly identifying students together in classes for the purpose of identity safety, and she wondered what my thoughts were about my son being intentionally placed in a class with the one other Black student in his grade level; although diverse in other ways, this elementary school was home to few Black students and families. We discussed this idea and the teacher shared the ways in which the school worked to leverage the idea of identity safety to support student belonging and inclusion.

At the time of this conversation, salient were a few identities of my own; not only was I showing up as a Black parent of a Black child in a largely non-Black school space, but I was also a teacher educator and emerging scholar whose work focused on the intersection of K–12 school contexts and identity development. Therefore, I brought with me a level of criticality and complexity to our discussion that day, while I also experienced a school considering identity safety and how they might begin to promote a safe learning environment for racially minoritized students.

What we do know is that school contexts matter in how students come to see themselves and the regard young people feel from others in school spaces. We also know that strong, highly regarded identities are associated with positive school experiences, academic success, and other school-related social and psychological outcomes. Therefore, each day schools have the opportunity to be places where diverse ways of being are not only present but valued and meaningfully integrated into the fabric and culture of what it means to do school. Schools can be intentional spaces that nurture the whole child—where school adults are a source of care and positive regard; where the curriculum is culturally relevant, sustaining, and inclusive; and where the structures, policies, and practices enhance rather than threaten cultural and historical ways of being. They can be places of psychological safety and opportune environments in which to learn and to thrive.

Since the day I was introduced to identity safety 10 years ago, much work has been done on how identity safe practices look in TK–12 classrooms. The most recent book in a three-part series, *Belonging and Inclusion in Identity Safe Schools: A Guide for Leaders*, builds on the authors' previous TK–12 classroom-focused identity safety work to create a guide for school leaders looking to learn about, and engage in, practices that support the development of identity safe school spaces. In the pages that follow, you will not only find references to educational and school leadership research but also professional experiences shared to ground the reader in how all educational leaders can engender a sense of belonging in service of student learning. During such a pivotal moment in our society and in the field, how fabulous that such experienced, deeply thoughtful scholar-practitioners are doing this work.

Shayna Sullivan, PhD
Dean
Alder Graduate School of Education

Prologue

Movements Creating Change

While the time for cultural transformation in schools is overdue, the time for change is ripe. The attention from movements such as Black Lives Matter, the brutal murder of George Floyd by Minneapolis police, followed by the largest protests in U.S. history have given us a raw view of the deep foundation and entrenchment of white supremacy within the police force and other institutions in this country. More people are now looking deeply at systemic racism. In concert with the Black Lives Matter movement, new and diverse voices have arisen to counter bigotry in support of racial equity. The protests, which include people from all backgrounds and walks of life, have filled the newsrooms and social media. We need to ensure this moment is not just a flash point that will fade in time. The goal is to realize meaningful conversations about race, to see them continue and lead to sustained change, especially among White people who may have little to no experience discussing race with each other or with people of color (Aaronson, 2020).

Listening to voices of Black and Brown and Indigenous people is an important and necessary first step. These movements are turning heads and changing outlooks across the United States. Cities and organizations are realigning their policies to support people of color. In the wake of George Floyd's killing, Interfaith Community Services (2020) in San Diego launched a Multi-City Racial Reconciliation Coalition stating that racial injustice is at the root of their work to address poverty, housing, health, employment, and education as well as all forms of racial injustice. In July 2020, mayors of 27 large and small cities across the United States wrote an op-ed about efforts to unravel "a long history of systemic racism and fighting for long-overdue equity for people of color—and Black people in particular" (Walsh et al., 2020).

Social justice activists, along with many leaders and educators, have been working for years to make substantive changes that shift not only attitudes and behaviors but the relations of power that prop up white supremacy. It is incumbent on us to "seize the time" and look deep into educational systems to halt the devastating pipeline to prison that has come to be seen as normal and inevitable by so many. It falls on everyone to disrupt patterns of inequity and "othering" with meaningful and sustainable changes.

The Pandemic: Panic and Opportunity

Behind these movements, and fueling them with a fierce intensity, the 2020 COVID-19 pandemic exploded into our lives and schools like a surprise volcanic eruption. The heat was felt everywhere, scattering our efforts and wreaking havoc upon our routines, while at the same time casting a glaring spotlight upon those conditions that disparage, exclude, and diminish opportunities for poor students and students of color. The pandemic also exposed the inequities that keep economically and digitally endowed families and students immune to more severe effects upon their education, health, and well-being. While COVID-19 shed light on these conditions, the effects of privilege for some and disadvantage for others have prevailed in the educational system in many subtle and overt ways, long before the virus hit.

Particularly for students living without health care, access to technology, and other resources, not to mention safe and healthy living conditions, the virus has exacerbated the disparities. These disadvantages have created a debilitating effect on performance, opportunity, and social and emotional well-being for the most vulnerable students. This downward spiral can easily damage the academic performance of all participants in the school, including students and staff. Stress, like all feelings, can be catching—especially among youth. To address this, in essence, is to uplift an entire school community, creating a culture that welcomes all members and supports them in their well-being and best efforts.

The pandemic has helped the nation awaken with a wider lens to the racial injustices and power imbalances present since the inception of our country, explicitly as a result of a cultural white monopoly guiding policies and attitudes. These same mindsets seen undermining equity can now be addressed within the schools in depth. In light of the Black Lives Matter movement, more White people have come to recognize that the real struggles endured by students of color have been hidden from view through a practice of colorblindness in the classroom that seeks to erase differences.

As educators, we work to investigate and root out structural inequities as well as challenge our inner realms of prejudice, implicit bias, and cultural blindness. We have the responsibility and opportunity to transform policies, relationships, and ourselves so that all students—including those facing entrenched inequities—are seen, valued, and supported to their fullest potential.

Renowned professor and author Linda Darling-Hammond (Darling-Hammond & George, 2020, para. 13) and colleagues pose a direct challenge to all educators. "Addressing inequality should not be an academic exercise or an isolated performative act—we who believe in educational justice must commit to the long-game of dismantling and replacing practices that have reproduced educational inequality over time. Just as high school sophomore Barbara Rose Johns waged a student walkout that culminated in a legal battle that would become *Brown v. Board of Education*, we must also act with courage to upend inequity in education. . . . How will each of us contribute to racial justice and educational equity now?"

Groundwork for a Better Future

With compassion and deference to the suffering created from the pandemic, COVID-19 nevertheless quietly portends an unprecedented opportunity bearing the capacity to transform our broken schools, because it has, in essence, cleared the stage for reconstruction. The tools for teaching and administering school operations have been leveled to an unknown status as educators grapple with the challenges of online learning, stripped of their former safeguards that were available in face-to-face interactions.

John King (2020), former Secretary of Education, recently suggested we make this a "new deal moment." We can take what we have learned in the pandemic and truly invest in schools where we highlight relationships and draw on students' identities. We can promote well-being and social and emotional learning as a portal for collaborative academic learning. If standardized testing is replaced by categories of proficiency with yearly learning capstones, if punitive discipline is replaced with restorative practices, and if the models of community schools are expanded with wrap-around services, we will realize a track for healing our schools.

It is up to each individual to make this more than a moment of heightened awareness and action. The opportunity to rebuild from scratch offers a unique level of freedom to choose differently. Schools are poised as important social interventions to leverage power and privilege into tools shared by all students, teachers, staff, and families. With that in mind, this book offers a systemic approach to implementing identity safe schools where the academic and emotional welfare of students are the centerpiece of our efforts, where the effects of white supremacy are confronted, and where we offer a pathway forward for our students. Feeling hopeful and encouraged, we ask our readers to join us with Linda Darling-Hammond (Darling-Hammond & George, 2020) when she asks, "How will each of us contribute to racial justice and educational equity now?"

CHAPTER 1

An Introduction to Identity Safe Schools

Introduction

Identity safe schools stand firmly in the belief that students of all backgrounds deserve a welcoming school environment that both recognizes and invites them to participate as fully and equally valued members of the classroom and school. When their diverse social identities are respected, they feel connected to each other and their community. The sense of belonging that arises works to negate feelings of alienation, indifference, and separation from others.

Indeed, "the problem of the 21st century is the problem of 'othering,'" john a. powell (lower case intentional) declares, encapsulating the bulk of our challenges under this label, which bears credence when he details its effects (powell & Menendian, 2016, para. 1). *Othering* can be described as the exercise of determining how one group is different from another, coupled with an intent to isolate and dominate the other group with constructs of inferiority. Whether expressed in global, national, or local contexts, othering occurs when one group experiences discrimination or exclusion due to their social identity (race, ethnicity, religion, gender identity, sexual orientation, disability, socioeconomic status, other forms of difference leading to discriminatory practices). The consequences are far-reaching, powell says, leading to a wide range of discriminatory practices, from microaggressions and bias-based bullying to acts of violence and hate, to even extreme cases of murder and genocide. He identifies white supremacy as the catalyst driving these reprehensible developments, based on the false belief that White people are superior. Harvard and Princeton studies show that 75% of White Americans hold subconscious biases with pro-White and anti-Black beliefs (Butler, 2014).

The Othering and Belonging Institute (n.d.) offers a path forward and away from acts of othering through "Targeted Universalism," which is described as an approach that sets universal goals for all people. The next step involves identifying targeted processes and strategies to fulfill the goals, determined by how different groups are situated within their cultural systems and geographic locations. Applied to education, Targeted Universalism calls on us to move beyond programs tacitly aimed at fixing kids or families—as if they were broken—to focus instead on fixing the "structural conditions and ways of relating to each other that contribute to persistent inequities in our schools and communities" (Osta, 2020, para. 1). Targeted Universalism "focuses on removing structural barriers, increases access to opportunities, and advances the well-being and thriving of whole communities of people" (Osta, 2020, para. 6).

Bettina Love (2019), author of *We Want to Do More than Survive: Abolitionist Teaching and the Pursuit of Educational Freedom*, proposes that educators approach their calling with the urgency of an abolitionist incorporating racial justice in that we expose and apply an authentic history of oppression and violence as well as resistance, joy, social change, and activism. She emphasizes that we not only love the students but also embrace and learn about their culture.

Systemic Racism and Schools

Since their inception, schools have served to replicate systemic racism, which is pervasive and expressed across all walks of society. This is evidenced in curriculum, policies, behaviors, and attitudes—both intentional and unconscious. It occurs in hiring practices that discriminate against Black and Latinx teachers, in the unfair distribution of resources and growing segregation in schools. It is perpetuated through the disproportionate suspensions and expulsions of Black and Brown students, which propel them into the "school-to prison pipeline" (Villenas & Zelinski, 2018). When low expectations and rote teaching persist, students of color internalize self-defeating feelings of inferiority (Dusek & Joseph, 1983; Lightfoot, 1978; Rong, 1996). Christopher Emdin (2016, para. 7) states that "teachers who hold within themselves perceptions of the inadequacy of students will never be able to teach them to be something greater than what they are. Teachers cannot teach someone they do not believe in."

Strides have been made over the past 100 years to counter these dismal practices. In the United States, historical events like the civil rights movement, Black Power, the women's movement, Gay Pride, and Black Lives Matter have served as aspirational developments working toward an equitable society. However, there has also been a backlash that has hindered progress: attacks on affirmative action, mass incarceration of Black people, resegregation, redlining practices in housing, holding children of undocumented immigrants in cages, and more. Countervailing forces have eroded public education by promoting vouchers that serve to further segregate students.

This failure for equity to manifest systemically is evident in both public and private institutions and policies, as well as our educational systems—in the latter, spanning from the elementary grades through college. While many people understand that students of color often do not receive an equal education, few realize the degree to which education is designed to maintain white hegemony. By the time students reach top universities, the disparity has reached high levels of exclusion. Legacy acceptances (students who get accepted to universities because family members have previously attended) offer a huge advantage to White students by not requiring top grades and scores. In a study that included 30 elite colleges, researchers discovered that students who enter with a legacy enjoy a 45% increased chance to get accepted (Bergman, 2020).

For students of color who break through those barriers and arrive on a college campus, the oppression does not necessarily end. A simple Google search reveals the common ritual of White students parading "blackface" at universities, including Virginia, Oklahoma, Tennessee, and California (Google, n.d.-a). At the University of Virginia (UVA), the practice has continued since the 1800s (Gates, 2019). This phenomenon was considered "normal" behavior by many Whites until recently and sends an ongoing and blatant message of white supremacy to White students, which can cause deep humiliation and trauma to Black students. In the last year, high school students in Minnesota, Maryland, Illinois, California, Colorado, and Boston either wore blackface at school events or posted blackface online, sometimes accompanied with racial slurs (Google, n.d.-b).

These systems, practices and attitudes of white supremacy are replicated when schools disproportionately honor White students by highlighting their accomplishments and honoring their culture—including holidays, heroes, and dominant historical narratives—while punishing students of color with an exaggerated number of suspensions and expulsions, failing grades, tracked classes, and over representation in special education. The pattern of favoritism is clear—it's not the result of an accident nor a random act. One principal described his daily dilemma when he observed "a row of Black students who have gotten in trouble, sitting in my office each day at lunchtime." The level of negative cultural bias that sent these students to the principal is deeply embedded in our culture, to the extent that often Whites do not see it, even while it exists as an ever-present reality for people of color.

Change is the only compassionate choice open for educational leaders who champion equity. Schools can and must do better. We can flip this script. Many studies have shown that when educators believe in the high potential for students of color, when students feel cared for and their identities valued, when the curriculum is challenging and rigorous with scaffolds and supports in place, achievement and well-being flourishes. (Flores-González, 1999; Hébert & Reis, 1999; Hilliard, 2003; Lee, Winfield, & Wilson, 1991). This encapsulates the vision for identity safe schools.

Dismantling systemic racism is work in progress by continually identifying, examining, and supplanting the white supremacist attitudes that produce these biases with narratives and practices that promote equity and inclusion. As we work toward creating an identity safe school, we seek to unravel the ideas of othering, implicit bias, and privilege with an intent to dismantle white supremacy, sexism, transphobia, and other systems of oppression. We embrace targeted universalism to right past wrongs and fill unrealized needs. We celebrate student identities with a joy and richness for all the forms of diversity available within our common humanity.

OUR STANCE: FOR WHOM DO WE ADVOCATE?

As we write this book during the unique days of the pandemic—coupled with large-scale protests against racism—we want to offer an explicit and clear articulation of our stance and purpose. Research on identity safety focused on the need to address pervasive stereotypes that plague students of color, particularly Black, Indigenous, and Latinx students whose academic achievement and well-being has endured continual threats from racism both inside and outside the school. We seek to redress these wrongs by supplanting systemic racism with systemic equity in the school. We address issues of intersectionality, as well. For example, we recognize that school experiences for a White gay student are not the same as experiences of a Black gay student, who—in addition to homophobia—suffers the indignities of racism. Identity safe research reveals that a non-colorblind climate of belonging and acceptance serves students of all backgrounds, especially those who are deemed to be different in some way. However, our content and many of our examples are intentionally designed to spearhead efforts to disrupt racism and white supremacy.

We offer this book to educators who seek to go deeper into these issues and create equitable policies by bringing identity safe teaching into practice across schools. We must serve these students, who have been targeted unfairly for so long. We believe the time is now.

PATHWAY TOWARD EQUITY

When schools seek to shift the balance of power to give voice and influence to the diverse members within our school community, when members are comfortable in their expressions to each other because they know they are valued, when they are welcomed with equal status and treated fairly in the school culture, we will have inclusion. Without this treatment, equity will not manifest. And beyond inclusion, there is an additional and intentional step up to become identity safe, which is specific to diversity. This quality embraces multiple perspectives in a community and supports the diverse needs of students, their teachers, and families. It acknowledges and honors a range of differences, including ethnicity, racial identity, religion, gender, and social groups.

Equity is reflected in student outcomes, when all students of all backgrounds are progressing at an equally high rate. We will know schools are equitable when outcomes are not predicted by race or any demographic factor, and all students receive the support they need to reach their full potential for learning and contributing. When we see equity expressed at all levels in a school culture, we can know our challenges will include finding ways to support the wills of the many who want to make contributions. Our time can be spent connecting diverse individuals and groups to leverage their support.

Identity safety has a particular flavor that can be seen, felt, and heard the moment we arrive on a campus. We will know equity has found a home when—in addition to high achievement of students of all races and ethnicities—we see a student stand up for a peer being bullied, or when students volunteer to raise funds for Special Olympics; when we see racial and gender diversity reflected in the student body government. Equity will triumph when high school students of all gender identities feel safe enough and motivated to join the LGBTQIA+ Alliance. These possibilities and more, when experienced within the school culture, are clear reminders that a school is successfully supporting identity safety.

Identity Safe Leadership: What It Is and Why It Matters

The work of identity safety emerged as a way to counteract the debilitating effects of stereotype threat. By grasping the pervasive damage of stereotype threat we come to understand the import for identity safety as an antidote, so we begin with an overview of the research. Theories of systems thinking and change management strengthen the efficacy when transforming an unsafe school culture to an identity safe one. We will interweave these ideas throughout the book, underscoring their interdependence.

STEREOTYPE THREAT

In his article "Thin Ice" (1999), Claude Steele defines "stereotype threat" as "the threat of being viewed through the lens of a negative stereotype, or the fear of doing something that would inadvertently confirm that stereotype" (para. 10). He goes on to add, "Everyone experiences stereotype threat. We are all members of some group about which negative stereotypes exist, from White males and Methodists to women and the elderly. And in a situation where one of those stereotypes applies—a man talking to women about pay equity, for example, or an aging faculty member trying to remember a number sequence in the middle of a lecture—we know that we may be judged by it" (para. 10).

Steele and colleague Joshua Aronson had previously developed studies to research the impact of stereotype threat and found that the simple fear of being judged by a negative stereotype can impair performance, inducing self-defeating behaviors from projected and perceived vulnerabilities (C. M. Steele, 2011). They designed one experiment to explicitly test stereotype threat by administering a test to both Black and White students using difficult items from the verbal Graduate Record Exam (GRE) in literature. Both Black and White students had been statistically matched and vetted for equal abilities via SAT scores. They told students that the test diagnosed intellectual ability, triggering a stereotype for Blacks that they were less intelligent than their White peers. They found that "when the test was presented as a test of ability, Black students performed dramatically less well than White students" (C. M. Steele, 1999, para. 17). When the exact same test was framed as a lab test that did not measure ability, Black students performed as well as Whites.

The Power of Stigma

"A Class Divided" (Peters, 1985), a *Frontline* TV episode better known as "Blue Eyes, Brown Eyes," is a classic film featuring a third-grade teacher from Iowa who created a simulation for her students to illustrate first-hand the emotional effects of racism on children of color. While we stress the urgency to refrain from carrying out a simulation like this that clearly targets children's esteem, we can learn from it. On the first day, the teacher required all brown-eyed children in the class to wear bulky collars around their necks to easily identify them. She proceeded to stigmatize them with comments attesting to the superior intelligence and ability of blue-eyed children. She hammered home the point that blue-eyed children are smarter, neater, and nicer than brown-eyed children, while the brown-eyed children shrank into their seats. The next day, she reversed her proclamation, telling them that she had lied to them the day before, the truth being that brown-eyed people were superior. "The brown-eyed people get five extra minutes of recess," she announced. "You blue-eyed people are not to play with the brown-eyed people." In both cases, the children deemed to be inferior took on defeated behavior, performing poorly both in and out of the classroom. Conversely, the "superior" children not only performed better but belittled members of the other group.

The video dramatically demonstrates how fast stereotype threat can impact behavior when a person is stigmatized. When the teacher initiated a phonics lesson with the stigmatized group, it took them 5.5 minutes to complete their task. Once they were freed from their collars, they finished it in a mere 2.5 minutes. The teacher informed them, "You went faster than I ever had anyone go. Why couldn't you get them yesterday?" A student replied, "It's about those collars." Another added "My eyes kept rolling around." The teacher chimed in, "And you couldn't think as well." Another collared student stated simply, "We're dumb." In just a single day of wearing the collars, these students internalized an entirely new and untested view of themselves as inferior and unworthy.

The threats that arise from treatment as a second-class citizen due to a person's background (race, class, gender, disability) can negatively impact performance even when individuals do not believe the stereotype applies to them. Their success can be thwarted by the fear that others will judge them by the stereotype. This is understood when realizing that the effect is not sourced from the low esteem of single individuals.

Negative messaging also shows up in external sources and includes information, both subtle and not-so-subtle, that members of an entire group are judged as "less than" other groups. These messages are so pervasive as to permeate the atmosphere to the extent that it is always "in the air." People of color hear messages that they are less intelligent, more violent, and even destined to live in poverty. Women hear messages of powerlessness and weakness, characterizations that proffer a misperceived and limited scope of options. Many additional research studies have demonstrated that stereotype threat damages the performance of people categorized by social class, gender, age, and many other stereotypes (C. M. Steele, 2011).

It is incumbent upon educators to adopt a proactive stance and guard against stereotyping that will affect their students. This includes those with autism and other disabilities, those who do not speak English as a first language, and those from low-income homes, as well as others who do fit white supremacist standards. Without proactive treatment to counter negative stereotypes, the unspoken messages that prevail include "You do not count" and "My teachers and peers will believe the stereotypes" and "It does not matter if I do not believe it. It will affect me." Being the subject of stereotypes also erodes student trust in their teachers and in their education. Counteracting and refuting stereotypes of all kinds, positive and negative, will open the space for authenticity and true value to emerge in identity safe schools.

IDENTITY SAFETY: DEFINITIONS AND RESEARCH

Research on stereotype threat offers yet another piece in the puzzle as educators seek to understand the causes of underperformance in their efforts to close achievement and opportunity gaps. Teachers ask for concrete, practical tactics to use in order to reduce and manage these identity pressures in real classrooms.

Claude Steele's wife, Dorothy Steele, also a researcher, understood the need to identify concrete ways stereotype threat could be reduced in practice. Along with her husband, she set out to identify an antidote to stereotype threat and supply teachers with approaches to counter negative and racially based stereotype threat in their classrooms, supplanting curriculum with a blueprint for positive, identity-based strategies. They coined the term "identity safety teaching" in which "teachers strive to assure students that their social identities are an asset rather than a barrier to success in the classroom. And, through strong positive relationships and opportunities to learn, they feel they are welcomed, supported, and valued as members of the learning community." (Identity Safe Classrooms, n.d.)

The Steeles gathered a team of Stanford researchers to observe and analyze the practices of teachers in 84 integrated elementary classrooms in an urban school district in Northern California during the 2001–2002 school year. The Stanford Integrated School Project (SISP) (D. M. Steele & Cohn-Vargas, 2013) engaged classrooms that had a makeup of at least 15% from each of three ethnic groups, Black, Latinx, and White. The researchers identified 14 behaviors, or "factors," representing a range of teaching strategies and approaches that researchers understood could lead to warm and inclusive classrooms, positive classroom relationships, a challenging and accessible curriculum, and diversity as a classroom resource.

The outcome for applying these conditions would, potentially, result in a classroom where all students could thrive and feel safe, leading to an experience that the Steeles and colleagues termed "identity safety," so named to emphasize the idea that people need to feel safe and free from threats to their identity in order to give their best performance. Trained observers, with negligible knowledge about stereotype threat or identity safety, visited each of the 84 classrooms. Two different observers visited each class three times each equipped with a classroom observation form detailing 200 criteria for their observations. Coupled with a student questionnaire designed to ascertain student comfort in terms of their sense of belonging, motivation to learn, perceived agency and interest in their work, and more, researchers resolved to identify the best paths forward for creating an identity safe classroom (D. M. Steele & Cohn-Vargas, 2016).

Their extensive data revealed in detail how identity safety practices influence student performance and a sense of self in a favorably significant way. They learned that students in classrooms where identity safety was practiced performed higher on standardized tests compared to students in lower identity safe classrooms. The correlation between how the students felt about school and their performance was also established with the student questionnaires. Those from identity safe classrooms enjoyed school more and performed significantly better than their counterparts.

The implications of their findings are promising for educators. Understanding how to address stereotype threat in the classroom in a way that creates happy learning places for students and teachers *and* addresses the negative impacts of systemic racism is a substantial win-win.

This bottom-up research model identified 14 factors that described specific behaviors of the participating teachers that resulted in creating identity safety in their students. The next question involved investigating ways to translate what was revealed in research and further describe the components of identity safety for teachers to apply in their classrooms.

Research on Identity Safety Continues

In 2006, I (Becki), along with Dr. Dorothy Steele's support, began my doctoral studies to describe the SISP identity safety factors in detail and identify effective ideas and approaches for classroom access. I worked for one year with a study group of elementary teachers to identify, organize, and describe what was learned from Steele's research. With Dorothy, we named four domains and condensed the evidence-based factors into 12 supporting components that captured the essence of the attitudes and behaviors observed in successful teachers from the research. We translated the concepts along with examples of concrete strategies to ease practical application in the classroom. Dorothy and I brought their ideas into a book for elementary teachers, *Identity Safe Classrooms, Grades K–5: Places to Belong and Learn* (2013). Working in the field with teachers from grades K–12, I heard secondary teachers requesting specific strategies for middle and high schoolers. I partnered with Alexandrea Creer Kahn and Amy Epstein, resulting in a second book, *Identity Safe Classrooms, Grades 6–12: Pathways to Belonging and Learning* (2020).

The four domains and 12 components of identity safety that serve as the framework for application of identity safe teaching in classrooms also serve as useful guidelines to transform all levels of school culture. Drawn straight from the SISP research, they are the bedrock of identity safety practice. We will highlight them throughout the book and apply them to the wider perspective for the whole school.

The Four Domains and 12 Components of Identity Safe Classrooms (D. M. Steele & Cohn-Vargas, 2013)

Domain 1: Student-Centered Teaching

1. Listening for Student Voices: To ensure that students are heard and can contribute to and shape classroom life

2. Teaching for Understanding: To ensure students will learn new knowledge and incorporate it into what they know

3. Focus on Cooperation: Rather than focus on competition, to support students in learning from and helping others

4. Classroom Autonomy: To support students in responsibility and feelings of belonging

Domain 2: Cultivating Diversity

5. Using Diversity as a Resource for Teaching: To include all students' curiosity and knowledge in the classroom

6. High Expectations and Academic Rigor: To support all students in high-level learning

7. Challenging Curriculum: To motivate each student by providing meaningful, purposeful learning

Domain 3: Classroom Relationships

8. Teacher Warmth and Availability to Support Learning: To build a trusting, encouraging relationship with each student

9. Positive Student Relationships: To build interpersonal understanding and caring among students

Domain 4: Caring Classrooms

10. Teacher Skill: To establish an orderly, purposeful classroom that facilitates student learning

11. Emotional and Physical Comfort: To provide a safe environment so that each student connected to school and to other students

12. Attention to Prosocial Development: To teach students how to live with one another, solve problems, and show respect and caring for others

Research on identity safety continues. Stephanie Fryberg (2016), professor at the University of Michigan and a member of the Tulalip Tribes, along with Mary Murphy (personal communication, September 20, 2018), professor at Indiana University, feature identity safety aligned with growth mindset in their research on creating culturally responsive spaces and belonging for all students. Stanford professor and director of the Learning Policy Institute (LPI), Linda Darling-Hammond and colleagues (Darling-Hammond & Cook-Harvey, 2018) focus on identity safety as an essential element in educating the whole child to create "a caring, culturally responsive learning community in which all students are valued and are free from social identity threats that undermine performance," explaining that "identity-safe classrooms promote student achievement and attachments to school" (para. 19).

Research on stereotype threat and its remedy, identity safety, have sparked further study as researchers develop identity safety experiments and case studies where positive contact and role models were found to promote identity safety (McIntyre, et al., 2003; Purdie-Vaughns, et al., 2008). In "How to Help All Students Feel Safe to Be Themselves," Ondrasek and Flook (2020) highlight an LPI case study at the Social Justice Humanitas Academy (SJHA) in the Los Angeles Unified School District (LAUSD). There, researchers observed trusting classroom relationships, attention to prosocial development, incorporating diversity as a resource, and other identity safety components in action, leading to improved achievement and a high graduation rate. Students who were surveyed reported that they "feel safe at school."

Making It Happen

GUIDING PRINCIPLES FOR AN IDENTITY SAFE SCHOOL CULTURE

In this book, we focus on bringing each of the components, and the guiding principles that support them, to life across a school campus—from the front office to the classrooms, yards, lunchrooms, and auditoriums—weaving them into a school culture to create safety and inclusion for students of all backgrounds, especially students of color and students with varied gender identities.

In the books *Identity Safe Classrooms, Grades K–5* (D. M. Steele & Cohn-Vargas, 2013) and *Identity Safe Classrooms, Grades 6-12* (Cohn-Vargas et al., 2020), we introduce identity safety as an antidote to stereotype threat and offer a detailed overview with vignettes and examples of teaching strategies for each of the domains and their respective components. We explain that identity safe teaching is an approach and not a program. We refer you to both those books for more information on teaching strategies.

To create a meaningful approach for implementation, we developed the identity safe components into a set of guiding principles that apply to both the classroom and the school. The principles draw from the components and are presented in a condensed form. Further in this chapter, we will elaborate on each of these guiding principles in their capacity to manifest the ideals of an identity safe school culture.

Identity Safety Guiding Principles

1. **Colorblind teaching** that ignores differences is a barrier to inclusion in the classroom.
2. **To feel a sense of belonging and acceptance** requires creating positive relationships between teacher and students and among students with equal status for different social identities.
3. **Cultivating diversity** as a resource for learning and expressing high expectations for students promotes learning, competence, and achievement.
4. **Educators examine their own social identities** to feel a sense of identity safety and convey that feeling to students, creating an identity safe environment for them.
5. **Social and emotional safety** is created by supporting students in defining their identities, refuting negative stereotypes, and countering stereotype threat, giving them a voice in the classroom while using social and emotional learning (SEL) strategies.
6. **Student learning** is enhanced in diverse classrooms by teaching for understanding, creating opportunities for shared inquiry and dialogue, and offering a challenging, rigorous curriculum.
7. **Schoolwide equity** flourishes for everyone in identity safe schools where the climate, the structures, practices, and attitudes prioritize equity, inclusion, and academic growth for students from all backgrounds. Leaders demonstrate emotional intelligence; attend to student needs; address racism, bias, and privilege; and serve as the architects of ongoing change.

These principles can be seen as individual trees in the woods. With the principles in mind, we can pull back to observe and manage the entire forest. From this vantage point, we can see where and how the principles are working together to support the greater culture that permeates the entire system. We can also identify the areas that need attention.

CULTURE IS EVERYTHING

In their article "Good Seeds Grow in Strong Cultures," Saphier and King (1985) describe a culture as the structure, process, and climate of values and norms that channel staff and students in the direction of successful teaching and learning. The culture of a school is the confluence of a wealth of moving parts that are continually interacting. Using the lens of systems thinking, we consider the way all aspects of a school are connected and impacting each other. In an identity safe school culture, many elements move and dance in harmony with all its parts, ensuring that learning takes place in the context of student well-being. The interplay of safety, inclusion, and acceptance forms a culture where every child has a place within it and feels safe in giving their best effort.

Identity safe leaders start by examining the existing school culture from a broad and comprehensive view. In nature, the regeneration of an ecosystem depends primarily upon the interactions of diverse creatures and plants; so does the health of our human ecosystem rely principally on our diversity and interdependence. When we think about the health of a tree, we don't limit our vision to the leaves or the branches. Topical treatment will not necessarily heal a sick tree, nor will it transform an unhealthy school culture. To get to the roots of the illness, we seek to understand in depth the extent that the system, or school, has intrinsically supported racist and biased attitudes, which are often embedded in quiet policies that seek deliberate camouflage from probing eyes. To find them and enact change, we dig deeper to investigate an entire range of practices and key into those that are provoking inequity. Identity safe leaders work in a continual process to transform school culture by taking a systems approach.

School leaders are required to attend to multiple levels of school operations simultaneously. Their lens encompasses all events and people in the community, from the student to the custodian to all materials and supplies, to helpful organizations outside the school. While at first glance this superpower may engender intimidation, it is a skill and, much like a muscle, it can and needs to be developed.

A fuller investigation of identity safety principles and applying them across the school as useful guides and resources can anchor our understanding for connecting the individual parts into a broader and more manageable view.

THE PRINCIPLES OF IDENTITY SAFETY AS A SYSTEMIC APPROACH (COHN-VARGAS, ET AL., 2020)

Principle One: Colorblind teaching *that ignores differences is a barrier to inclusion in the classroom.*

You have an opportunity to leverage your power to incorporate the voices of everyone in the school in a shared vision, and to do so is to invite their success and yours. Part of the vision involves the power of building trusting relationships where diverse identities are not ignored and all members of the community have a voice and feel they can contribute without leaving any aspect of their identity at the door.

Many educators—and sometimes entire schools—claim to be "colorblind" in an uninformed attempt to undo the effects of racism and bias. However, in a society that operates on a foundation of white supremacy, it is a mistake to think that racial differences and attitudes can be erased by ignoring them when these same attitudes are negatively influencing treatment in the justice system, housing, schools, and all social sectors. A colorblind school climate does not eradicate racism in the school, and will, instead, serve to bolster white supremacy. As we have shown in the section about stereotype threat, racist attitudes in the greater society continue both in overt and covert ways. Those who are different from the mainstream culture are acutely aware of it. Having their identities ignored can trigger mistrust, sap energy, and provoke feelings of anger, grief, inferiority, or shame. For White students, a colorblind environment allows them to maintain privilege. They often get away with petty crimes and other antisocial behaviors that are often dismissed by the phrase "kids will be kids." In many cases, they presume their gains are won fairly in a meritocracy, but in reality they often have many more options than students of color, and the deck is stacked in their favor. A colorblind environment serves to keep it that way.

SISP research found that colorblind classrooms negatively impacted student identity safety (D. M. Steele & Cohn-Vargas, 2013). An identity safe approach highlights differences in a way that validates diverse student identities, while searching for and rooting out inequalities with an honest commitment to address and supplant them with equity and inclusion. In subsequent chapters, we model ways to move from a colorblind to an identity safe culture.

Principle Two: To feel a sense of belonging and acceptance requires creating positive relationships between teacher and students and among students with equal status for different social identities.

Each student benefits from knowing that there are trusted adults on campus who care about them and their lives. Each adult needs to feel that the leaders have their back based in a culture of trust and respect. Every parent/caregiver deserves to feel included and valued.

Researchers have discovered that even children who have lacked care in early childhood can, by forming positive relationships with at least one person, mitigate

A Word About the Benefits of Diversity for White Students

When we talk of diversity as a resource, we refer to embracing students from all backgrounds—and we explicitly mean all races, including both students of color and White students. The inclusion of diversity in the curriculum helps to drive identity safety for all. A recent study in the journal *Child Development* (Society for Research in Child Development, 2013) demonstrates that students feel safer in school when they are educated in a diverse setting. Rather than teaching through a colorblind approach where some cultures are ignored, students who learn about different cultures and backgrounds feel a greater sense of comfort with their differences. It is important to understand that a growing body of research shows that White students benefit greatly from experiencing diversity in the classroom. We know that White students, as well as students of color at all income levels, enjoy increased motivation, critical thinking, and creative problem-solving from learning cooperatively alongside others with diverse backgrounds and perspectives. If we understand that *all* of our students are affected when *some* of them feel unsafe as a result of stereotype threat, then we are closer to grasping the level of synergy that flows between them. Some students will meet threats to their identities—or threats to the identities of other students in the classroom—with disengagement and discouragement, and still more will become aggressive and exhibit inappropriate or bullying behaviors. A safe environment is threatened for everyone when we ignore the identities of some (Wells, et al., 2016).

White students can develop the attitudes and behaviors that counter bias and racism while learning to accept students from many cultures and backgrounds. This will enable them to take a stand in fighting racism. Over the last four years, the voices of right-wing extremists, neo-Nazis, and racists have been amplified in mainstream media reports. An identity safe school can not only provide students of all backgrounds the skills and mindsets to navigate the world they live in and will work in, but also to feel a sense of hope and agency to be a full member of that world.

the effects of some of their earlier experiences (Werner, 1995). Children who suffer from continued negative stereotyping and biased treatment at school will often come to the conclusion that education will not serve them. With a long history of oppression, unequal conditions, and forced assimilation, many students and their communities have good reason to mistrust both the greater system of society and its brainchild, education, and by association those who work in it. As schools analyze their cultures, they can root out systemic tendencies that undermine trust and create winners and losers. The evidence is revealed in the grading and tracking systems that sort and select students, marginalize students of color, and subsequently limit opportunities that impact their future lives. Efforts to repair trust form a major part of system-wide culture and climate improvement.

A culture of equal status is grounded in cooperation and collaboration. Indigenous, African, Asian, Latin American, and other cultures have built collective societies that thrive on interdependence. When students come to us from these cultures, often their values and life experience are at odds with the individualistic values that drive competitive school environments in the United States (Hofstede, 1980, 1991). Incorporating more collaborative approaches, teamwork, and intentional efforts to understand the collective cultural values will create a space of belonging for students from diverse backgrounds. Integrating cooperation in classroom practices will also benefit students from dominant cultures who perhaps have not developed these values. In the SISP identity safe school research, fostering cooperation was an important factor that led to identity safety (D. M. Steele & Cohn-Vargas, 2013).

Each chapter in this book highlights the power of building trust, opening dialogue, promoting collaboration, and creating belonging for every adult and child in a school community.

*Principle Three: **Cultivating diversity as a resource** for learning and expressing high expectations for students promotes learning, competence, and achievement.*

Cultivating diversity is a way of life that permeates a school culture. In the SISP research, this factor was a defining quality that was evident in classrooms where students felt a greater sense of identity safety. Leaders can work to ensure educators are prepared to bring it into every classroom, to incorporate it in curriculum design and pedagogy, and beyond the classroom in hiring. Also, diversity can be prioritized in the process of selecting materials to purchase for the library and underscoring it as part of the wide range of schoolwide activities and after-school programs. It includes the installation and inclusion of rituals, symbols, presentations, and rules that reflect and honor the multiple cultures, languages, genders, and full identities of all students and their families. We serve our shared ideals in the conferring of titles and awards, the honoring of elders, and the construction of codes of behavior. With your attention centered on this goal, you can attract a diverse team to develop a vision and plan for cultivating diversity with safe practices integrated throughout the school.

By holding and promoting high expectations for adults along with students, identity safe leaders communicate and model a belief in the abilities of everyone in the community and support each person in reaching their goals. Just as high expectations with scaffolded support for academic progress have been found to improve achievement, holding high expectations for the way students treat one another improves the culture and climate of a school (Good, 1981). Often the role of disciplinarian falls to leaders. Bringing in an awareness of restorative practices on a schoolwide basis shifts the focus from punitive discipline to repairing harm and accommodating healing.

Cultivating diversity and high expectations are themes we delve into and highlight with examples throughout all chapters of this book.

Principle Four: Educators examine their own social identities to feel a sense of identity safety and convey that feeling to students, creating an identity safe environment for them.

To initiate the process for realizing identity safety and anti-racism, leaders, staff, and students begin by looking at their own identities, backgrounds, and values. The work for change includes recognizing and accepting our individual identities with all its attendant and marvelous complexities, and honoring the same in others. This includes uprooting internalized oppression and racialized and bias-based trauma. White people can seek to recognize the often hidden yet pervasive qualities of privilege, implicit bias, and white supremacist culture, and progress further to accept accountability for their own advantages and work for social justice. We want to highlight that we do not hold the assumption that White educators are explicitly biased or racist. We believe that most educators deeply care about their students and intend to be fair, including those who purport to be colorblind (D. M. Steele & Cohn-Vargas, 2013). We are saying, however, that white privilege is an embedded system worthy of personal investigation because it profoundly affects the lives of people of color (and their children). It deserves our attention. With an open mind, we are better qualified to serve needs in order to realize transformation for all students.

To aid in the undoing of these inhumane and destructive processes, leaders can begin by providing a forum for continual self-reflection as a regular practice. Staff, students, and families can engage in activities that encourage sharing identities with one another, and engaging in exercises to recognize and release old biases, attitudes, habits, practices, and structures that are inconsistent with compassionate, equitable systems (P. Noli & E. Porter, personal communication, July 22, 2020).

In Chapter 2 and Chapter 3, specific examples and vignettes will offer ideas for self-reflection processes and suggest protocols.

When we take an honest look at history to understand what brought us to this moment, we can learn why it matters. By examining patterns of overt (e.g., lynching, Jim Crow laws), and covert inequities including the "war on drugs" that led to mass incarceration of Blacks, we inevitably come face to face with the reality of how certain entrenched school protocols operate to both launch and perpetuate the pipeline to prison system.

Principle Five: Social and emotional safety is created by supporting students in defining their identities, refuting negative stereotypes, and countering stereotype threat, giving them a voice in the classroom while using social and emotional learning (SEL) strategies.

In the SISP research (D. M. Steele & Cohn-Vargas, 2013), attention to prosocial development emerged as an important factor practiced in classrooms where students felt identity safe. This attention to prosocial development is fostered through SEL instruction but goes beyond teaching social and emotional skills. It embraces an environment where students are treated with respect and in turn are supported in feeling that who they are and what they think matters.

Prosocial development is fostered by supporting the physical, emotional, and intellectual well-being of each individual. In Chapter 3 we will offer strategies to ensure adults in the school are prepared to meet SEL needs as well as reduce the presence of implicit and explicit bias. In Chapter 5 we will explore ways to expand the school into the community to serve the many needs of families and to support the SEL and well-being of the students.

Principle Six: Student learning is enhanced in diverse classrooms by teaching for understanding, creating opportunities for shared inquiry and dialogue, and offering a challenging, rigorous curriculum.

The SISP research highlighted a constellation of factors that lead to student agency in classrooms where students felt identity safety and achieved at higher levels. These included *listening for student voices, teaching for understanding, fostering cooperation,* and *student autonomy. Identity Safe Classrooms, Grades K–5* (D. M. Steele & Cohn-Vargas, 2013) and *Identity Safe Classrooms, Grades 6–12* (Cohn-Vargas et al., 2020) are steeped in strategies and examples of how to design student-centered instruction to promote rigorous learning and student agency. By working with staff, leaders' tangible support will make this a reality by ensuring that educators have the resources and training they need to provide an innovative and rigorous and inquiry-based curriculum with critical thinking and project-based learning. In Chapter 3, we give more examples for adult learning to ensure educators are prepared to teach in a way that promotes Principle Six. In Chapter 6, in the section "Starting the Year Together: A Schoolwide Effort," we offer some entry points for launching student-centered identity safe practices in the classroom.

Principle Seven: Schoolwide equity flourishes for everyone in identity safe schools where the climate, the structures, practices, and attitudes prioritize equity, inclusion, and academic growth for students from all backgrounds. Leaders demonstrate emotional intelligence; attend to student needs; address racism, bias, and privilege; and serve as the architects of ongoing change.

Leaders can incorporate multiple fields of knowledge from many sources in goal setting, planning, implementing, evaluating, and improving the school. Involving diverse stakeholders (including students) in decisions will garner support from all school groups and mitigate resistance. Throughout the process, leaders navigate their communities through sustained efforts by asking hard questions, opening dialogue, listening attentively, and incorporating anti-racist curriculum. When conflicts erupt among members of the school community, leaders take bold steps to draw on mutual empathy that springs from listening, understanding, and applying fair treatment. This process can allow people the breathing room and support to become accountable for their mistakes and repair any harm done.

To foster a strong culture, leaders build on diversity as a resource in the many schoolwide activities, daily practices, and rituals where students and adults have a chance to shine. When these routines authentically reflect the full community's cultural assets, a collective and healthy group identity can be established.

Attending to the broad view with an eye on all aspects of the school culture stands out as the single most powerful way to transform your school. You most likely will find many positive aspects of your school climate as you first explore your own beliefs, then branch out to consider the effects of the practices, policies, and people in your school upon identity safety (e.g., friendly teachers, effective teaching and learning, positive discipline practices). You may also discover areas that are lacking and in need of attention.

A few possible areas can signal a need for change in order to become identity safe.

Consider how you might change some of the conditions below:

- A staff of predominantly White teachers with mostly people of color as paraprofessionals and custodial staff

- A disproportionate number of White students in advanced placement and a disproportionate number of students of color in special education

- Staff who feel uncomfortable discussing race with each other (or with students)

This overview is central to your role as a leader in an identity safe school as you develop an eye for equity in all aspects of culture and climate. Throughout each of the chapters, we will highlight ways to infuse and implement an identity safe culture in your school, closing the gap between ideas and practice.

Drawing From Identity Safe Research and Equitable Practice for Change

Thus far, we presented the research that undergirds the concept of identity safety, shared the components that lead to identity safety, and applied it to a set of principles that can guide your school. Working together to forge a shared and transparent theory of change will help tremendously in defining the path to becoming an identity safe school. Developing a theory of change starts with thinking about how and why transformation is needed and what can be done to realize the desired changes in your school environment. From there, the process includes attracting diverse stakeholders, drafting long-term goals, and working backwards to identify how to reach the goals. In that way, all stakeholders understand the link between the current collective performance and what you can accomplish together as you transform your efforts into an identity safe experience for all involved.

A WORD ABOUT THE PROCESS OF CHANGE

The leaders from Interaction Associates (2019) posit that to make enduring change requires a three-pronged focus on *results, process*, and *relationship*. If these areas are not in balance, then changes will be short-lived—if they make it off the ground at all.

Results

Transformative change is about results arising from a set of goals and a plan of action that leads us forward. However, without an effective process, results are sporadic and disorganized at best. Also, if there is too much focus and pressure to get results without considering relationships, people can become brutally competitive or highly critical. To achieve an identity safe school culture, we keep our eyes on this goal, make a plan, monitor it, and note progress as we advance.

Process

Change efforts that lead to results require attention to process—how we are doing and what we are doing—throughout planning and implementation. If the process is inclusive of the voices and ideas of diverse stakeholders, it is more likely to realize success: a greater span of perspective and knowledge will inform the work, and invested participants will work harder. Nevertheless, too much focus on the process can lead to endless hours spent in meetings without a successful conclusion or foreseeable results, which is frustrating at best. Additionally, without attention to relationships, people who are left out of the process will not feel represented and will not commit to making needed changes.

Relationship

Finally, forging respectful relationships based on acceptance and compassion will create positive experiences, motivating people to enroll and commit to the work for desired outcomes. Unless relationships are positive, the best intentions will be tainted with doubt and a lack of trust. Supportive and positive relationships are an essential ingredient for change, but they need to be incorporated into an inclusive process that leads to sustained results.

Identity safe school leaders keep their eyes focused on student needs and academic and social and emotional growth of students, as they develop an inclusive process and build relationships of trust and equal status. We will take the discussion of how to create transformational change further in Chapters 2 and 7.

IDENTITY SAFE PRACTICES SUPPORT A RANGE OF STUDENT IDENTITIES

Identity safe practices are also greatly beneficial to students who are stigmatized for a variety of reasons beyond race. Their needs are met as their identities are validated and by ensuring they are not subject to harassment, bullying, and exclusion.

The identities and roles of women and men are changing across the world. As children grow up, they come to learn about and experience themselves as gendered beings, absorbing the societal stereotypes. School can play a part in breaking down barriers that limit females in reaching their full potential and limit males in developing the capacity to express feelings and vulnerability. An identity safe school can serve to challenge societal norms that inhibit children from freely expressing their gender identities. As part of our practice, we take the time to consider how we model for and communicate about gender with students.

For LGBTQIA+ students, "Don't ask, don't tell" is akin to colorblindness, erasing their identities and harming their well-being. To see yourself reflected in the curriculum and portrayed as valued members of society is essential for LGBTQIA+ students and those who are questioning gender identity and sexual orientation. Gay-Straight Alliances have done so much to support these students in school. However, often the validation of LGBTQIA+ identities is never touched upon in the classroom. These students will come to feel identity safe when educators incorporate curriculum and literature that addresses gender differences, when they meet LGBTQIA+ role models, and when their identities and gender expressions are openly acknowledged and accepted as part of their daily lives across the grades.

Immigrant children and English learners have specific academic needs to be able to fully participate in the classroom community. Efforts to draw from their cultures, validate their languages, and celebrate bilingualism as an academic and economic advantage, as well as provide English language development (ELD) pedagogy, offer them access to classroom life.

Physically disabled, learning disabled students, and students on the autism spectrum each have unique learning styles. Often, they are stigmatized simply by the special education label. Yet, there are so many aspects of their social identities that can be celebrated and integrated into their classroom experience. Their unique academic needs can be addressed while giving them opportunities to contribute and fully share in classroom life.

Students with religious backgrounds that do not match the majority of students also benefit from an identity safe environment. Muslim students report frequently being called "terrorists" and Jewish students describe having had coins tossed at them. Often, adults are not aware until an incident occurs that impacts the entire school. In an identity safe environment, these students will not feel the need to hide their identities or put up with teasing and bullying. The values that are expressed and continually articulated will promote empathy and understanding across these and many other differences.

Given its prevalence among students, the causes of and resolution for trauma deserve our attention and study. Without comprehensive understanding and trauma-informed practices, identity safety will not be possible. We will examine trauma in general before focusing on racialized trauma.

IDENTITY SAFE SCHOOLS INCORPORATE TRAUMA-INFORMED PRACTICES

The ACEs (Adverse Childhood Experiences) (Centers for Disease Control and Prevention [CDC], n.d.) longitudinal study delivered a warning to educators and health providers that 70% of the U.S. population has experienced some level of adversity by the time they reach school age. The study revealed the long-standing impact of trauma on health and relationships. Children growing up in segregation and poverty, in particular, are found to have endured greater negative impacts upon their health and well-being.

Self-regulation refers to a person's capacity to control thoughts, feelings, and behavior. In a Duke University report (Murray, et al., 2016), *Self-Regulation and Toxic Stress Report 4: Implications for Programs and Practice*, it states that self-regulation plays a significant role in a person's well-being, producing effects that last a lifetime. The capacity to self-regulate positively impacts all aspects of health, including physical and emotional health as well as social and economic status. Conversely, Hamoudi, et al. (2015) explain that when adversity manifests as children are developing a sense of agency, the process and the development of self-regulation is disrupted. When exposed to toxic stress for long periods of time, a child's stress hormones become dysregulated with long-lasting effects—not only to physical and mental health, but extending as well to a person's spirit and zest for life. If we do not feel seen and valued, we are especially prone to being triggered into a fight–flight–freeze response in which self-regulation is extremely challenging. In classrooms that are not identity safe, this plays out with students who cannot focus, lack impulse control, get into frequent conflicts, or have trouble learning and retaining new information.

Students who arrive at our schools after experiencing childhood trauma need even greater doses of guidance and support to allow them to adapt and thrive in school. With the right attention, they can make great strides. Interdisciplinary teams of teachers, counselors, and paraprofessional staff can learn about and help students through somatic and self-regulating practices such as yoga and mindfulness. Social and emotional learning in the classroom and counseling groups can help them manage their emotions. We can scaffold their experiences as they learn to trust themselves, affirming and attending to their internal sensors and responding in healthy ways to both stress and threats. A caring relationship can improve achievement for students who have experienced trauma. Community school models with wraparound services can address some of the external stressors of poverty and unsafe environments.

All our best efforts cannot resolve these issues, however, without addressing the root causes of trauma. Looking deeper to create an identity safe space, we consider the ways racial and other forms of discrimination cause trauma. The ongoing threats to a person's (or child's) well-being as a result of supremacist policies and beliefs generates racialized trauma. Over time, white supremacy can produce extreme effects on people subjected to daily microaggressions and abuses. Our bodies retain and reenact history, passing on both our trauma and resiliency to new generations. In *My Grandmother's Hands*, Resmaa Menakem (2017) writes about the power of culture, describing a process where our bodies actually absorb the expressions of culture, including trauma and its mitigating cousin, resilience. His grandmother had short stubby fingers from picking cotton, beginning as a four-year-old child. He describes the trauma stored in her body as visceral, a cultural byproduct of white supremacy. The trauma induced from the cotton burrs cutting her fingers was matched by the way they healed. Her fingers adapted to the constant injuries with a new shape: stunted but tough and prepared for the daunting tasks ahead.

Discrimination experienced by a child—or by a child's parents—catalyzed by media coverage of unarmed Black and Latinx people being shot by police or others becomes a significant source of anxiety and stress. A destructive barrage like this will in time impact a person's ability to self-regulate.

Measuring the Impact of Racism on the Health of Black People

In an interview on CNN (Zakaria, 2020), Harvard Public Health Professor David Williams described the causes of the disproportionate death rate from COVID-19 for Black citizens. Williams explained this as part of a pattern evidenced over the last 100 years where Blacks have a higher death rate than Whites for every leading cause of death (e.g., heart disease, diabetes, hypertension). In addition to the impact of poverty, Williams and colleagues have done significant research on the impact of discrimination on the health of Black people at all socioeconomic levels. In one 2018 study, researchers identified the states where unarmed Black men were shot and killed by police. They found that mental health outcomes worsened for not only friends and family of the deceased but for the entire Black populations across the region for the following three months.

In order to determine the impact of what Williams describes as everyday incidents where Black people are treated with disrespect, given poor service in stores, or addressed like ignorant children or in condescending manners, he developed the "Everyday Racism Scale" (D. Williams, 2016). The scale is a tool designed to capture feelings of devaluation and day-to-day indignities suffered repeatedly by Black people. Using it, researchers found that discriminatory treatment causes stress that shows up in higher infant mortality rate, high blood pressure, and heart disease, and it can predict premature mortality.

Researchers J. M. Williams and Bryan (2013) studied African American students who achieved at high levels and found specific factors associated with both their achievement and their engagement with school. A stand-out factor involved their access to at least one warm and caring adult who knew them well. This can include a positive relationship with a teacher, coach, principal, or counselor, as well as peers and school friends. Even when negative factors threatened their well-being, in some instances, peers motivated one another to keep trying. When educators held them to high standards, when they taught lessons that linked to their interests, learning was accessible and interesting. Some of these students also benefited from athletics, clubs, and other extracurricular activities that drew them to school. In another study titled "The Long-Run Impacts of Same Race Teachers," researchers at Johns Hopkins University and American University found that if Black students had only one Black teacher by third grade, they were 13% more likely to enroll in college. That statistic jumped to 32% if the student had two Black teachers (Camera, 2020).

It is part of a leader's role to raise the awareness of adults on campus to these conditions and offer strategies for addressing them in and outside the classroom. Trauma-informed practices include mindfulness, somatic practices, and other tools for helping traumatized students learn. As part of creating an identity safe school, we can ensure staff come to understand the impact of trauma as well as racialized trauma and take steps to address it (Menakem, 2017).

Rising to Challenges/Avoiding Pitfalls

This book is a call to action to step up to the ongoing challenge of creating identity safe schools. In each chapter we define specific ways to rise to this challenge and stay the course. This chapter focuses on the importance of knowing and understanding the root causes of inequities in our society and schools, and in refuting white supremacy and stereotype threat, without which we are ill-equipped to promote change. For optimal results, we encourage leaders to dig deep into the principles of identity safety to both comprehend and appreciate their power to transform an entire school. These pages are dedicated to showing you how to accomplish this.

As we embark on the path of equity, we aim to keep a vigilant eye open for common pitfalls. A common mistake among educational leaders involves treating equity as a separate practice from teaching and learning. This occurs in schools with many students of diverse backgrounds, as well as those with a majority of White students whose educators often do not feel this topic is relevant for their population. This pitfall unfolds through "drive-by" equity workshops that happen once—sometimes after a racist incident—and then are forgotten by the leaders until another racist event rocks the school.

Change cannot find fertile ground through episodic or superficial treatment. An ongoing exploration and discussion of equity is insufficient without engaging actions to dismantle inequitable practices and policies. If staff participate in diversity workshops that ask them to self-examine without investigating the impact of implicit and explicit bias on students, unpacking systems of oppression and understanding power, privilege, and equity will not develop.

Equity-focused work is initiated on an interpersonal level before leading to concrete actions and steps to ensure success. Leaders support and monitor educators in this courageous work to carry it—complete with concrete strategies—into their practice. On the other side of the scale lies a well-intended but overwhelming desire for action following a controversial or distressing event, such as an act of hate. An attitude of panic or disquiet can overshadow a deeper awareness of the issues, often leading to rushed and harried solutions. Unless educators examine the historical antecedents and broader concerns, changes will be superficial and short-lived.

Another common quick fix is the hiring of a "diversity consultant," coordinator, or "dean of diversity" as the sole representative to reflect the diversity of the student body. Without engaging the entire school community, these efforts can be meaningless and/or can place the burden of change on one person. Also, placing people of color into token roles or positions is not only unfair to those persons but is a recipe for marginalizing the issues and stunting the change process. Leaders can diversify hiring, draw in families, and invite their voices into the leadership process.

A pitfall to be avoided occurs when members of one ethnic group are pitted against another. Sometimes referred to as the "oppression Olympics," this process describes a competition for "who has suffered more." These attitudes are neither healthy nor healing. Leaders can work to ensure that compassion is not viewed as a pity party. They can make it clear that the suffering of each person or group should not be compared with another person or group. We model and encourage all shares with a spirit of humility and acceptance.

While the path toward equity can involve these and other unanticipated pitfalls, it is still a meaningful process to witness empathy and compassion grow and strengthen our connections. We will guide you through the processes that both mitigate and heal those tense moments, creating opportunities for mutual growth.

Closing the Gap Between Ideas and Action

In this chapter we presented the research on stereotype threat and identity safety and the domains and components that emerged from the research. This is foundational to understanding the principles that guide implementation. The rest of this book will present ways to take these ideas and put them into practice in your school. We present approaches to examine identity safe systems that are at play in the school.

Chapter 2, "Leadership for an Identity Safe School," describes the power of equity-focused leadership along with the skills and habits of identity safe leaders.

In Chapter 3, "Adult Learning in Service of an Identity Safe School," we present identity safe intrapersonal, interpersonal, and institutional staff learning experiences as well as structure and routines that draw from research on adult learning.

In Chapter 4, "Data and Assessment for an Identity Safe School," we highlight identity safe practices for gathering, analyzing, and using data as well as strategies for formative assessment and grading.

In Chapter 5, "Identity Safe Partnerships With Families and the Community," we describe ways to support and involve parents/caregivers and partner with the greater community.

In Chapter 6, "Coherence and Congruence: Schoolwide Systems and Activities to Support Identity Safety," we highlight an identity safe approach to additional systems: classroom practice, prevention and intervention, behavior and discipline, staff wellness, and schoolwide activities.

In Chapter 7, "Planning and Implementing Schoolwide Identity Safety," we offer an inclusive process for planning the path forward for the whole school.

The process of working to dismantle white supremacy and creating social justice becomes a mission of courage, more meaningful through our collective effort. In each chapter, we will offer concrete suggestions for moving from ideas into action.

How to Use This Book

Our first two identity safe books (D. M. Steele & Cohn-Vargas, 2013; Cohn-Vargas et al., 2020) focused on approaches for teachers in classrooms grades K–5 and 6–12. We provided a wealth of specific strategies across the domains and components that emerged from Dorothy Steele's (2012) identity safe teaching research. This book will not replicate the material in them but rather will develop the ideas for application at a schoolwide level. Educational leaders can enjoy multiple access points for implementing identity safety in this book. We recommend that you read the introduction completely. Once you have determined where your staff and school can reap the highest benefit, you may choose to either read sequentially or, after assessing both your areas of strength and areas for growth, approach the related chapters accordingly and apply the identity safety ideas and principles within. You can return to and access different chapters at different times in an order that addresses your needs. As your understanding broadens, and when you see a culture of identity safety taking root in your school as more people climb on board, you will be able to enjoy many self-perpetuating benefits that define a caring community. You can also join with your staff or with colleagues to engage in book study groups, which can greatly expedite implementation with shared understandings promoting ideas and action. Share this book with other members of your school district and community to invite contributions and talents outside your school and widen the influence of an identity safe culture.

HOW THE BOOK CHAPTERS ARE ORGANIZED

- Each chapter starts with a section titled **Why It Matters,** detailing an aspect of schoolwide identity safety supported with research about why it is important. Aspects of an Identity Safe School Culture are also highlighted in this section relevant to the topic of the chapter.

- **Making It Happen** follows, which includes specific examples and vignettes demonstrating how to implement the ideas. For this, we offer what we call *examples and non-examples*, providing both positive strategies as well as examples to help us avoid falling inadvertently into traps of implicit bias and practices that exclude others. We will highlight the ways educational leaders may unintentionally sabotage their efforts through unconscious acts or colorblind behavior, and we laud examples of identity safe practices.

- **Rising to Challenges and Avoiding Pitfalls** is a section featuring some of the more complex aspects of identity safe leadership. Here, we focus on potential mistakes—and highlight some of our own that manifest when we neglect to operate with an identity safety lens.

- In **Closing the Gap Between Ideas and Action,** we summarize some key points in the chapter and present ideas for implementation.

- **Check Yourself** questions are included in each chapter to challenge our thinking as we reflect on our practice.

- **Using the Tools** ends each chapter with an activity for leaders that will also serve to move the work forward for their school. The tools we identify (reflections, surveys, and self-evaluation tools) can be used in study groups with other leaders, or independently for introspection. Either way, they are designed to support leaders in identifying and evaluating progress in order to advance to new levels of understanding and practice.

ABOUT OUR TERMINOLOGY

In identity safety, each word we employ conveys our belief system and attitudes regarding race and equity. We have been very intentional in our use of terminology, while recognizing that language about race and identity and labels that are commonly used in schools are continually evolving. To that end, we take care to emphasize the organic and transformative nature of identity, and by extension, the acronyms and terms that describe them. We represent them here as a moment in time while recognizing the freedom for them to change as new identities unfold within the natural medium of identity discovery. Because identity is fluid and flexible, the words we choose or that others impose on us require that as leaders, we continue to create an ongoing space for dialogue and understanding, to unpack the power of language. A tenet of identity safety honors the choice for people to self-identify, regardless of external perceptions of one's culture or group membership.

For our work here, we chose to capitalize the racial designations of Black, Brown, White, and Indigenous. We use the term "Black" to indicate people of African American, Caribbean, and African backgrounds. The term "Latinx" refers to people with heritages that draw from Mexico, Central and South America. We take note that some Latinx people are Black or Asian, and we honor their self-designation. The term "people of color" indicates Black, Latinx, Indigenous, South Asian, Asian, and people of mixed heritage.

We use the term LGBTQIA+ (an acronym for Lesbian, Gay, Bisexual, Transgender, Queer, Questioning, Intersex, Agender, Asexual, and additional emerging identities). We use the word "they" for people who identify as gender neutral or transgender and have selected that pronoun for personal and public use. In another usage, they/them/their can describe an individual (e.g., Each student can choose the book that they want). This usage is accepted by the *Merriam-Webster Collegiate Dictionary* (Merriam-Webster, n.d.). This language is more inclusive and is being used increasingly in common parlance.

We frequently refer to equalizing status in the book. By this we mean efforts are made to ensure that people of varied social identities are afforded an equal measure of respect and value, and they are treated fairly. Efforts are also made to undo policies and procedures that perpetuate inequity.

With an intent to express inclusivity, we chose to use the comparatively lengthy term "parent/caregiver" to describe parents, grandparents, foster parents, and all the people who serve as guardians of our students. Finally, we have opted to frequently use the word "educator" to ensure we are including all educational roles including teacher, administrator, paraprofessional, counselor, coach, and others.

WHO ARE THE EDUCATIONAL LEADERS WHO WILL BENEFIT FROM THIS BOOK?

This book is for anyone and everyone in a school community who thinks about and cares to take action to influence the school culture. These are individuals who are willing to become architects for identity safe spaces, both in and outside the classroom. Leaders can emerge from any group within the school community, including roles both traditional and less so. Principals and assistant principals, superintendents, directors, and teachers are likely candidates, but parents, paraprofessionals, and even community leaders can successfully catalyze and lead efforts to affect change.

The Many Paths to Leadership

Principal leader: Lorraine Monroe (1997), an African American woman, founder, and former principal of the Frederick Douglas Academy in Harlem, transformed her school through opportunities for personal and academic growth resulting in 98% of students attending college.

Campus supervisor leader: Janet worked as a campus supervisor at a large elementary school. Beyond keeping students physically safe, she helped them feel pride in their identities. On one occasion, she organized a luncheon where students read their poems to the mayor. On another occasion, she brought students to meet the Black Caucus in the state capitol.

Teacher leader: After the protests for the police murder of George Floyd, Kelly Palma, a high school teacher, approached her principal and asked for a staff meeting devoted to discussing the impact of racism. That led to Kelly facilitating that meeting and extending it into a four-part series on microaggressions, implicit bias, and comfort zones. They plan to continue the professional development into the next semester.

Parent leaders: Black parents at Design 39, a school in San Diego's Poway district, formed a group called "Small and Mighty" in an effort to improve belonging and inclusion for their children. They approached their principal, Joe Erpelding, and together created training for the teachers, addressed the district principals at a meeting, and held online discussions with the parent community, which led to ongoing efforts to better serve Black students within the district.

Student leaders: In response to a sexual harassment incident at their Richmond, California, high school, a team of peer leaders designed and led a Gender Awareness Day with the whole school community. The day was an extremely powerful learning experience for students, staff, and parents/caregivers and has since become an annual event.

This book is for anyone within a wide variety of roles in the school community who is willing to approach identity safety with a long-term commitment. This person will be ready to include many voices, inviting others to contribute and participate in decisions, ask the hard questions when needed, and facilitate transformation. In other words, anyone with the will to do so can step forward.

Check Yourself

Throughout the book we pose many questions for readers to ask themselves and to reflect, and we also provide *check yourself* questions. We believe that to move beyond the status quo and investigate fairly some of the widely held illusions that our society holds for all groups requires us to challenge ourselves to probe more deeply.

- What am I doing to refute and counter stereotypes and address stereotype threat with students?

- What can we do to learn about systemic racism and uproot it in our school?

- Are we providing role models that demonstrate people of all backgrounds and gender identities in nontraditional careers?

- Are we helping students gain the necessary social skills to treat one another with respect and be prepared to have healthy consensual sexual relationships?

- Are we teaching history from the perspectives of people of color, women, and LGBTQIA+ members of society?

Using the Tools

Stepping Into the Work

The very crux of what it means to be a school leader who orchestrates within the community with magnanimity, deference, and grace for all its members is epitomized in the principles and practices of identity safe ideas. This book is intended to introduce you to them, and educational leaders can then further avail themselves of the many resources in each chapter. These resources will carry you further toward a deeper understanding of all the aspects for an identity safe school. Take the time to learn more about identity safety, stereotype threat, privilege, microaggressions, and anti-racist education, and you will prosper in your ability to inform all your actions in a way that will resonate with and benefit those who depend on your support. You can use the following questions to reflect on your practice as an identity safe educator and leader and refer to them as you read the book.

Educate Yourself

1. How can you broaden your education about identity safety? What topics are still unfamiliar to you? Which ones have you studied but may need to update or explore further in order to address it with full cognizance in your school?

Ask Yourself

1. What are your areas of strength as a leader?

2. Can you identify areas where you will benefit from more growth?

3. What will you do to bolster your areas of growth?

Know Your School Community

1. Who do you consider your allies at your site?

2. Who have you not reached out to yet? How can you connect with these persons?

3. Who are your mentors or people you can confide in either at the school or in your personal life?

4. How can you frame all community members in a positive light when they are the topic of discussion?

5. How can you guard sensitive information in ways that respect those for whom the information affects?

Assess Your School for Identity Safe Practices

1. In what ways does your school already embody identity safe principles? Consider classrooms, the schoolyard, and your school families.

2. What areas on your campus can you recognize that need attention? Where does it feel unsafe, and what can you do?

Assessing your school will be more fully examined in Chapter 7.

Pace Yourself

You can start small and grow. Change can be a slow process, depending on who is on board and the level of change that is needed. Especially in the beginning when meticulous attention is required, it can make perfect sense to take it a step at a time. To begin, you can ask yourself

1. What are your starting points?

2. How will you measure progress?

3. What entry points can you use in your school practices and policies to initiate and implement different aspects of identity safety?

Entry points for identity safety are explored fully in Chapter 6.

In each case, these processes will lead to changes that positively impact your entire school community, including students and families from all backgrounds. Students of color, those from low-income families, and others who have experienced stereotypes due to their English learner status, students in special education, and those with other differences may recognize considerable benefit. White students and those from privileged backgrounds will also gain substantially, both academically and emotionally, from the caring environments of identity safe classrooms.

 Available for download as a full-page form at https://resources.corwin.com/BelongingandInclusionISS

Leadership for an Identity Safe School

Introduction

Leadership styles are as varied and unique as the number of people willing to lead. Given dedication and conviction, the personal style of leadership for any leader can carry identity safety forward across the school community. Strong leaders empower staff to support students in thinking creatively and independently, using their knowledge, skills, and determination for reaching their highest potentials (Blankstein, 2004; Nieto, 1998; Noguera, 2003). The link between education and equity is upheld by every child's right to learn and the need for an educated citizenry in a democratic nation (Banks, 2005; Darling-Hammond, 1997; Kozol, 2005; Ladson-Billings, 1999).

Identity safe leaders wear many hats, orchestrating within each role to create a positive climate and establish pathways for student voice and agency. They create conditions for the inclusion of all voices and foster a climate that is anti-racist and anti-oppressive. Creating equitable assessment systems, they guide and mentor staff. They facilitate continual professional learning and engage students, staff, and families in decision-making. Their words and deeds are in sync, and their vision leads to identity safe students of all backgrounds who achieve at high levels. This includes students with special needs, English learners, and those who require alternative modes of instruction. Each child is provided the resources needed to scaffold their learning.

As our world rushes toward change at an exponential rate, and as the United States advances toward the year when White people no longer constitute the majority of the population, more educators are recognizing the urgency to cultivate diversity within the school system. Identity safe leaders will discover themselves ahead of the curve as they build their schools into learning organizations fostering equal status and opportunity for all students. These leaders build awareness and prepare their staff with an equity lens, promote culturally relevant teaching methods, and confront racism and all forms of bias directly and with confidence.

Leadership for an identity safe school is grounded in the seven principles of identity safety, outlined in Chapter 1. We restate them in this case, as they pertain to leadership:

1. **Colorblind teaching** that ignores differences is a barrier to inclusion in the classroom.

   Leaders learn how to avoid the colorblind trap for themselves and staff, modeling openness about their own backgrounds. They encourage all members of the school community to participate with their full social identities salient. When leaders articulate this principle and share its purpose, staff will be more likely to embrace and enact it with students.

2. **To feel a sense of belonging and acceptance** requires creating positive relationships between teacher and students and among students with equal status for different social identities.

   Leaders have a unique opportunity and responsibility to foster belonging and acceptance for everyone. They are often the ones who are first to become aware of newly enrolled students, families in crisis, and other factors that can create potentially isolating conditions for children. They also know which students are repeatedly subject to exclusion or bullying and need support. Leaders work with staff to restructure school policies and traditions in order to nurture positive relationships and equalize status.

3. **Cultivating diversity** as a resource for learning and expressing high expectations for students promotes learning, competence, and achievement.

   In identity safety, diversity is a resource for learning in all curricular areas. Educational leaders ensure its application through professional learning about culturally relevant pedagogy. Leaders also make resources available from primary source curriculum banks to classroom libraries with expository and fictional sources for every grade level and subject. They lead staff and parent/caregiver dialogue about race and help teachers learn to facilitate these conversations with their students. Leaders draw from the cultural capital of all their students and families to enrich the school culture. Leaders hold high expectations for students and staff, giving positive feedback that communicates belief in their potential. These skills can be taught to educators so that they will be able to translate them into their practice with their students.

A powerful way to cultivate diversity for learning is to diversify staff to mirror the student body. Students benefit in many ways from being around adults who look like them and are likely to share many of their values and cultural practices. The presence of staff of color not only provides meaningful support to students but also can serve to change the conversations in staff meetings with discussions that guide decision-making to include the interests and needs of all students.

4. **Educators examine their own social identities** to feel a sense of identity safety and convey that feeling to students, creating an identity safe environment for them.

   This process of unpacking social identities centers on race, culture, gender, and economic status, as well as religion, age, and other influences that have shaped who we are today. We begin with ourselves and then work with everyone in our community to build awareness, understanding, and readiness to overcome stereotypes, biases, inequitable policies or structures, and other constraints related to our social identities. We build an environment in which people of all social identities are valued and embraced as their full selves. Leaders can take part in this process and provide time for staff members to safely reflect and choose what to share within their comfort zone.

5. **Social and emotional safety** is created by supporting students in defining their identities, refuting negative stereotypes, and countering stereotype threat, giving them a voice in the classroom while using social and emotional learning (SEL) strategies.

   Leaders can ensure that their staff recognize the powerful alliance between academic achievement and a culture of social emotional support. The cognitive and affective parts of ourselves are constantly interacting when we learn. As leaders develop prosocial skills and engage in positive relationships, including the ability to collaborate, they prepare students for school and beyond. The identity safe leader models and practices positive social and emotional skills, understands trauma-informed practice, and supports staff in integrating social and emotional learning throughout their curriculum.

6. **Student learning** is enhanced in diverse classrooms by teaching for understanding, creating opportunities for shared inquiry and dialogue, and offering a challenging, rigorous curriculum.

Identity safe leaders demonstrate strong instructional leadership as they work to ensure student-centered teaching practices, which include teaching for understanding while upholding rigor, challenging leaders to secure a robust curriculum tailored to students' needs. These leaders are well versed in curriculum and instruction and stay abreast of new research and best practices. They are open to meaningful feedback from data, surveys, and personal interviews from all stakeholders. They use it to inform their practice, adjusting for optimal results to support rigorous teaching and learning in identity safe ways. They are adept at facilitating staff in collaborating to meet the wide range of academic needs, thereby devolving from an old model of top-down authority where methods and desired results were merely dictated.

7. **Schoolwide equity** flourishes for everyone in identity safe schools where the climate, the structures, practices, and attitudes prioritize equity, inclusion, and academic growth for students from all backgrounds. Leaders demonstrate emotional intelligence; attend to student needs; address racism, bias, and privilege; and serve as the architects of ongoing change.

Equitable policies and practices can be a galvanizing force to help reverse the effects of long-standing racist school systems. Leaders give attention to how resources are fairly deployed to support achievement for students of color. They ensure disciplinary practices are not biased. They provide English language services for students and establish policies to address racial slurs and prevent bullying and teasing. They equip schools with gender-neutral bathrooms and allow transgender students to use bathrooms that match their gender identity. They ensure that staff get the training and resources needed to develop and thrive as culturally responsive educators.

Strong leadership spreads identity safety at an exponential rate, but this doesn't mean change relies solely on one leader. Successful leaders establish multiple helms with copilots to accommodate the myriad needs of the community in service to the students. Distributed leadership structures, such as role-alike teams and multistakeholder school councils, will further expand how the school is shaped by the voices and knowledge of the community. As we stated in Chapter 1, influential leaders may not always hold positional power; rather, they leverage their roles to influence change.

A review of research (Leithwood, Seashore Louis, Anderson, & Wahlstrom, 2004) for how leadership influences student learning states that

> successful leadership can play a highly significant—and frequently underestimated—role in improving student learning. Specifically, the available evidence about the size and nature of the effects of successful leadership on student learning justifies two important claims: 1. Leadership is second only to classroom instruction among all school-related factors that contribute to what students learn at school, . . . and 2. Leadership effects are usually largest where and when they are needed most. (p. 5)

To the second point, the report explains, "Existing research shows that demonstrated effects of successful leadership are considerably greater in schools that are in more difficult circumstances. Indeed, there are virtually no documented instances of troubled schools being turned around without intervention by a powerful leader. Many other factors may contribute to such turnarounds, but leadership is the catalyst" (p. 5).

In addition to the two claims stated above, we identify in the "Why It Matters" section two significant reasons why leadership matters specifically in an identity safe school: the importance of an ethical stance reflected in all our actions and the power of equity-centered leadership. We also consider some of the different challenges faced by White leaders and leaders of color.

In the "Making It Happen" section, we describe the leadership stances (the stands we take that reflect our attitudes and beliefs) that serve us for the impetus and motivation they provide to all of our decisions. They include equity consciousness, cultural humility, a growth mindset, and compassion. We also consider the skills and competence—which can often be gained from practice—that we believe will help move your school toward identity safety. This includes self-awareness, listening and engaging others, relationship-building, instructional leadership, problem-solving, and consensus-building and change management. While leadership is a broad topic with many books written about it, we have opted to target specific stances and skills most needed for an identity safe school. We then add approaches for working with staff, which include diversifying, supervising, and retaining staff. In Chapter 7 we offer examples of planning processes on how to achieve an identity safe campus.

Why It Matters

ETHICS AND EDUCATIONAL LEADERSHIP IN CHANGING TIMES

According to Michael Fullan (2001), the imperative of rapid changes (which can encompass societal and governmental upheavals, or cultural changes within a single school) necessitates leadership that is capable of incorporating moral purpose, understanding change, developing relationships, knowledge-building, and coherence-making. In an identity safe school, leaders direct their moral compass toward student learning and social and emotional needs, which form the basis for every decision. Relationships guide all interactions, placing it within a leader's purview to prioritize building strong relationships with groups and between individuals.

Fullan (2001) describes moral purpose as a leader's motivation to seek positive outcomes for all stakeholders. Moral purpose starts with a clear understanding of one's own values and a willingness to examine how they manifest in both small and large decisions, affecting all their actions (O'Neil, 1996). The identity safe leader is guided by a primary attitude of compassion and fairness, coupled with a desire to contribute to the well-being of others. With a world in flux, a leader works to at once understand the change process, adapt to the constantly changing conditions, and build coherence into the process while remaining a solid and steady support for others. Leaders keep their ship afloat, continually tracking newly arising information while also serving as an anchor for their stakeholders. Fullan (2001) compared a thriving learning organization to a living system where entities actually experience the most risk during times when they are static. He suggests that when conditions of threat push organisms to the brink of danger, an effective leader will lead to the times when they experiment, mutate, or reorganize and renew themselves to survive.

For identity safe educators, their internal vision and moral compass, which guides them toward diversity, equity, and inclusion, can help them prioritize to determine what is most important. Our compass guides our intuition, good will, and judgment in the wake of the external pressures, unintended consequences, and mandates that continually bombard us.

In Chapter 1, we address "othering" as a habit of categorizing individuals and groups based on identifiable and manufactured differences with an intent to establish superiority as well as manipulate and dominate those categorized as "other." Identity safe leaders seek out the nuances of how othering operates in subtle and not-so-subtle ways in systems. By taking into consideration historical and cultural aspects of the impact of white supremacy, we work to mitigate the inappropriate use of power and privilege (Bogotch & Shields, 2014).

Likely all of us have seen the impact of a weak leader. The weakness may lie in an inability to communicate accurately, compassionately, or fairly. In other cases, a leader may neglect to follow through on projects or promises. The results can be devastating—in a short time, the culture of a school can erode, morale plummets, and even a staff exodus can ensue. The evidence can be seen on the tense faces of staff, and eventually it takes its toll through the erratic behavior of students, ultimately affecting their achievement.

Conversely, a dynamic leader with a strong moral compass can transform a school from a place where nobody wants to work, where parents/caregivers do not want to send their children, to a place where parents/caregivers are lining up to attend. How can a leader accomplish this? It starts with building trust, in showing the community you care, that you are willing to take hard stands and keep your promises. If you reach out to involve students and families, they will join you to forge a shared vision—one based on identity safe practices, anti-racism, and educational equity. Then, together you can nurture a school culture based on a collective vision. The school community wants to see that you can effectively manage operations and resources, remove obstacles, and solve problems while empowering teams to ensure student success. Powerful teaching and learning are not simply the results of expert principals who espouse a vision of desired results but rather teams of educators who are empowered to work together.

ETHICS AND EQUITY-CENTERED LEADERSHIP

All duties ascribed to an administrator gain an added ethical dimension when viewed through an equity lens. This dimension does not require harder work or more time but rather illuminates all decisions and school interactions. This applies to everything from curricular planning, student referrals, discipline, and disciplinary hearings, and to interactions such as yard and hallway supervision. Administrators also use their equity lens as they recruit and hire, and establish meeting and training topics and activities. Their lens is adjusted as well when they supervise teachers and make decisions about tenure.

Positionality, Power, and Privilege

It is not enough to claim identification for not being a racist person. "Not being racist" describes a passive position that does nothing to alleviate real-world conditions for racism.

> The opposite of racist isn't "not racist." It is "anti-racist." What's the difference? One endorses either the idea of a racial hierarchy as a racist, or racial equality as an anti-racist. One either believes problems are rooted in groups of people, as a racist, or locates the roots of problems

in power and policies, as an anti-racist. One either allows racial inequities to persevere as a racist, or confronts racial inequities, as an anti-racist. There is no in-between space of "not racist." (Kendi, 2019, p. 9)

Identity safe leaders understand this difference. There is no middle road for taking a stand against racism. Yes, it does entail some of the hardest work to initiate and sustain change, but on the other side of that bridge lies some of the most rewarding experiences available for educators: a community aligned with the same values, working toward the same goals—not in spite of, but in celebration of their differences. Toward this end, we engage in self-reflection and develop self-awareness on how power, privilege, and oppression impact us personally as well as historically. Regardless of our identity markers, we have all grown up in a racist system. Like fish who are accustomed to living in polluted waters, we often do not see it. Taking a stance as anti-racists, it behooves all leaders to look deeply at positionality and privilege.

Whether you are a person with positional or influential power, you need to carefully consider how power in itself affords privilege. This requires your consideration on how to use it. We all have power over some situations and lack power in others. We do well to hold ourselves in check with the authority assigned to us and consider how to best use our measure of power to elevate the voices of others. At other times, we use our voice to speak the truth to power while standing for fairness and social justice. The process of tackling issues of equity and anti-racism is challenging for all leaders, but it is worth considering some particular challenges faced by leaders of color and different challenges that White leaders face as they undertake school transformation.

Leaders of Color and White Leaders Face Different Challenges

According to a survey of superintendents (Modan, 2020), White males dominate the field. The number of superintendents of color rose from 5% in 2000 to 8.6% in 2020. The number of female superintendents rose from 13% in 2000 to 26% in 2020. Site leadership is dominated by White males as well, while classrooms are dominated by White female teachers. These numbers leave us with a long way to go to mirror the population these leaders should represent. Many leaders of color walk a tightrope in retaining employment and negotiating with systems that often place many stumbling blocks in their path. Hiring teams often use the phrase "it's just not a match," which allows them to pass over a Black or Latinx principal candidate without having their personal biases challenged. A 2017 Harvard University study showed persistent racial discrimination in hiring against Black and Latinx Americans with little or no change over the last 25 years (Quillian, et al., 2017).

In 2020, Vice President Kamala Harris was the first woman of color to represent a major party on the presidential debate stage. A *New York Times* article titled "Kamala

Harris and the 'Double Bind' of Racism and Sexism" (Astor, 2020) depicted the challenges she faced, which ranged from name-calling by members of the opposing party to relentless criticism that she was too strong or opinionated. The article described how she had to walk a fine line between stereotypes of women as the weaker sex and an old racist trope targeting the "angry Black woman," characterized as emasculating, aggressive, and hostile. Identity safe schools seek to diversify the field of school leadership, revising hiring practices and refuting the stereotypes and double standards applied to leaders and all educators of color.

Considerations for Leaders of Color

Brandy, a Black leader, was promoted from teacher, to coach, to principal in a school in Arizona where she had worked for 15 years. The first year as principal, she found herself constantly having to prove herself to the parent community. They often asked intrusive questions about her credentials and experience, ignoring the many years she had given to their community that led to her selection as principal.

For leaders of color, personal understanding of the experiences and perspectives of people of color, as well as awareness of racist tendencies or implicit bias from Whites—including those with authority over them—will help in considering in advance ways to handle sensitive situations or additional pressures. A Black principal may be accused of only caring about Black students. A White parent may complain that efforts to create equitable conditions for students they perceive as different from their own will detract resources and advantage from their children. Leaders can educate the community that equity will not lead to a zero-sum game with winners and losers. A win for any subgroup or even one person in this context is a win for all.

Self-reflection provides a space for leaders of color to unpack tensions and build resilience for responding to the biases of others, as well as recognizing their own biases. In the book *Flipping the Script: White Privilege and Community Building*, Donna K. Bivens (2005), author of the chapter "What Is Internalized Racism?," writes,

> As people of color are victimized by racism, we internalize it. That is, we develop ideas, beliefs, actions, and behaviors that support or collude with racism. This internalized racism has its own systemic reality, and its own negative consequences in the lives and communities of people of color. More than just a consequence of racism, then, internalized racism is a systemic oppression in reaction to racism that has a life of its own. In other words, just as there is a system in place that reinforces the power and expands the privilege of White people, there is a system in place that actively discourages and undermines the power of people of color. (p. 44)

It's easy for a leader of color to feel alone in an educational setting where White staff dominate. It can help immeasurably to connect with others outside your place of work, if needed, to establish a community. You can benefit from participating in support groups and networks such as the National Alliance of Black School Educators (https://www.nabse.org/), Education Leaders of Color (https://edloc.org/), the National Indian Education Association (https://www.niea.org), Latinos for Education (https://www.latinosforeducation.org/about-us/), and Asian American Youth Leadership and Empowerment (https://www.aalead.org/).

Considerations for White Leaders

For White leaders, attending to power and privilege is foundational for an identity safe school. A White leader holds both white privilege and positional authority. By acknowledging white privilege and taking steady action to ensure equal status and opportunity for all community members, a White leader builds trust for their positional authority. When white privilege goes unaddressed, this trust is fragile or missing, particularly when working with people of color and other historically marginalized groups. White leaders can come to understand that white privilege is always in play. Even when they don't intend to leverage it as power, it remains. This is expressed first and foremost by the very fact that a White leader holds a position of power in a system that systematically denies that access to people of color (Jones, 2020).

Cultural humility, an invaluable tool for White leaders, describes an interpersonal stance that centers on understanding and responding to aspects of cultural identity and experience that are most important to others (Waters & Asbill, 2013). White people are generally not raised to "see" racism or to see how color defines many aspects of experience and opportunity in society. During the spring 2020 racial justice uprising, many White people became newly aware of systemic racism, an awareness that people of color do not have the option to avoid. Cultural humility acknowledges these gaps in awareness and knowledge and directs them to start from a place of listening and witnessing.

White leaders can take a multifaceted approach to listening and witnessing to avoid inadvertently placing the burden of teaching on a small number of people of color that they work with or serve. This includes sustaining representative, diverse stakeholder structures discussed throughout this book, such as parent/caregiver advisory councils, racial and other types of affinity groups, and broader community dialogue and activist networks. White leaders can also listen and witness—and use what they read and watch—to seek, hear, and respond to a diverse range of voices.

For identity safety to thrive, White leaders work to model and assist other White people to develop a positive racial identity. In her 1992 book *A Race Is a Nice Thing to Have*, Janet Helms outlines a six-stage framework of positive White identity development. White leaders represent and encounter development all along this spectrum, from the person who doesn't see themselves as White and embraces colorblindness, to the person committed to evolving through steady action to be anti-racist. Books such as *A Race Is a Nice Thing to Have* (Helms, 1992) and *How to Be an Anti-Racist* by Ibram X. Kendi (2019), as well as training such as offered by Embracing Equity (https://embracingequity.org/) and Showing Up for Racial Justice (SURJ) (https://www.showingupforracialjustice.org/) are invaluable resources for leading this critical aspect of the work.

One White Leader's Journey

Joe Erpelding was raised in a Catholic family in a white neighborhood. It was all he had known before his father sent him to an intermediate magnet school where he met students from many different backgrounds and ethnicities. He feels grateful today for that exposure to different cultures, yet nothing prepared him for the day when he was a principal at Design 39, a TK-8 grade elementary school, and was approached by Chas, a Black parent. Chas told Erpelding that Black students were being called the N-word and asked, "What are you going to do about it?" Joe thought (with a measure of trepidation in light of his inexperience), "What am I going to do about it?" He decided to bring together the Black parents in the school for a meeting to discuss the issue. He was nervous, but he understood himself as a person willing to be "led by challenge," and with this attitude, he approached the room where they were to meet.

This became the first meeting of many for Joe and the "Small and Mighty" group of Black parents, as they came to be known. They took Joe under their wing, and by his testimony, taught him much. They began with the understanding that they were going to engage in "real talk," and not allow the truth to be hijacked from an overabundance of politeness. Joe knew he needed an education. Amon, a member of the group, informed Joe that "there are two Americas," and explained what it meant for his son and himself to simply leave the house and go somewhere, anywhere, in their car. They had to make certain that they had their driver's licenses and insurance cards ready to grab and show in case they were stopped by the police. They also had to remember, as Black males, to shuffle their feet in a parking garage so as not to surprise or frighten anyone. One of the parents told Joe, "I don't need you to talk for me, I just need you to stand by me." Joe learned that as a White male, he could use his positional power to bring opportunities to the group. He did, and they accomplished much together, which is detailed in Chapter 5. Joe and the Small and Mighty parents continue their work in the district because, as Chas stated emphatically in an online Town Hall meeting with the parent community, "At the end of the day, it's about our children."

For White leaders, attending to their power and privilege will better attune them to the needs of students whose backgrounds are different from theirs. They can increase their awareness of those times that they display implicit bias or express microaggressions, and work to change their attitudes and behaviors. Attending to these sensitivities, they will also be better prepared for moments when they receive "charged" feedback implicating them as racist or advocates of racist policies or attitudes. A centered, anti-racist approach can enable them to listen and refrain from defensive and reactive responses, or fall into traps of white fragility (DiAngelo, 2018). Furthermore, once leaders acknowledge privilege, they can use it to benefit identity safety for all.

Challenging Our Biases

Educational leaders of all backgrounds can become attuned to biases within themselves and others—the latter with an intent to observe, educate, and mitigate when necessary. The responsibility for learning about the experiences of people with a host of targeted social identities (gender, social class, disability) and intersectional identities extends to all of us. In service to our self-reflection, asking questions can help identify blind spots, which includes uncovering personal perspectives that pertain to people outside our social or identity group.

When working to create identity safe schools, it is important to acknowledge the diversity that exists within every group, including race, ethnicity, and culture. Gender identities, for example, are varied in all ethnic groups. Among Blacks, there are African Americans, African immigrants, Caribbean Blacks, and more. Among Latinx, we find people born in the United States and immigrants from Mexican, Central American, and South American countries—each with different customs and traditions. Asians also have varied backgrounds from many different countries and experiences. Indigenous people belong to many tribes. Lumping and labeling people into homogenous groups invites unsubstantiated assumptions that lead to stereotyping.

People from all ethnic groups engage, at times, in biased attitudes and behaviors within their group. Examples include some communities of color that have grown up with colorism, the attitude that lighter skin is more beautiful and acceptable, or terms like "FOB" (fresh off the boat) and "ABC" (American-born Chinese), which are used by some members of the Chinese American community to emphasize social hierarchies. Leaders can also deepen their understanding of the complexities of intersectionality for oppressed identities, such as a transgender/Latinx person or a Black/Muslim. With a keen eye on what we want to accomplish, we can uncover and work to rectify the subtle and not-so-subtle inequities, both real and perceived, that emerge as we lead diverse communities.

As we take on the challenge of identity safe leadership, we keep our moral purpose and our commitment to equity-centered leadership in our minds and hearts at all times. By openly acknowledging our positionality as leaders—and our awareness of the power and privilege it affords us—we will be ready to take on the challenge of leading a diverse community. As we work to actualize these commitments, we enhance our allyship with youth and adults. From here, we examine how identity safe leaders can make it happen.

Making It Happen

When we view everything through an identity safe lens in our work, certain attitudes, stances, and skills will naturally present themselves. In this section, we will identify the most important attributes in this regard as you calibrate your own lens and take action. You can select those traits first that you feel will most benefit your growth as an equity-minded leader.

We have selected some specific areas of focus for stances to adopt while prioritizing for identity safe school transformation. From there, we target specific skills needed by an identity safe leader seeking to make transformative change. We conclude the section with a focus on the leader's role in human resources.

THE STANCES OF AN IDENTITY SAFE LEADER

Our stances determine how we show up in our lives, in our work, and in the world. They actuate our frame of mind, opinions, and the words we speak. They guide our decisions. Stances that speak to identity safety include the following:

- **Equity consciousness:** An awareness and commitment to equity and social justice.

- **Cultural humility:** Awareness of multiple perspectives with an intent to understand and respect differences in backgrounds and beliefs.

- **Growth mindset:** An understanding that everyone is continually growing and learning and gaining knowledge as they go. A leader's growth mindset stance serves as a model for others.

- **Compassion:** An attitude and a way of seeing and being with ourselves and others where we seek to alleviate harm and suffering (Greater Good Science Center, n.d.).

Equity Consciousness

Identity safe leaders develop an awareness of the level of equity and inequity present in behaviors, policies, settings, organizations, and outcomes. In identity safe schools, diversity as a resource is manifested by giving students plentiful opportunities to share their life experiences in multiple classes and over the span of their entire school years.

Identity Safe Practices at Humanitas Academy

A Leadership Policy Institute case study (Ondrasek & Flook, 2018) about the Social Justice Humanitas Academy in Los Angeles Unified School District (LAUSD) describes how students are offered many opportunities to integrate their identities and lives into the content of the curriculum. In one example, ninth graders do a deep dive into their personal histories and consider them in the context of what is going on in the world. In one example, students read *Always Running*, a memoir by Luis Rodriguez (2005), where the author describes his youth on the streets of East L.A. After reading the book, students wrote essays analyzing how the author overcame the obstacles in his life and became self-actualized (one of their school's core values). Their essays identified "cultural wealth—including aspirational, familial, and navigational capital—and grit as important resources for overcoming trauma and achieving self-actualization. Their essays highlight the types of deep engagement that culturally responsive pedagogy can foster" (Ondrasek & Flook, 2018, para. 29).

In 2018, when the case study was completed, Humanitas students enjoyed a high graduation rate, with over 80% of the students achieving college and career readiness. In a district survey, Humanitas students reported feeling safe at school, a positive sense of belonging, and acceptance at school. Ninety percent said that "adults at my school treat students with respect," and 88% indicated that they "feel they have a voice in decision making," compared to only a quarter of students in the rest of the district (Ondrasek & Flook, 2018, para. 33). Ondrasek and Flook (2018) observed that "identity safety doesn't emerge from just one approach. With a multitude of practices in place—such as those at Humanitas—students from diverse backgrounds can come to understand that their social identities are wholly compatible with educational achievement, and that their unique perspectives add value to their communities, both within the classroom and beyond" (para. 35). In concert with this sentiment, Juan Miramontes, a senior at UC Berkeley, is quoted on the Humanitas website stating, "The academics got me here, but it is the values and love SJHA instilled in me that gets me through" (Humanitas, n.d.).

Identity safe leaders provide for the expression of diverse voices and perspectives in every aspect of school life. This includes noticing which students are called upon to speak and which ones sit silent in their classrooms. Safeguarding fair choices for students to participate on the debate team or enjoy representation on the student council are within the scope of an identity safe leader. When they see a discrepancy, they can work to increase access and representation.

Nancy, a principal in Wisconsin, recounts,

> There used to be a lot of hand-wringing that there were hardly any students of color in Advanced Placement classes. I posed the issue to the subject matter departments and asked them to come up with solutions. The English Department returned with a proposal to stop tracking all incoming ninth graders. We had pushback from some parents who were worried that mixed ability groupings would dumb down curriculum and set their children back. I assured them that all classes would embody high standards. This was just a first step for us. We will monitor carefully and see what worked and what we need to tweak. I am hoping other departments will follow.

Egalitarian structures, where all voices are heard in mixed-ability groups, show everyone that their thoughts, ideas, and opinions matter.

This recognition for group diversity and integration of specific student identities into the curriculum and classroom practices will promote a sense of equity and equal value for all.

Cultural Humility

When we engage in cultural humility, we understand that we don't know everything there is to know about other cultures, and we humble ourselves with that presumption. This means we clear out any of our own preconceived inner biases, not just once, but throughout our lives as new ones arise. Only then are we prepared to listen to others—and keep listening—for experiences are always in flux. We allow for the changing sensibilities and ideas others express and share about their cultures as new events and circumstances develop in their lives. We remain open and listening.

This process begins with understanding ourselves in regard to culture. We consider our judgments—we search for and identify our implicit and explicit biases—and we seek to suspend them and avoid assumptions about people from other cultures and backgrounds. We respectfully approach people who are different from us with an open mind and an interest in learning more. While we aim to treat people of all social identities with kindness and compassion, we recognize that we have much to learn from people who do not share our social identities. Orienting toward compassion for others is a way of opening our hearts and minds to see, understand, and empathize with a sense of humility. It provides us with a willingness to presume nothing and a desire to learn. Many well-intentioned efforts by White people to be culturally responsive operate from a perspective of whiteness as a norm, without realizing that people of color are often treated as the "other." White leaders can acknowledge power imbalances and seek to rectify them. They can work to understand how that might affect people of color and their responses to White leaders. The stance of cultural humility requires a lifelong commitment to self-reflection on our attitudes, beliefs, and actions.

Growth Mindset

When we nurture a growth mindset in ourselves, we cultivate a habit to remain open and flexible, always learning and growing. When new circumstances or information arise, we develop a mindset to receive the new input and integrate it with and balance it against what we already know. This can lead to innovation and many new ideas, while we adjust and learn from our mistakes as well. In this manner, we not only are able to mature our thinking and plans, but as leaders we are positioned to support both adults and students around us to develop their cognitive and emotional intelligence—as well as their talents and abilities—by encouraging their efforts to learn. With a growth mindset, we focus on the process and the journey, not simply the outcome. When we confront obstacles and make mistakes, which is inevitable as we lead and manage a school, we seek to learn from them while we avoid pointing fingers and blaming others. We take accountability for our actions, share our vulnerabilities, and aim for transparency with our communities.

When leaders model a growth mindset, they set the stage for classroom teachers to follow suit. The stance can become a way of abiding in flexibility for everyone. According to Carol Dweck (Cohn-Vargas, et al., 2020), when identity safe teaching is integrated with a growth mindset approach, students are able "to continually grow and reach their highest potential."

Compassion

Author Kristin Neff (2020) writes, "Compassion engages our capacity for love, wisdom, courage, and generosity. It's a mental and emotional state that's boundless and directionless . . . available to every person simply by virtue of our being human" (para 21). Orienting ourselves toward compassion is manifest in three ways: compassion toward others, receiving compassion from others, and compassion for ourselves (Cohn-Vargas et al., 2020). All three ways lead to deeper understanding and acceptance and healing. As we turn "toward each other," we exercise the capacity to support and nurture one another. Compassion is essential for establishing a climate of identity safety. Without it, a leader's relationships with staff, students, and the community will experience a reduced impact on both their work and their creative energies. A stance of compassion adds great value for stabilizing the sometimes unpredictable challenges that can crop up in the change process. It provides us with a lens to view all exchanges and events without fear, and it prompts us to approach others with language that affirms, assures, and strengthens everyone's stance to keep the faith and persevere.

Moving beyond personal stances that lead to identity safety, we examine the skills that will help leaders rally others to stand with them. When stakeholders are on board, an identity safe leader will support the team with skill-building, designing, and managing change processes that will move the school ahead.

SKILLS OF IDENTITY SAFE LEADERS

To be a leader of a complex system is challenging. We are each naturally endowed with aptitudes. Other competencies are gained from study, practice, and experience. We all excel in different ways. Some leaders enjoy interpersonal skills that enable them to motivate others, bringing groups of people together to create a sense of team, or—even better—a sense of family. Some are great at delegating tasks; others excel as dynamic speakers. Yet still more are attracted to data and use it to drive toward concrete results. Some are clear thinkers in a crisis or shine as problem-solvers. It isn't necessary to perform well in all areas when we begin, but ultimately strong interpersonal skills, in particular, are needed to manage change. It is within each of us to activate our established skills, learn new ones, and realize our untapped potential.

Personal leadership refers to the qualities that leaders manifest through social and emotional intelligence, which is not exclusive to any particular style of leadership or personalities. Each leader develops their unique style for expressing these valuable proficiencies. When we feel comfortable with our own range of emotions, we are better equipped to recognize and respect the feelings of others, promoting their ease and ours. People quickly perceive our reception of them, which will direct their responses. The moment we face students and their families, they can feel our sense of worth for them. Our desire to understand them will allow us to receive them in a way that they feel seen and heard. Strong personal leadership skills include relational and communication competencies needed for connecting with staff, students, families, and the community. This also includes the capacity to attend to student needs while dealing successfully as a conduit between the district, the community, and the staff. Our skills also help us to accept feedback without becoming defensive. We are ready to step up and effectively call out and redress bias and speak truth to power, including supervisors and other district leaders. Here are some of the skills and abilities that contribute to identity safe schools, which we shall address in the following sections:

- Self-awareness

- Relationship-building

- Listening and engaging others

- Instructional leadership

- Problem-solving and consensus-building

- Change management

Self-Awareness

Taking time to cultivate the practice of self-reflection launches the process for becoming an identity safety leader for students of all backgrounds, races, gender identities, religious affiliations, as well as all forms of intersectionality. As a continual practice, self-reflection guides leaders in all of their functions (Horng, et al., 2009). This laser focus, especially as it is practiced in the long haul, strengthens the confidence and courage needed to take strong stands on behalf of students and staff, or when a member of the community is targeted by bigotry or hate.

When we create a thoughtful space alone with the breathing room to build our resilience, we can better realize the tools we need to create a positive school climate. We are better prepared to address the microaggressions, counter negative stereotypes, and resolve conflicts that will certainly arise. Each person finds their own method of self-reflection. Some like to keep a journal, others do quiet meditation, while still others choose to talk through their thoughts and feelings with a confidante. The latter can make a great difference when we find a trusted friend or mentor with whom to process our reflections. We can share complex situations with them, checking for balance and clarity. They can also offer trusted and personal feedback as we work to improve ourselves as leaders.

An aspect of self-reflection for identity safe leaders involves shifting our internal focus to our own social identities. This prepares us to respond to the identities and social-emotional needs of students and staff with compassion and agility. In our self-examination, we unearth beliefs and attitudes, and we examine them for evidence of implicit and explicit biases. Most often, these biases were formed as children, before we developed the cognitive abilities to question their validity. We can, however, question them now. In service to our self-reflection, we shed light upon our blind spots by remaining alert to our passing thoughts and feelings and catching those moments when we hear ourselves judging or stereotyping a person or a group who is different from us. These watchful exercises are beneficial for leaders of all ethnicities and backgrounds. In effect, we clear our own inner canvas, gaining the clarity to bridge toward understanding the perspectives of people outside our social or identity group. We learn about others and remain ever ready with the courage to listen and speak up, openly expressing our vulnerabilities and protecting the sensitivities of others. Our growth in this skill set empowers us to address biased behaviors wherever we find them. We are better prepared to strengthen our capacity to acknowledge and learn from mistakes, take accountability for our actions, and attend to how others perceive us. In turn, this empowers us to better understand ourselves in a healthy cycle that reinforces our abilities to respond to the social-emotional needs of others appropriately. Reading books by anti-racist educators and attending self-awareness workshops and study groups also greatly assist the process of building awareness and a compendium for the large and varied social identities that can exist within a community.

In the "Using the Tools" section at the end of the chapter, we have identified a series of questions that will help you in this process. In Chapter 3, we describe self-reflective processes for staff, and in Appendix B you can find an additional Staff Self-Reflection Activity.

Relationship-Building

In Chapter 1, we highlighted the power of positive relationships as an essential ingredient that impacts every aspect of leadership. Additionally, relationships with and among students emerged as a key identity safe teaching component from the Stanford Integrated Schools Project (SISP) identity safe research (D. M. Steele, 2012). The same applies with adults. Many leaders are adept at the skill of building and sustaining positive relationships. For all relationships to be identity safe, we seek to foster acceptance, inclusion, and mutual respect in the context of a collaborative culture.

Leaders cannot execute the entire transformation of a school alone. By creating collaborative structures and processes, they empower stakeholders as shared participants in school change. Leaders are able to welcome a range of contributions to a learning organization, sharing in the habit of adapting and adjusting. By drawing on teacher leaders, TSAs (teachers on special assignment), mentors, and master teachers, leaders can empower a growing team to work on extending identity safe practices. Together, they can work with the staff to incorporate behaviors that will lead to well-being, equal status, and agency for students. Team members can be trained to model effective practices for their colleagues. Often, a respected colleague can make all the difference where other approaches may fail.

A Team Effort to Make School Safer for Transgender Students

When identity safe leaders have strong relationships with their staff teams, they are more likely to be successful when working to unpack practices that harm students and undo unfair policies. For example, at one school in Illinois, a survey alerted the principal that transgender students did not feel safe at the school. However, much of the staff had limited knowledge and experience for understanding and supporting transgender students. The principal invited a consultant from a national organization, Gender Spectrum (https://www.genderspectrum.org/), to lead a professional development session with staff to increase awareness of transgender student experiences and the challenges facing them. Following the session, leaders—together with several teachers—held a focus group with several transgender students. The focus group discussion revealed that students who had changed their names to match their transitioned identity felt uncomfortable from their first day in a new class when the teacher read their name off the roster, because it was their former name, which no longer represented their identities. The school's data system had not allowed students to change from the names that were listed when they first enrolled in school as children. The focus group leaders went back to Gender Spectrum to find out what other schools had done to reset their data systems. Using this new knowledge, they contacted the company in charge of their data system and were able to make the name changes and create a safer space in school for transgender students.

Relationships are nurtured through many different interactions—formal and informal—as well as when confronting challenging situations (e.g., giving support to a staff member who is having difficulty, or when grappling with a crisis). Strong relationships that engage with trust and bridge differences begin with listening.

Listening and Engaging Others

Identity safe leaders connect with students, staff, and the community by employing deep listening skills. This leadership skill is parallel to the SISP component called *listening for student voices*, which we apply here to include the entire school community (D. M. Steele, 2012). We can intentionally strengthen our capacity to actively listen to a range of student, staff, and community voices. Listening with humility includes attending to the words as well as the nonverbal cues—gestures, facial expressions, and tone of voice. We seek to listen in a nonjudgmental fashion and take care not to interrupt as we create meaning from a person's ideas, experiences, points of view, and the stories they share with us. We check for understanding by asking clarifying questions, paraphrasing, or summarizing to invite mutual understanding.

Louise Waters shares her wisdom and experience from her long career as an equity-focused educational leader, teacher, principal, superintendent, and education professor. In this story, she relates her motivation to start a "listening campaign," which she initiated in her first years as principal in the San Francisco Bay Area. The school accommodated a wide range of diversity, with 40% of the students' families earning incomes below the poverty line, and no single ethnicity greater than 20%. Most families came from immigrant backgrounds. She says,

> Although I had lived in the community for 15 years, I undertook a listening campaign in order to see through my new eyes as a principal. During the summer before school opened, I met individually with each staff member to listen to their hopes and fears, and hear them describe the school's strengths and weaknesses. I also held a series of parent meetings—some general and others specific to each ethnic/language group. The information I gleaned was invaluable. It allowed me to find the landmines and points of commonality and to begin to build trust. It also helped me frame my first staff meetings, knowing the points of entry, early wins, as well as issues to defer. Allies I acquired then kept me apprised of hot topics, smoldering tensions and opportunities over my eight-year tenure.

For Waters, the listening allowed her to understand the different needs of the immigrant students and break down stereotypes. She explains,

> Before my interactions, I knew the communities had different needs and experiences but I knew little about the particulars or the tremendous variations within each group. Most of the Afghan families were refugees but some came from the educated elite whose parents spoke English. Often these students outperformed their American peers, particularly in math. Others had been Mujahedeen living through war and refugee camps with limited formal schooling, and perhaps with family members still unaccounted. The needs of the particular students were different, and that range was repeated in the other immigrant groups. Listening taught me to be wary of generalizations.

Waters's listening campaign led to the development of language academies where students strengthened their primary language skills in Spanish, Tagalog, Farsi, Vietnamese, and Punjabi. The English speakers learned Spanish. She concludes, "Before the Language Academies, I had very little knowledge of the cultures, the expectations for schools and teachers, or the experiences of these families, and the knowledge I needed to adequately respond to their students' needs."

Leaders also work to strengthen listening skills across the school community. In one charter network, leaders adopted a set of equity principles to anchor listening and engagement in every meeting, discussion, and decision:

1. Cultivate equity consciousness, including awareness of subtle bias and inequity. Become aware of the level of equity and inequity present in behaviors, policies, settings, organizations, and outcomes.

2. Engage in self-awareness and reflection. Foster an understanding of one's identity, values, biases, assumptions, and privileges.

3. Listen to, and elevate the voices of the most marginalized and most affected.

4. Respond to biases and inequities in the immediate term. Connect small "micro" issues to "macro" context, framing equity as a larger social issue.

5. Identify and undertake equity action(s). As you consider action, include your thinking and processing from Steps 1–4.

Throughout this book, we circle back to the topic of listening. You will find references to cultivate active listening with staff in Chapter 3, and with families and the community in Chapter 5.

Instructional Leadership

An identity safe leader recognizes that the ultimate goal for students involves providing access to teaching that will lead to their authentic learning and progressing. The SISP (D. M. Steele, 2012) research demonstrated that when students feel identity safe, they perform better academically. The research identified four academic components that lead to identity safety for students: *listening for student voices*, *teaching for understanding*, *focusing on cooperation*, and *student autonomy*. Identity safe leaders keep these components in mind as they develop an ambitious vision of academic excellence. This vision is rooted in rigor with high expectations, supported by appropriate scaffolding, and inspired by the goal of leading the students toward opportunities and choices to further their education and, ultimately, find meaningful careers. Using deeper learning strategies, students probe their ideas, formulate questions, and critically analyze solutions. Aisha, a high school English teacher, specifically asks her students, "Can you take that idea a bit deeper to help us understand your thinking?" Randy, a third-grade teacher, asks, "Who can look at the problem in a different way and tell us why you think that?"

These leaders are also aware that this instructional vision can only be accomplished when students' social identities are wedded to a strong academic identity by educators in and outside the classroom. To realize this, educator performance, data analysis, and a shared commitment to equity each need consideration. Leaders empower staff, students, and parents/caregivers with a voice in developing and realizing the instructional vision.

A Tale of Two Districts

Researcher and author Pedro Noguera (2017) carried out a case study with multiple districts that included an extensive analysis of several efforts to close achievement gaps. Here we highlight two districts: the Ocean School District in California (a pseudonym) and the Brockton High School in Massachusetts, whose name was not changed because various articles celebrate their achievements.

Ocean School District, CA

In the Ocean School District, White students constituted over 50% of the school population, with smaller numbers of Asian, Black, and Latinx students. Noguera explains that for over 20 years, the district had engaged in a variety of efforts to address the achievement disparities between the White and Asian students, and the Black and Latinx students. However, the district was unable to make sustained change in the gaps nor significantly improve academic outcomes for Black and Latinx students. Their 2015 case study uncovered a staggering 43% of Black students and 40% of Latinx students enrolled in special education, in contrast to only 8% of White students. Noguera explains that the study revealed a series of factors impeding change: a "high rate of turnover in leadership at the district and site level; a failure to implement and evaluate new initiatives aimed at improving teaching; a lack of fidelity in implementation; political distractions; and a wide variety of institutional obstacles." Most importantly, the study found that there was a lack of clear and consistent focus on how to deliver high-quality instructional support for all students. They also found that most teachers were not using critical thinking strategies or deeper learning activities.

Brockton High School (BHS), MA

With a student population of 4,200, Brockton High School has a student body that is 60% Black (including African Americans, Africans, Haitians, and Cape Verdeans), 22% White, and smaller percentages of Latinx, Asian, and mixed students. Seventy-six percent come from low-income families, and they have a large immigrant population. In 2002, the school was ranked lowest in the state. Over the next five years, teacher leaders formed a restructuring committee focused on deeper learning, which engaged in strategies that mirror the following identity safety components:

- Teaching for Understanding: higher-order thinking activities and a literacy focus that includes analysis of literature.
- Listening for Student Voices: open-response writing where students express what is meaningful to them.
- Focus on Cooperation and Student Autonomy: Project-based learning, Socratic seminars, and other collaborative activities; adults also collaborated closely in improvement efforts.

Steadily, the school improved with a coherent and consistent focus on deeper learning. With 97% of students progressing to higher education, BHS was awarded Bronze Medals (in 2008, 2010, 2012, and 2013) in the Best High Schools Rankings by *U.S. News & World Report* and has been recognized as a National Model School by the International Center for Leadership in Education for 11 consecutive years (Noguera, 2017).

My (Alex) journey toward formal school leadership began swiftly. As the beginning of the school year preparations began, one of our site leaders left due to personal circumstances. Three weeks before the school year began, I was approached by our principal to step into an instructional leader role. That year, the school was faced with a daunting task. The year prior we struggled to get our appropriate accreditation, and our student achievement results were not reflective of what we knew our students were capable of achieving. Under considerable pressure, the staff had one year to get a handle on things or it would have implications for our ability to offer a school program. In order to create focused change and build a strong instructional foundation, I engaged the school community around embracing backwards lesson planning, common and frequent assessments, and building a school culture anchored in personal pride and success.

Identity safe leaders also consider the unique instructional needs of all individuals and groups, including students on the autism spectrum, those with learning and developmental disabilities, as well as students with ADHD. They also institute trauma-informed practices and provide a continuum of services including counseling (see Chapter 6). Seeing beyond labels to find each child's gifts and talents, raise achievement levels, and increase belonging are all necessary and meaningful for treating the whole child. Not a single one of them belongs exclusively to a characterization defined by a label, which promotes a fixed mindset about them. They each embody unique perceptions, ideas, and intelligences that set them apart. An identity safe instructional program stems from an understanding of child development; their unique social, emotional, and cognitive needs; as well as their gifts and abilities. Then, we can focus on developing their strengths, addressing their needs, and fostering continuous improvement.

Without a staff's shared and vested commitment to instructional improvement, students will not realize their highest potential. Identity safe leaders train, support, and promote staff to address *listening for student voices, teaching for understanding, focusing on cooperation*, and *strengthening student autonomy* in their classrooms. Students can then experience identity safety, feel successful in school, and give their best efforts.

Problem-Solving and Consensus-Building

One kindergarten teacher would often remind her students that "problems are our friends," in the hopes of reframing the many problems and dilemmas that life places before us into opportunities to learn. For educational leaders, even that upbeat statement can ring untrue under the weight of so many great responsibilities. Still, this kindergarten teacher may have an encouraging message even for us, because there are concrete ways to break down complex issues into friendlier—and still realistic—paths for realizing solutions. And it pays to remember that we do not make this journey alone. There are many voices that assist in the decision-making process, and our role often involves garnering the support and leading our teams with an eye on both equity and fair treatment.

Problem-Solving for Identity Safe Schools

University courses will never fully prepare us for every type of problem that will cross our path as educational leaders. Interaction Associates (2019), referenced in Chapter 1, offers simple guidelines for tackling issues and solving problems. Here, we describe specific considerations that impact schoolwide identity safety. These steps can be adapted to addressing problems both small and large:

- **Identify the issue:** What is the problem or concern? What are its root causes, and why is it important to address? How does it relate to identity safety? Where do we stand with it at the moment?

- **Set a goal:** What are you trying to accomplish? How will it impact stakeholders of all backgrounds? How will you know the goal is achieved?

- **Determine a path of action:** Have you involved or received input from all stakeholders in the creation of the plans? Are your plans realistic? Have you mapped intermittent goals to help measure progress?

Preparation:

- **Participation:** Which stakeholders need to be considered as you determine the path? How will you consult and involve them? How will you include the voices of people who are not often heard? Surveys, focus groups, and informal conversations can help identify who needs to be consulted and how they can participate in making the decision.

- **Data:** What data do you need to gather to better help you understand the problem?

- **Context:** Explore the organizational context: What else is going on in the school that could impact the effort you are making? What unintended consequences may emerge along the way?

- **Stakeholder analysis:** Imagine how the change effort will impact each person (teachers, students, families, etc.). What would make it a win for each of them?

Problem-solving steps—reaching agreement can result from either or both of these perspectives:

- **Vision space:** Reach an agreement on a vision for the future. Imagine what it would be like when the problem is solved.

- **Problem space:** Reach an agreement on the problem. Legitimize the different perspectives, analyze the problem, and agree on some root causes.

Move to identify solutions and a plan for implementing them:

- **Solution space:** Generate possible solutions, evaluate and discuss, and agree on the resolutions.

- **Implementation space:** Agree on an action plan with steps to solve the problem. Plan for how to evaluate implementation.

School leadership places a wide range of problems on our plates along with the responsibility to address them. While most problems are relatively easy to handle, we are, at times, confronted with situations that we never could have imagined. Experiencing a huge crisis can rock a school, but ultimately, we learn as much from our successes as our failures. All situations become opportunities to learn and grow. Our emotional competence will carry our courage as we face adversity, obstacles, crises, and emergencies.

Targeted by Hate: Two Very Different Approaches for Problem-Solving in a Crisis

A Gay Teacher and a Missed Opportunity to Teach and Heal

Marley worked as an athletic director at a Catholic school in a small town. She describes the night when someone followed her home, waited until she was in bed, and then smashed her car with an ice pick. She recalls the events, stating,

> Next, the school was spray-painted with my name and anti-gay slurs, and I received letters that contained threats to kill and eviscerate me. I know now I was attacked for being a lesbian in a Catholic school environment—for being my truest self. But you see, I've never looked at life that way. I just did my best to serve the kids, and I believe that I did a good job.

In her role, Marley built many strong relationships with students, but other students openly used anti-gay slurs.

She continues,

> The Head of School really cared about me. He was a good man and was horrified by it all. I think he fought to keep me there even when other leaders maybe didn't want that type of publicity. The police were involved, but never solved the case. I asked for security, but that never happened. Eventually the effect of the trauma drove me to leave my position.

Marley wished that school leaders had spoken openly about the crimes against her rather than cover them up. She lamented that while the newspaper wrote blatantly about the crime that occurred, the school did not inform the students about the events, leaving them to learn about it through the news and rumors. She also felt that the personal relationships she had developed with her students would have caused them to be compassionate toward her. As she says, "When you know someone who is gay and have a good relationship with them, you are more likely to stand up for their rights."

The school did provide a modicum of professional development on prevention of biased-based and other forms of bullying, but as Marley put it, "In my opinion, it wasn't helping where the problem was. Clearly, there were issues within the student population." Marley felt that the awareness of diversity needed to be addressed directly with the students and that teachers needed training to facilitate student dialogue.

(Continued)

(Continued)

A Transgender Student and an Education for a Community

A transgender student was bullied and brutally beaten up on the school field after school. In minutes, a video was sent to a large number of students. Rapidly, the whole school became aware of the incident through social media. The principal took immediate action to support the student and take disciplinary action against the attackers. The following morning, he gathered the entire staff in an emergency meeting before school. Then he addressed the school over the loudspeaker, expressing a strong stand against violence, bullying, and acts of hate toward transgender students, or any student for that matter. He sent a letter to the parent/caregiver community with a similar message. Later in the week, he held a Town Hall meeting to explain what happened and revealed his plans to take action and ensure a similar incident would not happen again. He facilitated a restorative justice process, beginning with the students who were responsible for the bullying. He provided opportunities for them to learn, understand, and repair the harm they caused, and ultimately, change their attitudes and behavior. This process culminated in a healing circle in which these students listened to the student (and two accompanying allies) who had been the target of their bullying, apologized, shared their new understandings of the root causes of their harmful actions, and outlined the steps they would be taking to try to repair harm. These steps had already been informed through adult mediators by the student who had been bullied.

In the next few weeks, the principal began educating the staff. He brought in a guest presenter who gave an overview of gender identity—describing a deeply held sense for some of being male, female, or a different gender independent from their biological sex (Baum & Westheimer, 2015). Then he brought in a panel of staff, students, and family members who shared stories about feeling invisible at times and not valued as their gender selves. In sharing, they created a comfortable and compassionate zone for staff to ask their questions and learn from the experiences of their guests.

The school site council took action to integrate these improvement goals in the school's three-year plan. The principal's efforts even reached the level of the district school board, who developed new policies to ensure that students who are born into one gender, but who identify with another, can use the restroom and locker room that best suits them. They also can choose the pronoun of their preference, dress in a manner that matches their sense of gender identity, and join sports teams that match their self-identified gender.

Consensus-Building for Identity Safe Schools

Equity-focused leaders work to bring the school community together as they navigate through conflicts and dilemmas, making needed adaptations (Blankstein, Noguera, & Kelly, 2015). When at all possible, they use consensus-building processes when making decisions that affect students. An identity safe campus is the result of a team approach where everyone is contributing to student well-being with the aim of getting all stakeholders on board to make it happen. As part of fostering a solution-oriented culture, identity safe leaders use facilitation skills with the group to create a safe environment for evoking a range of opinions and discussing them in a nonjudgmental manner. Posing dilemmas and encouraging alternate ways to view, analyze, and solve problems fosters engagement and creativity. Through modeling and teaching conflict resolution strategies, leaders facilitate difficult discussions with confidence and care. We approach these exercises as an art and a science, engaging both our intuition and knowledge.

As an art, we seek to read and understand the responses and reactions of the group or person in front of us, focusing on their points of view. When leaders have strong individual relationships with participants, they have already created a culture of listening, connecting, and working through different perspectives respectfully. This means that difficult decisions can find smoother paths to resolution.

The science of consensus-building involves a set of techniques and methodologies. The process includes brainstorming and openly considering and discussing many ideas and differing perspectives. The goal is to come to shared understanding and an agreement on how to move forward. It often requires compromising and discovering decisions that everyone can live with. There are many methods for coming to consensus (e.g., multiple voting or using sticky dots that allow participants to narrow decisions down). The consensus process may take more than one meeting, with multiple discussions and successive adjustments for everyone to arrive at a place where they feel comfortable and can embrace the decision. Questions to ask and remember about this process can include the following:

- Did the process and organization include all stakeholders with an interest in the outcome?

- Is it driven by a shared and meaningful purpose?

- Does it follow respectful norms for engagement and conversation?

- Is everyone engaged and contributing?

- Are varied data points used to arrive at solutions?

- Are participants encouraged to challenge assumptions and explore alternatives?

- Were significant efforts made to find creative responses to differences?

- Has consensus been sought only after fully exploring all ideas and interests?

Change Management

Change processes can be messy at times; however, they yield both advantage and opportunity for those primed to recognize it. Margaret Wheatley (n.d.) signals the tremendous potential that we can access during times of great chaos. She highlights scientific discoveries from chaos theory and quantum physics where "chaos is natural . . . and relationships are what matters, even on a subatomic level." She points out that leaders need to recognize the "intricate webs of cooperation that connect us." (para 1).

Identity safe leaders begin a change process by checking their own assumptions to clear a path for listening with compassion and understanding. As we have detailed in consensus-building, they empower all members of the school community to participate and contribute. They support their communities to adapt to change with flexible attitudes, and they work in teams to implement a theory of change that results in deep and sustained transformation. In Chapter 7, we offer specific steps for a process to transform your school into an identity safe space.

Timing is an integral aspect for implementing successful change. It's important to consider the best time to introduce change for the most favorable reception. You may ask if your community isn't already reeling from other changes. Are you noticing any nuances that may undermine your efforts in spite of the hard work? For example, are teachers arguing amongst themselves? Consider the morale of staff and families—are they amenable to change? Would it make a difference to address a hesitant person or group before proceeding?

Carol Weiss (Theory of Change, n.d.) popularized the concept of a "theory of change," challenging organizations to articulate and describe their assumptions and processes, outlining the steps needed to actualize long-range goals and outcomes. In Chapter 1, we highlight the importance of weighing the results you are seeking—or the vision—in the context of the change process, and holding it alongside your continually evolving relationships with all stakeholders. Ask staff about their beliefs regarding transformational change while you, and they, seek to meet identity safety goals that will lead to accomplishing your shared vision. Relationships are your key to tapping into their emerging perceptions and can offer direction for guiding people toward producing the conditions needed to reach your goals.

Often the process of change begins with the low-hanging fruit—in other words, those efforts that are likely to be successful. Creating change in meaningful, yet swift, ways shows everyone what is possible. In shifting the culture of the school, I (Alex) believed that student participation would be essential for the success of this process. While some adults at the school were uncertain about our collective ability to boost student achievement, I was confident that our students could and would rise to the occasion. I knew I could talk to students, and they would listen and respond. Now an administrator, I used my former teacher–student rapport to recruit high social status male students who had the potential to influence their peers about test-taking. I asked them what they knew about standardized tests, showed them our school's performance, and looked at scores from various schools across the city. Nobody had ever talked with them before about the tests, the scores, and their meaning. Without prompting, the students responded that they not only did not know how important the tests were externally, they knew they could do better because they "did not even try." We worked collaboratively together to create a short presentation that they could share with the student body.

At our weekly schoolwide Family Meeting, the students shared information about how our school was working to improve and also talked about the power of pride in one's work. In addition to having opportunities to grow in the classroom, we launched a schoolwide "SWAG" (Students Who Achieve Greatness) initiative. We wanted all students to see how they would be celebrated for their academic growth and highlight ways they had contributed to the school community.

At the same time, I began working with the faculty, but not all teachers were on board. One particular teacher with strong instructional skills was quite vocal, asserting that he did not think standardized tests were of value and worthy of focus. As I had done with the students, I reached out to some of the teachers who were effective with other teachers and students. Reframing the conversation to focus less on standardized tests and more on student learning helped this veteran teacher achieve exceptional results in his classroom. Consistent with the change theory process, we began the steps for backwards mapping, specifying where we wanted the students to be by the end of the semester. From that point, improvements were both marked and rapid.

Louise Waters describes applying a theory of change that she refers to as "disruptive incrementalism." *Disruptive* points to changes intended to disrupt the status quo in service of the larger equity mission. In order to realize sustained change over time—change that impacts all students—it must impact the organizational structure. *Incremental* refers to attending to the process of implementation—a "go-slow-to-go-fast" philosophy that is designed to maximize the chance of success. The steps, whether within one school or an entire district, include the following:

1. **Pain point:** Identify a felt need for which there is high consensus and that aligns with an important structural change to advance equity.

2. **Local Exemplars:** Identify elements of the change that are already in place and highlight these and their champions. Involve these staff members in designing the larger change.

3. **Call to Action:** Explicitly frame the change and urgency in the school's equity goals.

4. **Early Success:** Move ahead with the teachers, departments, or schools most interested and ready. Ensure early success with strong support and problem-solving when issues arise. Use early adopters to develop systems that make it easier for later adopters to succeed. Acknowledge and compensate early adopters for codifying their work.

5. **Ongoing Communication:** Invite and address fears and problems before and during the implementation and continue to share lessons learned and successes system-wide.

6. **Flexibility:** Allow flexibility in the timeline and model within parameters. Be clear about the boundaries and rationale.

7. **Transparency:** Be transparent about any financial implications and invite people to participate in anticipating and creatively addressing potential downsides.

Waters described using disruptive incrementalism as it manifested in real time when she served as superintendent. Her district was planning for a move from five to six periods a day. At first, many teachers expressed reservations about the impact on their teaching and preparation load. However, over the preceding year during her annual one-on-one conversations, Waters listened as staff raised significant concerns about limited electives and the few chances students had to retake failed courses. This was particularly acute in relation to special education students and English learners, both of whom had additional support classes filling slots in their schedules.

Based on her discussions with teachers, Waters framed the shift from five to six periods by sharing the student needs that staff had identified. She highlighted the graduation and college readiness disparities exacerbated by their tight schedule.

She also shared staff and student concerns that a tight program offering only core courses did not allow students to discover and develop their passions, or dive deeply into culturally relevant classes. Drawing on shared goals and areas of common discomfort or frustration created a safe arena for expression and an openness to the possibility of change. She then invited faculty from the school in the district that was most interested in the six-period day to help her develop and pilot the initial model. Over time, teachers from other schools saw the effectiveness of the change and buy-in increased. Allowing flexibility with the model and a two-year timeline encouraged more to come on board. She also explained how the change supported financial sustainability. A portion of those savings were returned through a salary schedule adjustment.

Waters shares, "While it took two years to move to a six-period day, it was done with little of the rancor common to such endeavors. Moreover, staff emerged energized to design electives and intervention supports that benefited students."

As leaders navigate the transformation of their schools into vibrant learning organizations, they can help the entire school community seek coherence and stability within the constant disequilibrium of a rapidly changing environment through supportive and compassionate exchanges. A consistent approach in this manner will empower collaborators to continually seek out creative solutions, especially in light of opportunities that also tend to crop up during the change process as they work and learn together. These perks further bond everyone to each other and their shared vision.

By taking the time to examine the theory of change as it is applied specifically to your school and circumstances, you can evaluate the steps that will guide the identity safe school process. By applying disruptive incrementalist steps, you can identify the obstacles to overcome, build on local strengths, and achieve early successes.

LEADERSHIP AND STAFF

Linda Darling-Hammond reminds us that diverse and well-prepared teachers are among the most important factors in creating a positive climate that supports the whole child (Darling-Hammond & Cook-Harvey, 2018). Tuned-in leaders address staff needs with the same vigor and attention they afford their students. They realize that teachers are the most powerful conduit for student identity safety. In Chapter 3, we describe ways to introduce teachers to identity safe teaching practices through professional learning. In addition to training and supporting teachers to perform in their classrooms, identity safe leaders work to *diversify*, *retain*, and *supervise* staff in order to anchor those initial efforts.

Diversifying Staff

As described in Chapter 1, students benefit greatly and have been found to achieve at higher levels when they have educators who look like them, share, and understand their backgrounds. Students and families will always find trust easier to embrace when they see members of their own ethnic or social group working in key positions within the schools. Efforts to increase the representation of Black teachers and administrators—as well as others from diverse backgrounds—will not only greatly support the students and their families but can also deeply influence the whole faculty's commitment to equity when they experience and understand the perspectives of the diverse voices within the school community. Strategies for diversifying the educator workforce ultimately must reach beyond individual school sites with efforts that include large-scale initiatives with forgivable student loans for potential candidates, as well as providing for service scholarships and residencies that encourage student participation in the application process. However, leaders at the site level do not need to wait for these efforts and can diversify their sites through developing partnerships for student teaching with local universities with diverse teacher candidates. They can support their school's alumni and encourage paraprofessionals from the community to become credentialed teachers. Extended attention can reap many solutions.

Retention of Staff

Staff retention rates serve as a barometer for measuring teacher satisfaction, indicating the presence of a positive culture and work environment. People choose to stay in jobs where they feel their ideas and contributions make a difference. Site administrators are uniquely positioned to increase a sense of efficacy and team spirit throughout the day by offering a few words, a note, or a passing comment to

Teacher Residency Programs Expand Diversity

Teacher residency programs provide a powerful opportunity to solve the critical need for diversity within schools. Alder Graduate School of Education (https://aldergse.edu/), for example, partners with districts and charter management organizations statewide to identify and prepare prospective teachers from local communities to serve in yearlong placements. This innovative model allows for school organizations to attend to pressing challenges like teacher shortages while ensuring that local teachers are supported and prepared with cutting-edge theory and clinical application opportunities.

encourage the personal efforts of staff members. A little effort can go a long way toward developing relationships in and among the school community.

People notice whether you have their back—or not. During hard times when conflicts arise, such as when a teacher is confronted by a hostile parent, the support of a leader can make a huge difference for them. When Jen, a second-grade teacher and a lesbian, became pregnant, she was unsure how to inform her students and families. As her pregnancy progressed, the students started asking about the baby's daddy. She approached the principal, who promised to "have her back," telling Jen to send anyone with concerns directly to her. The next time the topic came up in class, Jen informed her students that her baby would have two mothers. All parents/caregivers, except for one, were fine. She referred that unhappy parent to the principal, who kept her word and supported Jen by meeting with the parent and supporting Jen, who was grateful that the principal had come through for her.

Identity safe practices that value diversity and support adult identities contribute greatly to a collective feeling of belonging and a shared commitment to the students. As mentioned, expressions of staff appreciation can take many forms during a single day, including a kind word in the hall, a verbal recognition at a meeting, or a mention in a staff bulletin or parent newsletter. Sometimes, a formal teacher recognition event, or media coverage of meaningful school activities, can deliver much-valued appreciation. While identity safe leaders take special care to notice who may be performing well and accomplishing wonderful things, they also make sure not to miss teachers who may be moving about in their quiet universes and are rarely acknowledged. These individuals may even shy from attention, yet they can still enjoy an approach from their school administrator with a word of gratitude. Identity safe leaders are careful not to treat some staff as "favorites," working to mete out recognition fairly.

Supervision of Staff

School administrators are tasked with the complex process of supervising and evaluating teachers who are new to the field, as well as experienced and veteran teachers. Mentoring, coaching, and other support greatly benefits new teachers during those challenging first years as they discover their sea legs. Identity safe administrators hold high expectations for accountability, supported by their efforts to help all teachers under their supervision meet the specific needs of students. It is their responsibility to provide honest and useful feedback with explicit recommendations in evaluation conferences. Encouraging feedback is effective for teachers in the same way it is effective for students. Teachers enjoy hearing "I believe in you; I hold a high standard for your student-centered teaching and achievement, and I will offer support for you to get there."

I (Kathe) have experienced many standard evaluations in my tenure as a teacher. I've saved them as encouraging reminders for doing what I love. The best ones were those that specifically listed the behaviors, attitudes, management, and hands-on curriculum techniques that I used with my students. Taking the time to complete an evaluation with thoughtful observations and comments can bind a teacher to the process through positive recognition from the administrator. It creates a vested interest for teachers to continue to give their best efforts.

When teachers are struggling, the site administrators provide concrete suggestions to help them grow. When a teacher has been supported over time, but the efforts do not translate into positive student outcomes, leaders have the daunting task of releasing an untenured teacher, or helping a veteran teacher to face the fact that it might be time to retire. Sometimes coaching a person out of the profession is a blessing for them as well.

With supervision and monitoring, wise feedback, and a team approach in a collaborative and identity safe culture, teachers grow and thrive. In Chapter 3, we share how to develop an adult learning community.

Rising to Challenges/Avoiding Pitfalls

When choosing to be a leader, most of us have signed up for the challenges that leadership brings, motivated by our deeply held values and beliefs. We rise to take on a new role and fill a need. We recognize and take responsibility for our mistakes and failures, gaining the courage to stand tall and persevere. These qualities carry us through some of the pitfalls we face along the way. While challenges sometimes accost us from all sides with constant demands and (sometimes) contradictory district expectations, we use our moral compass, stand firm, discover the best course of action, and lean into our courage.

Neglecting to Consult Others

A common trap involves moving forward without consulting interested or vested stakeholders. For the larger decisions especially, discussing the issues with leadership teams or advisory committees will allow you to discover what they think and feel. They will share good ideas that might not have occurred to you, as well as some innovative solutions to problems. For input from the larger community, the use of surveys and focus groups to hear varying perspectives will invite their investment (see Chapter 7). For smaller decisions, gathering several trusted stakeholders together to gauge their opinions will keep you from the trap of an input-free decision. While most educators will agree with the identity safe teaching principles in theory, changing structures to realize change may still engender resistance. Consulting about even small adjustments will preclude much conflict and can help you choose the best path to achieve the changes.

Adopting a Growth Mindset and Learning From Mistakes

As a leader, mistakes are inevitable experiences. One of my (Alex) greatest regrets as a new leader was neglecting to attend to the emotional components of change. While many of the staff were my colleagues and I enjoyed their respect, not everyone was invested in the plan I put forth. Making things more challenging, I initially relied on a compliance-oriented strategy to support our efforts (collecting lesson plans and using a rubric to give feedback). Needless to say, this did not work. Midyear after surveying staff, I realized that they were open and invested to look at student data and their plans, but they found time as a barrier. Introducing a professional learning community format shifted the compliance focus to one of learning and collaboration and restored the feeling of trust my colleagues had for me. This effort—common lesson planning—paid dividends in our school's ability to better support the needs of our students. That year our growth was in the top 0.5% in our entire state. As a leader, I learned the important lesson of creating the conditions for change, collectively developing structures and practices to support professional autonomy, and creating space for reflection so that as a team we could grow together.

A Painful Lesson

Louise Waters shares a painful lesson she learned as principal.

My clerk was upset about an African American family new to nearby subsidized housing. A month in, they had already amassed a number of tardies. Family services was working with them about attendance, and I had personally reached out to the mother to try and build a relationship. The clerk was frustrated that they had not turned in complete immunization records for two of the three children. She explained that after multiple requests, the mother refused to do anything more, saying she didn't care about the consequences. Reluctantly, I took the School Resource Officer (SRO) as I went to inform the mother that we had to disenroll the students per state law. She was livid. Why the continual harassment? She had given all of the records to the clerk. Why was one child OK and the others not? She showed me the originals. Obviously, the clerk had either misplaced or failed to copy all of the information. Seeing this as a problem family that did not care, she had demanded rather than asked for the paperwork. As tensions escalated both sides got angrier and more entrenched. And I bought into the story. I could have simply called and inquired. I could have visited without the SRO and the presumption of guilt to learn what happened. My prior personal outreach seemed hollow and contrived—just one more White clerk and principal who didn't care about her family. The relationship I was trying to foster was shattered. A few minutes of listening could have prevented this wild escalation and the months of work to reconnect.

Closing the Gap Between Ideas and Action

An identity safe school is always a work in progress. However, it is important to identify and celebrate growth and progress along the way.

ON THE PERSONAL LEVEL

The path to equity consciousness and emotional intelligence is a continual growth process. It is a given that you will make small and large mistakes along the way, so do not get discouraged. Bouncing back from failure with a growth mindset will help you as you encounter both internal and external obstacles. Here are a few thoughts to help you assess and strengthen your values and actions:

- Continue to study and learn from others to deepen understanding, and have your fingers on the pulse for leading-edge ideas for equity, change, social justice, and education.

- Engage in self-reflection to identify your strengths and blind spots as a leader. Set personal goals to enhance your emotional intelligence.

- Develop listening skills and seek to empower and build strong relationships.

- Identify a mentor/coach or trusted colleague to work with you as a confidant and thought partner.

ON THE SCHOOL-WIDE LEVEL

Here are a few ideas to ensure that you're living up to your vision, mission, and identity safe school goals:

- Work with staff to develop a common language for identity safety and proficiency in equity-focused cultural and systemic change processes.

- Align problem-solving, consensus-building, and change processes to the identity safe principles.

- Diversify staff to mirror the school and provide ongoing supervision and support.

Check Yourself

- To what degree am I aware of my own power and privilege? How can I exercise my power to amplify the voices and increase access for others?

- What are my blindspots? How can I work to become aware of them in the moment?

- Have I spoken up to my supervisors and/or the school board when I see unfair policies or practices that harm students? Why or why not?

- Have I reached out to include the students and adults who are least connected to the school, or have I tried and then given up? How can this be done?

- Does the diversity of the staff mirror the student population? If not, how can I recruit and provide supportive working conditions for more diverse certificated and classified staff members?

- What can I do differently to contribute to the identity safety and academic identities of students in each of these groups: Black and Brown students, LGBTQIA+, English learners, immigrants, special needs, and traumatized students?

Using the Tools

Self-Assessment Template

With an asset-based approach, how do we gauge our strengths and our social and emotional assets? What areas require more attention and effort? Here are a few questions to ask yourself as you reflect on your social and emotional intelligence:

Self-regulation:

1. How do you manage yourself amidst the many pressures of our role?

2. How do you manage your reactions when we are put on the spot or attacked?

3. How do you balance your work life with our personal lives?

Empathy:

1. How do you feel empathy for others? Do you try to imagine how it feels to walk in their shoes?

2. How do you express compassion for others?

3. How do you model acceptance people with a range of gender identities and racial backgrounds?

Internal Motivation:

1. What motivates you?

2. How can you motivate others?

Social Skills:

1. How do you communicate with others? Are you transparent? Do you share information with your constituents in a way that is truthful but does not cause them to feel worried or panicky?

2. How do you express anger or frustration in direct, but calm ways, without blaming or attacking?

3. How do you mediate conflicts between students and adults?

4. Do you have the courage to speak up when you witness staff mistreating students or one another? How?

5. Do you have the courage to speak up to your supervisors and district leaders when you witness unfair policies? How?

6. How do you face crises and emergencies?

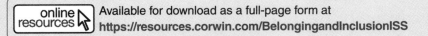

online resources ᐅ Available for download as a full-page form at
https://resources.corwin.com/BelongingandInclusionISS

CHAPTER 3

Adult Learning in Service of an Identity Safe School

Introduction

Some of my (Kathe) best experiences as a teacher were the shared ones with my colleagues and our students. One that stands out for me was the day when one of my classroom parents, June (a pseudonym), who was a high school writing teacher in the district, brought her students to pair with my third graders for an afternoon of writing together with the high school students modeling and inspiring the younger ones. Working both together and with our students, we created a newsletter for a fictitious community living in a self-sustaining dome on the ocean floor. When they met that afternoon, the fun felt richer watching the enthusiasm and bright eyes around the room. June and I cast knowing glances and smiles back and forth as we witnessed the connections forming between them. Afterwards, we published a newsletter about the project that was shared with both our parent communities. Aside from ushering in a layer of satisfaction when we take those opportunities to share the love, collaboration between colleagues increases our efficacy for learning as we borrow, exchange, and research information to support our projects and each other.

An article from the Center for Teaching Quality states that "analysis of survey and interview data from teacher leaders provides additional evidence on what existing literature has shown is true of all teachers: that collaboration among teachers paves the way for the spread of effective teaching practices, improved outcomes for the students they teach, and the retention of the most accomplished teachers in high-needs schools" (Berry, et al., 2009, p. 2, para. 3).

When the entire staff connect to learn about identity safe practices, we can enjoy the cooperating talents and contributions of all players as they invent and co-create systems to apply identity safe principles for the whole community. Margaret Wheatley (2000, p. 341, para. 2) writes,

> As a living system self-organizes, it develops a shared understanding of what is important, what is acceptable behavior, what actions are required and how these actions will get done. It develops channels of communication, networks of workers, and complex physical structures. And as the systems develop, new capacities emerge for living and working together.

Wheatley asks leaders to "forego fear-based approaches" (para. 2) and support staff teams in guiding their own growth. She adds,

> This highly localized change activity does not mean that the organization spins off wildly in all directions. If people are clear about the purpose and true values of their organization, their individual tinkering will result in system wide coherence. In organizations that know who they are and mean what they announce, people are free to create and contribute. A plurality of effective solutions emerges, each expressing a deeper coherence, an understanding of what this organization is trying to become. (p. 342, para. 4)

Effective models for identity safe professional learning occur in a variety of partnerships between teachers and teachers, and teachers and administrators, which enhance the learning experience as each group contributes their unique perspectives to the whole.

In this chapter, we focus on ways to create the conditions for educators to learn and grow in the service of creating identity safe spaces for students. Leaders can attend to the learning needs of educators using the principles of identity safety to guide the work.

1. **Colorblind teaching** that ignores differences is a barrier to inclusion in the classroom.

   "Many school reform efforts are based on limited understandings of racial equality and as a result are likely to exacerbate inequality rather than lessen it," writes Amanda Lewis (2003, p. 193, para. 3). She continues, "Thus, it is quite appropriate and, in fact, desirable to encourage in our students an aspiration for a world in which color doesn't matter, but only as part of a larger curriculum that helps them understand that race continues to matter and that only through our collective hard work will it come to matter less" (p. 196, para. 1). Without exploring issues of identity and race, educators may falsely believe that they are not discriminating and are giving every student equal treatment, oblivious to differences (Delpit, 1995; Lindsey, et al., 1999; Paley, 1979). However, in a colorblind school environment, students and educators alike can unintentionally perpetuate and experience a default identity defined by stereotypes (Lewis, 2003). For equity to prevail, it is imperative that educators understand how a colorblind mindset causes damage. When identities are ignored, educators' and learners' gifts, cultures, stories, goals, and dreams are not fully seen. Some may feel compelled to deny a part of their identity to be accepted (Gaertner & Dovidio, 2000). Colorblindness can threaten belonging and trust, which in turn diminishes the mind's readiness to learn. When a school's adult learning system includes "basic training" around the dangers of colorblindness, educators gain a foundation for learning and sharing ways to acknowledge different identities without stereotyping or singling out students, their families, and other staff members. When educators understand why this is harmful, it can increase their will to create a non-colorblind environment.

2. **To feel a sense of belonging and acceptance** requires creating positive relationships between teacher and students and among students with equal status for different social identities.

A positive climate among staff, which shows up in respectful, helpful, and welcoming relationships between them, is a requisite first step for transferring identity safety into their classrooms with their students. Adult learning systems can amplify positive climate and equal status by fostering identity safety and promoting it in study groups, teaching, and staff teams. Coaching and pairing new teachers and staff with veterans for mentoring partnerships provides entry for the new teachers to also enjoy collegial relationships. These kinds of collaborations create a warm adult climate that can easily ripple out to the entire school community with students enjoying the benefits.

3. **Cultivating diversity** as a resource for learning and expressing high expectations for students promotes learning, competence, and achievement.

Diversifying staff to reflect the ethnicity of the student body and fostering a warm and inclusive environment among everyone sets the tone for acceptance. In this context, leaders promote multiracial and multicultural understanding, and they model and teach identity safe agreements and routines for interactions and open dialogue. Examining group dynamics and power relationships is a crucial first step in cultivating diversity and equity, because inequitable practices are often deeply ingrained in traditional ways of operating (Kouzes & Posner, 2002). This also includes considering ways to validate all staff contributions and to equalize status in terms of value between classified and certificated staff roles.

Continual explorations into the personal beliefs and identities of staff, along with providing platforms to dialogue about race and integrate culturally responsive teaching and curriculum into their classrooms, will lead to growth. Staff will be able to air ideas and feelings as well as their fears—the latter, a necessary step toward more complete understanding and consensus. The journey toward identity safety gains strength and momentum when they engage together.

From there, deprivatizing teaching (an approach where educators open their classroom doors to one another and freely discuss their practice) allows educators to share identity safe practices and hone them in their classrooms. Leaders can support these efforts by providing resources for a wide range of multicultural curriculum and materials that offer counter-narratives to traditional historical accounts. Diversity can then grow deeper roots and understanding when staff meet for shared study and team planning throughout the year.

4. **Educators examine their own social identities** to feel a sense of identity safety and convey that feeling to students, creating an identity safe environment for them.

Opportunities for educators to reflect on their own identities, racial as well as gender, religion, culture, and other aspects of their social identities—coupled with a compassionate intent to recognize, accept, and understand the myriad influences upon them and use it to reduce their biases—prepares them to support their students in a similar vein. In the process, they learn about the identities of other staff members, creating a broader understanding that can translate into more compassion and caring that spreads exponentially across the school.

5. **Social and emotional safety** is created by supporting students in defining their identities, refuting negative stereotypes, and countering stereotype threat, giving them a voice in the classroom while using social and emotional learning (SEL) strategies.

   Leaders of the adult learning system can model and teach many of the practices and routines recommended for use with students to boost belonging and safety. Through open dialogues and reflections about race, staff can deepen their awareness of and readiness to confront and respond to stereotypes and microaggressions. They can learn and practice individual and group reflection, create guidelines for sharing, and hear different experiences and perspectives. These opportunities will strengthen their understanding about themselves and others, as well as build their readiness as educators to support belonging and safety for all students.

6. **Student learning** is enhanced in diverse classrooms by teaching for understanding, creating opportunities for shared inquiry and dialogue, and offering a challenging, rigorous curriculum.

   Schools have their historical roots in the factory model, where children are viewed as raw material. Selective knowledge was thrust upon them through rote repetition in preparation for accepting unquestioning obedience and dull work on assembly lines. Twenty-first-century teaching frameworks highlight creativity, innovation, critical thinking, problem-solving, communication, and collaboration, as well as social and cross-cultural skills (Belanca & Brandt, 2010). Although much has changed for the better over the years, the underlying assembly-line structure is still present in many unexamined practices. During the years of "No Child Left Behind," rote learning was accentuated, particularly in urban schools. Many current teachers who graduated from preservice programs during that time were never taught other methodologies. Research on identity safety highlighted the power of student-centered teaching, where students are not treated as automatons but are constantly interacting and questioning. Educators need time to explore the connection between constructivist teaching and identity safety, examine the latest research, and develop strategies to integrate any needed direct instruction on-ramps to deeper learning.

7. **Schoolwide equity** flourishes for everyone in identity safe schools where the climate, the structures, practices, and attitudes prioritize equity, inclusion, and academic growth for students from all

backgrounds. Leaders demonstrate emotional intelligence; attend to student needs; address racism, bias, and privilege; and serve as the architects of ongoing change.

A strong leader develops an inclusive infrastructure that empowers teams to involve others in planning and participation in decision-making. Transformational leaders strive to create an atmosphere of trust and dignity, where all members of the learning community have ample opportunity to realize their full potential (Kouzes & Posner, 2002; Murphy, 2000; Senge, 2000). This level of treatment is required to unpack and address societal inequities and oppression and understand how they are played out in schools. The leader also incorporates an asset-based approach that focuses on a student's strengths as opposed to a deficit mindset that views negative aspects and weaknesses. By incorporating a positive mindset into every area of the school (e.g., academic and behavioral interventions), every student is assured that a constructive outlook will affect all decisions made on their behalf.

A positive climate where diverse adult and student identities are valued strengthens staff stability, leading to increased retention, which spreads a feeling that this is a great place to work. Leaders exemplify openness, compassion, acceptance, and a can-do attitude to motivate and involve staff. Empowered staff members will work together to solve problems, reach consensus on important decisions, and change structures and policies to ensure equity and identity safety.

In this chapter, we share strategies to bring adults, who embody many different roles (teachers, administrators, paraprofessionals, counselors, and other staff), together for a concerted effort to create an identity safe school.

1. We draw from adult learning theory to involve them in shared learning.

2. We show how to build collaboration where mutual integrity imparts the feeling that all team members feel valued and trusted. We ensure that staff feel identity safe themselves, enabling them to include one another in efforts to actualize it for students.

3. We describe areas of self-reflection, dialogue, and study to address identity, anti-racism, and the reduction of stereotype threat and bias.

4. We provide formats and structures for shared learning.

With a focus on adult learning, we examine ways to build staff capacity to create identity safe spaces. When we introduce platforms for them to process at the intrapersonal, interpersonal, and institutional levels, we use these three integral steps to provide a full and meaningful identity safe school culture. We then explore effective structures, routines, and rituals for adult learning with and about identity safety, including strategies for educators to bring these principles to life with their students.

Why It Matters

The transformation to an identity safe school happens when a committed staff understand and engage in validating all student identities. When a school operates as a learning organization, educators are honing their craft and sharing it from room to room. To succeed, educators develop technical and adaptive skills for three levels of action: *intrapersonal*, which involves examining their own identities, values, and beliefs as well as considering the implications for implicit bias, microaggressions, and stereotype threat; *interpersonal*, where they explore identity safe processes through relationship-building, collaboration, and professional learning; and *institutional*, where they participate in processes to analyze data and reflect on and change policies and practices that perpetuate inequality and white supremacy. We will elaborate on these action levels later in this chapter.

Identity safety becomes an anchor that stabilizes the change process when intrapersonal, interpersonal, and institutional levels are integrated in a comprehensive, systemic, and ongoing adult learning effort. Adults, like students, thrive in an identity safe learning community. A safe and caring adult community who self-reflects, shares best practices, continually learns, and works together for schoolwide equity will lead to a collective willingness and capacity to share it with their students.

A District-Wide Equity Team: Seven Years of Collaborative Inquiry

When I (Becki) served as curriculum director, I invited educators to participate in a district-wide equity team as a voluntary ongoing study group. We met monthly for seven years. Together, we explored our attitudes and beliefs as part of an intrapersonal self-examination. At the interpersonal level, we reflected on our relationships

(Continued)

with students, parents/caregivers, and colleagues. We studied issues of race and gender and the history of oppression. We examined ways to reverse the damage caused by erroneous racialized views of intelligence, eugenics, and stereotype threat. On the institutional level, we used district-wide data, surveys, and focus groups to examine structures and systems. We also reviewed new research and evidence-based practices. We invited Dorothy Steele to share her Stanford Integrated Schools Program (SISP) research, and consequently the equity team became an incubator for identity safe teaching. We brought Claude Steele, Carol Dweck, and Pedro Noguera to present to the larger education community. Members of our group emerged as leaders and played a role in strategic equity-focused initiatives. Each of these levels contributed in essential ways toward equity and identity safety for our students.

Autonomy and Engagement in Adult Learning

Andragogy, popularized by Malcom Knowles (1973), advances adult learning theory that accounts for internal motivation and establishes the learner in the driver's seat. Adult learners perform best when they are in charge of their learning. Interactive processes and cooperative activities promote participation for expressing agency. Varied learning modalities capture interest and speak to the strengths of different adults, increasing opportunities for personal expression. The SISP research highlighted autonomy and cooperation as two important components of identity safety (D. M. Steele, 2012). The more educators feel autonomy in connection with cooperation and collaboration, the more they are likely to share these qualities with their students.

There is always a lag between what is learned from new research and reaching the capacity to use it in professional learning environments and classrooms. In other words, we do not always run our faculty meetings using best and latest practices for teaching and learning. Adults respond well to many of the same engagement strategies that we promote for use in their classrooms. What works for their students works for them. Modeling for and presenting pedagogy that draws from more recent brain research, inquiry-based learning, and teamwork will equip educators with the technical and adaptive capacity to replicate it.

Before they practice with their students, however, they benefit from experiencing it firsthand. In our experience, educators respond exceptionally well to identity safety because it intimately addresses one of our deepest motivations: to feel belonging and acceptance.

Making It Happen

Kouzes and Posner (Leadership Challenge, n.d., paras. 1–6) defined the qualities of a committed leader saying, "Model the way, inspire a shared vision, challenge the process, enable others to act, and encourage the heart." The spread of identity safe practices among staff members relies on a collegial atmosphere with high levels of trust, supported and facilitated by their educational leaders and mentors. It accelerates by drawing on master teachers and supporting their leadership skills (Lieberman, et al., 2000). When staff are empowered and enabled to work together through an established sense of trust, they will delegate tasks to one another to improve efficiencies and share knowledge, successes, and obstacles in an enjoyable and supportive environment—and without fear. This can fuel a collective confidence to explore problems in depth, going the extra mile to investigate, discovering elements they had not known or considered, and collaborating on solutions.

A COMMITTED LEADER SETS THE STAGE: BETTER TOGETHER

Transforming a school begins with a leader who models good listening and demonstrates caring, honesty, and integrity. Leaders also inspire a safe atmosphere by sharing from their own self-inquiry process and by revealing personal vulnerabilities at appropriate times. Admissions of fallibility encourage staff to share truthfully with others, allowing for mistakes to inform their practice, and encouraging a sense of full acceptance among them.

As identity safe leaders approach schoolwide change and the requisite adult learning to actualize it, they seek to know and understand the values, attitudes, and capacities of their staff. Attending to the individual personalities and identities, relationships, and social networks invites their interest. When leaders consider individual teaching styles and the ways different teachers connect with their students, as well as the morale and general climate and culture, they gain insight for the most effective approaches for motivating and guiding them. These appraisals also allow leaders to consider ways that different individuals react to change, such as whether they support or resist new ideas and strategies, and how they might react to the principles of identity safety.

Leaders can ask themselves questions about how well they know the adults on campus and use the knowledge to work with staff in ways that prepare them for an exploration into equity and identity safety. Understanding the identities of staff will help leaders consider staff readiness and openness for exploring issues of identity. Questions to open an understanding can include the following:

- What are the backgrounds and identities of each staff member?

- How do individual staff members feel about their own lives, their sense of agency, and achievements?

- How do individual staff members show respect and interact with each other, their students, and families?

Tracking prior professional learning experiences and previous dialogue about race, gender, and other aspects of difference will help leaders know where to begin sensitive conversations about identity with them. Questions such as these can help leaders broaden this understanding:

- What previous equity goals have been in place, and what has been done to achieve them, and by whom?

- What types of diversity- and equity-focused conversations and professional development have taken place in the past, and how did the staff respond to these sessions?

Understanding the level of trust between staff members and observing how they work together will allow leaders to see where to start in developing or extending a culture of collaboration. Questions to inform about trust include the following:

- Do staff members frequently and voluntarily work together as a team? Do they create plans together? Do some co-teach?

- What are their social connections beyond their grade level and department within the school?

- Do race, gender, age, income level, or other demographic factors play a role in connection and communication among staff?

- Do certificated and classified staff interact with mutual respect?

Acquiring a deep knowledge of the staff and the ways they work together will empower leaders to make the content relevant to them by using the knowledge to tailor approaches for their reception. Among the greatest tasks we can perform for staff as educational leaders involves engendering their trust in us. The process of trust-building has different starting points for different leaders. Some leaders rise within the ranks of the school itself, where members of the school community are familiar with them. Others are hired from outside sources, sometimes displacing former beloved administrators.

A New Leader Enters During a Difficult Time

I (Alex) moved from my teacher role to dean and then principal in the same school at a time when the school was struggling. For many reasons (turnover, access to curriculum, infrastructure to support student and staff needs), student achievement was suffering. We found ourselves in the position in which things needed to change quickly. We knew that if nothing shifted, there was a possibility we would have to close the school. Our first act, as a school community, was to diagnose what lay at the root of our challenges. Getting clear about the root causes provided a stable platform for working and learning together to strengthen our program and transform student outcomes.

An important step in the process included engaging in clear, transparent, and frequent communication. Being on the brink of closure brings understandable feelings of instability and concern among staff. As a member of the staff but new to a position of leadership, it was essential to create consistent ways to connect with our staff community. This included weekly bulletins, consistent communication and feedback structures during our weekly professional development, and making it a point to connect with individuals on a one-on-one basis. Eliciting and responding to staff feedback and needs built critical trust so that as we embarked on change processes around analyzing and responding to student data, collaborative lesson planning, or common classroom culture actions, we could do so in a manner that allowed us to make mistakes and learn together as a community. We saw positive growth take hold with students, and as changes became evident, the threat for school closure disappeared.

Surrounding staff members with positive approaches and reminders of their shared vision helps to keep goodwill and spirits aloft, and builds their trust in us. When professional learning activities become safe places for everyone to share, educators will be more amenable to attend staff meetings, instead of running in the other direction. Equalizing status and listening to the perspectives of those in varied staff roles promotes both safe sharing and greater support for students.

Leaders set the stage for trust among staff members through modeling, as well as compassionate and investigative efforts into their identities and interactions to discover best approaches. By developing a unified culture with attention focused on staff concerns, talents, and challenges, a team spirit grows.

IDENTITY SAFE ADULT LEARNING AT THE INTRAPERSONAL, INTERPERSONAL, AND INSTITUTIONAL LEVELS

Intrapersonal: Staff Self-Reflection

At the intrapersonal level, educators' confidence with their own identity—feeling comfortable in their own skin, so to speak—strengthens the willingness to support and transmit a similar feeling to their students. In Chapter 2, we encourage leaders to become more in touch with their own identities and beliefs. Self-reflection will also greatly benefit staff teams and can be presented in a variety of ways.

Activities that allow educators to reflect on their many—and often complex—social identities is meaningful and heightens bonds of connectedness among staff. Appealing to people to write about a set of identity-focused questions provides them with a process for accessing their inner landscapes. Afterwards, offering an opportunity to safely choose what to share with a partner or the larger group can deepen a sense of acceptance and trust. Sometimes, a person's reflections will elicit deep emotions. Encouraging expression of sensitive and appropriate sharing both during and after group sessions helps participants feel supported in heartfelt ways. Compassion extended within the group demonstrates to all that their leader understands and fully accepts who they are. We are complex beings, but the process of opening up our feelings draws out understanding and creates a shared sense of community.

Personal reflections provide a safe path for drawing out individuals and can be used as a comfortable exercise in regular meetings, or as an icebreaker for a longer session. For example, sessions can begin with writing or a partner-share about a theme or topic, drawing from what Kris Gutierrez and Barbara Rogoff (2003) call "repertoires of practice." They explain that when someone shares their specific traditions, rituals, and practices, their personal experiences serve to illustrate their ethnic identity, instead of allowing other people's assumptions or stereotypes about them to lead. Experiences vary from person to person, even among individuals from a similar ethnic or religious group. Attention to these variables offers leaders an opportunity to provide for the unique and personal cultural expressions of staff. A simple icebreaker can set the tone, such as "share how your family celebrates winter holidays," or "what were your favorite foods you ate as a child?"

In identity safety, we never define other people's identities for them, even and especially if we may have harbored preconceived notions about their identities. We can always discover very different perspectives among people with similar backgrounds, as identities are impacted by innumerable factors (e.g., cultural backgrounds, languages, intersectionality—when someone has two or more oppressed identities, people with mixed heritages and racial backgrounds, and people in transition from one gender identity to another). We are also influenced by our childhood experiences (where we grew up, relationships with our parents/caregivers, our religious upbringing, traumatic experiences) and adult experiences (e.g., marital status, professional life, travel experiences). To add to the complexity, our identities are in a continual flux as we grow and change throughout our lives.

While race is a social rather than biological construct, in general, our Westernized society has continued to view racial categories and identities as fixed (Gannon, 2016; Lewis, 2003). Leaders benefit from knowledge that identity development presents as a continuum. Working with staff to unpack their own experiences of racial identity development will open new pathways of self-reflection and understanding. Our job is not to categorize people but rather to create spaces for people to reflect on their identities in the service of connecting and belonging.

Find staff self-reflection tools in Appendix B: Identity Safe Staff Self-Reflection Activity and Appendix C: Identity Safe Classroom Practices: Teacher Self-Assessment.

Interpersonal: Building Trust and Collaboration Among Staff

At the interpersonal level, we extend the idea of cultural proficiency to include awareness of an array of social identities including gender, language, and religion. We also apply identity safe practices to physical, mental, and learning differences. In a climate of trust, staff will be ready to explore, accept, and grow their understanding of these proficiencies. Margaret Wheatley (2000) reminds us that "the only way to make sustainable change is when the leader trusts the constituents and facilitates their coming together, the exploration, and the attempts to change as 'a dance and not a forced march.'" (p. 346, para. 1).

Building that culture of trust happens over time in day-to-day interactions as the faculty learn to work together interdependently, sharing their fears and hopes and unifying their commitment to identity safety. Trust grows as the staff feel their colleagues and administrators have their backs. In my (Alex) experience building trusting relationships, making the time and space for feedback to inform my practice, combined with tools of change management, worked substantially to shrink and manage the change process. I feel this is one of the most crucial elements to consider when seeking to promote identity safe practices with staff.

Norms for Collaboration

Setting norms for collaboration will ensure equal participation, especially when teachers are making decisions that impact them and their students. When teams review and master skills together for setting objectives, or brainstorm processes that allow many ideas to come forward with methods for narrowing solutions and reaching consensus, a desire for further collaboration naturally ensues. By forging shared agreements in advance, they are more likely to honor them in practice. If a person breaks one of the agreements, most often they simply need a reminder of the norm. Staff teams can work together to develop agreements and post them where all can view at every session. It is not an exercise of overkill to highlight them briefly before every meeting, emphasizing their import and updating them to stay relevant. Agreements keep members on track as the agenda moves forward.

Norms for Collaboration

1. Share the air. Ensure all participant voices are included.

2. Listen to and respect all people and ideas—even when you do not agree.

3. Take risks and try new things.

4. Practice being open-minded.

5. Speak up and say "Ouch." Let others know if you have been harmed or offended.

6. Say "Oops" to acknowledge your mistakes and be open to learn from them.

NOTE: Facilitators can define the "ouch" moment, explaining that if any participant feels hurt, offended, or uncomfortable, they are invited to express the feeling to the group. They can also explain the "oops" perspective, which encourages a person who has committed a microaggression—at times in response to an ouch moment—to be accountable and apologize.

Deprivatizing Practice

Another key element for collaboration includes deprivatizing practice, which involves unlocking the practice of teaching behind closed doors by supporting teachers and staff to invite colleagues into their classrooms to observe. Afterwards, educators can debrief and share impressions through safe and instructive dialogue that supports growth. Determining a particular theme in advance provides a focus for the observations. Prior to the observation, everyone agrees to supportive methods for giving feedback so observed teachers do not feel judged or evaluated, thus protecting their vulnerability and encouraging participation. Leaders can facilitate a day of observation by hiring two rotating subs who move from classroom to classroom, releasing teachers in turn to observe each other and follow up by sharing impressions. I (Kathe) enjoyed welcoming a second-grade teacher, who was struggling in his first year on the job, into my third-grade classroom to observe my classroom management techniques. He took notes and later decided what strategies appealed most to him. I shared my tips for mastering them, then spent a different afternoon observing him in his classroom as he translated the techniques into his own style. It was a rewarding exchange that reminded me how often new teachers tend to struggle unnecessarily in their classrooms without being noticed, and how easily it can often be fixed.

This approach can be similarly applied to support staff serving in specialized roles such as counselor, school manager, teacher on special assignment, campus supervisor, or parent/caregiver engagement coordinator. Staff in more singular roles can collaborate across school sites for peer observation and dialogue.

See Appendix D: Identity Safe Classroom Observation Form.

Interpersonal Dialogues about Race, Bias, and Diversity

A conversation between multiethnic groups of people about race, bias, and diversity is one of the deepest and possibly more daunting topics that a leader can undertake with staff, yet it is necessary for a full level of identity safety to be realized. A safe school culture necessitates that certain truths be addressed on a personal level to acknowledge when bias and racism are present. Thankfully, preparation and attention to certain details can usher in the right environment for safely engaging adults in these conversations. Leaders can access various approaches for entering into dialogue, with the goal of raising consciousness with a commitment to equity and social justice.

Humans often experience grief, anger, or shame in contemplating racial injustice endured, ignored, and/or perpetrated. For people of color, close proximity to White people's blindness to these injustices—and to white privilege, as well—can be very upsetting and at times feel more like re-injury rather than progress. This feels more true when White people become caught up in defensiveness or shame. Racial affinity groupings (R. King, 2018) can provide responsive, safe spaces for sharing and dialogue. Restorative practices for sharing our stories and experiences, hearing and honoring all voices, and working to repair harm are powerful tools. Direct teaching about the history of oppression can open minds and hearts, particularly for people with gaps in awareness of structural oppression and power and privilege.

Connecting across differences helps us develop compassion and understanding and is a life force for overcoming racism. I (Amy) recall an experience at an elementary school in which 99% of the students were Black and Latinx and 95% of the teachers were White. The prior year, I had helped launch a Family Resource Center at the school with staffing that was 50% parents/caregivers and 85% people of color. There were many culture clashes and a sense that teachers were highly resistant to seeing or talking about race and racism. With support from the principal, we engaged an outside facilitator for anti-oppression work. At first, the work was very halting and had a strong "us versus them" energy. The turning point came during a full-day cultural sharing event. The facilitator led us in randomly assigned small groups to draw and share our cultural identities. "Culture" was defined broadly to provide access points for all. Many of the White teachers, while not geared to discussing race, talked passionately and authentically about their Irish, Italian, largely working-class roots and histories. This sharing of personal identity and experience deepened a sense of shared vulnerability and safety, and it seemed to soften and connect the group. In the subsequent full-group share-out, there was a stronger sense of caring and compassion. Then Dorothy, an African American parent staff member of the Family Resource Center, bravely shared her experience of feeling diminished by a teacher handing her back a flyer she had made, filled with corrections made in red pen. She spoke about feeling unsure that she was welcomed or valued. Suddenly the teachers "got it." Their personal connections with Dorothy seemed to take precedence, and empathy rose up in the place where defensiveness had stood. One by one, teachers shared that they had not seen the power dynamics at play but now did. Many apologized and resolved to do better. This marked a true sea change at the school in being able to talk about and work through racial divides and inequities.

We believe that meaningful dialogue about race includes all of these perspectives, but not all at once. Attending to the needs, impressions, and general receptivity of the participants will inform which approaches may serve best and might include a combination of approaches or a predominance toward a single one. Facilitators remain steady and alert to support and guide the group with needed information and rules for engagement. Fostering acceptance and open-mindedness will generate goodwill that is often needed to inspire trust and active listening, which is vital for these discussions. Once a safe base is established, leaders can move to the harder, more substantial work that includes facing the real effects and damages in people's lives as a result of systemic racism.

We recognize that some discomfort is inevitable in an authentic exploration of difficult topics.

While it must be handled skillfully, the efforts are worth it. An in-depth conversation about personal experiences with race and culture can be a powerful key for unlocking misunderstandings, creating compassion, and promoting trust. Indeed, personal identity experiences shared within the group can provide the portal for a safe and deep understanding of discussion topics suggested later in this section and an understanding for the many ways that students are personally affected.

We can work to dismantle white supremacy together by mutually recognizing and sharing its presence in our lives and the lives of our staff and community. As leaders, our own confidence and trust in the efficacy of our identity and others will inspire strength and convey the feeling that vulnerabilities in the group will be protected. This rings true for leaders of all ethnicities and backgrounds. We begin with our personal sense of identity, creating trust and a space for safe, truthful sharing. Admittedly, it will require sharp attention and active compassion to carry out such discussions—and comfort may not manifest at the outset—but the only way to get to the other side, as they say, often means going right through the middle. But there are riches on the opposite shore, which makes the journey invaluable. It is important when you do share yourself to your group that you keep it real. Share your sense of identity in a way that exposes a measure of your inner landscape, because you will ask them to do the same. Here are questions that you can pose to the group to get conversations started, after you have modeled a few yourself:

- How are you experiencing your race or ethnicity in your life?

- How often do you think about race or ethnicity?

- Have you experienced a situation where your race or ethnic identity contributed to your discomfort? How about toward a sense of joy and pride?

- How do you think uncomfortable situations about race or ethnicity should be handled?

- What does courage mean to you in the context of race and ethnicity?

- Have you observed problems with race and ethnicity within this school?

- What practices or gestures contribute to your emotional safety and the expression of your culture?

- How can we act courageously together? How do we support one another in accepting our differences?

Before embarking on personal journeys with staff, leaders establish rules of engagement upon which everyone agrees. These can include the following prerequisite actions:

- Create a safe space by establishing confidentiality

- Give participants time to reflect on their thoughts before responding

- Encourage deep and active listening. Allow a few moments of silence after each share to ensure understanding and comprehension. At times, paraphrase the content of the share or message until the person indicates that it's correct. Shares are given in the first person for personal expression, never the "you." Leaders can open shares with a vulnerable exposure from their own experience. More on listening is presented in the section on "Formats: Built-in Routines, Rituals, and Listening Protocols" later in this chapter.

- Promote emotional safety. Let participants know that they are not there to point fingers or blame, only to share experiences of our identities within the context of our families, communities, and general society. Feedback is encouraged but limited to expressions of understanding or questions for clarification. Judgment is not on the table.

We strongly believe that identity safe spaces cannot be created without holding honest dialogue about race and oppression. As you embark, consider what your staff have already done in the past. Recognize that it is okay to feel discomfort when uncovering truths about the deeply rooted history of oppression and/or when revealing personal experiences with race and ethnicity. It is unlikely you will achieve closure in one session, or even a number of sessions, but the long-term view will serve you. The mutual and simultaneous appreciation of value in one another and our identities during these sessions does not disappoint. The recognition of our shared humanity brings a satisfying and motivating energy to all our efforts.

Facilitating a Challenging Discussion

I (Kathe) presented a workshop with Becki in Billings, Montana, for the national gathering of the organization Not in Our Town (https://www.niot.org/) to celebrate the 20th anniversary of the community coming together to stand up to a racist hate group that had been terrorizing Billings's citizens and their families, particularly Blacks and Jews. The townspeople of all races and religions had come together to end the hate, effectively running the hate group out of town. In our education workshop at the gathering, one member brought up the use of the N-word and his disgust with it. It was a guarded moment. Group participants were from many states across the country. Their ages, races, and experiences were diverse, and the group included teachers, a principal, a police officer, and some students. At first, the tension was palpable as different members expressed what the word meant to them. Some anger surfaced, but we kept talking. While other items on the agenda were swept off the table, we could sense that this one clearly held more import as everyone leaned into the circle we had formed with our chairs.

After initially expressing strong opinions, and being reminded of our community agreements, people started listening, really listening. Everyone was invested. The Black police officer and the White principal each expressed an extreme distaste for the word, but they eventually opened up to hear a student, who explained that no offense was intended when his friends, all Black, used it with each other. A Black woman told him she thought the word carried the seeds of hatred and should never be used. He received her words with quiet respect. A White student, who initially shared that she used the word with her many Black friends who had told her she was one of them, now realized that the word was offensive, and promised to quit. We offered appreciation for the level of vulnerability expressed in the room, which provided a platform for a newly acquired trust in stepping into sensitive topics between diverse peoples. It was an important first step for realizing that a safe atmosphere can be found for conversations between those of different races, generations, and social standing on topics about race. We believe harmful language including the N-word should be excluded from educational contexts. Leaders need to be vigilant to uphold identity safe spaces for everyone.

The gains of trust and a deeper sense of awareness from this level of interpersonal sharing and dialogue about race is extended to exploring topics that uncover and address conditions that have created and continue to perpetuate racism and bias. Some of those topics include

- reducing and eliminating implicit bias;

- understanding and mitigating stereotype threat;

- learning about history, including oppression as well as the resistance to it and movements to end it;

- studying anti-racist and abolitionist educational theory, pedagogy, and practice;

- understanding the backgrounds of the different cultural groups in the school community;

- practicing culturally responsive teaching;

- supporting LGBTQIA+ and gender nonconforming students;

- understanding the immigrant experience and meeting needs of English Learners (ELs) students;

- supporting students with disabilities;

- facilitating conversations about race with students; and

- dismantling white supremacy.

Examining Implicit Bias

One school leader engaged staff in taking the Harvard Implicit Bias Test (Project Implicit, n.d.) on their own without obligating them to share results. Following the test, they embarked on a conversation about implicit bias and their reflections on the process of discovering unconscious biases within themselves. The conversation continued with an exploration of research on effective ways to eliminate these biases through empathy, and countering and refuting stereotypes.

These discussions occur over time and can be woven into ongoing work with the expressed goal of having them lead to action in our classrooms. While we believe it is best to be proactive rather than wait for a crisis moment to open these dialogues, we acknowledge there are some critical incidents requiring an immediate response. Below are some examples we have observed in some of the schools we have supported:

- An incident where a second grader called a peer the N-word that became the subject of hostile e-mail exchanges among parents and sparked tension in the community.

- A middle school student who drew a caricature of his Palestinian teacher on the wall with the caption "terrorist."

- An autistic student who was brutally beaten.

- A high school student who drove to his school with confederate flags waving from the back of his truck.

Incidents such as these do not mean that the school has failed in its equity efforts. Rather, they can happen anywhere and at any time. Whether they happen or not isn't the question, but how they are handled and resolved matters most. With conflict resolution and mediation strategies in hand, a leader is ready to move through difficult moments with courage and commitment to the students. Because of the sensitive nature of these incidents, dialogue about race can greatly benefit both staff and students, and sometimes an experienced outside facilitator can provide a safety net for venting deeply felt expressions.

Institutional: Examining and Changing Practices, Procedures, and Policies

As part of seeking transformational change, school leaders go beyond talk about racism to invite staff to join in seeking solutions to situations and practices resulting from institutional bias and racism. When we critically examine climate, behavior, and academic data, teams can make honest appraisals of active and unfavorable conditions in the school and resolve them using a systemic approach. Solutions might include taking steps to diversify staff to mirror the student population, improving access to higher-level courses, and rectifying policies that have maintained an unfair advantage for some students over others. The Equity Literacy Institute (n.d.) defined a set of skills and abilities that build staff capacity:

1. The ability to *recognize* even the subtlest biases and inequities

2. The ability to *respond* skillfully and equitably to biases and inequities in the immediate term

3. The ability to *redress* biases and inequities by understanding and addressing them at their institutional roots

4. The ability to *actively cultivate* equity by applying an equity commitment to every decision

5. The ability to *sustain* equity efforts even in the face of discomfort or resistance

These skills are developed and woven into the process of applying the principles of identity safety in every aspect of the school's operation.

The institutional level encompasses a range of small and large decisions, including some that appear deceptively simple. The overriding fact here is that no one right answer exists that can support staff in grappling with a dilemma and assigning equal status to all voices. When educators embark on a collaborative approach to institutional transformation, they consider all factors by using data, monitoring changes, and making adaptations. One high school principal worked with her leadership team to determine the distribution of Title I and other federal funding to leverage equity for students. The team opted to focus on the needs of an influx of students who had recently arrived from Yemen. A war had been tearing that country apart, and many students had previously attended school only for partial days. Older students did not arrive with transcripts of their credits. District data showed that 66% of Yemini students were not on track to graduate (Oakland Unified School District, n.d.-a). They discussed how Yemeni families are not categorized as refugees by the U.S. government, so they do not qualify for federal refugee programs that help families transition.

After a long and thoughtful discussion weighing all the options, the team decided to hire an Arabic-speaking parent liaison, purchase curricular materials about Yemini culture, and provide staff training to support students and families. In Chapter 4, we offer some team processes for analyzing data and making improvements. In Chapter 7, we describe processes for moving a school through an institutional change process toward identity safety. A trusting climate, positive relationships, and a shared commitment to place students at the heart of our work will make room for these changes to occur.

Keeping an Eye on the Ball: Finding Equitable Solutions Together

In one high school, controversy erupted over changes to a popular robotics science program. Students of color pointed out that the program mainly consisted of White students. The students explained that their middle school had not offered the coursework to adequately prepare them to meet the program's entrance requirements. The students from feeder schools in the more prosperous neighborhood had taken the necessary courses while they had not. Initially, the program leaders resisted adjusting entrance requirements, stating that they did not want to lower standards for the program, even though that would have allowed more students of color to enroll. Even worse, program administrators claimed that by lowering entrance requirements, the unprepared students would not succeed in the program. However, some staff members pressed forward with their commitment to apply an equity lens to respond and redress the problem. The staff continued to grapple with these perspectives and ultimately came to consensus on an equitable solution, reducing entry requirements and offering tutoring for those who had not received the prerequisite coursework.

STRUCTURES AND FORMATS FOR PROFESSIONAL LEARNING

Identity safe practices lend themselves well to a variety of professional learning models because they form part of a holistic approach, a way of teaching and interacting, and not a program with fixed steps. Many teachers are already quite adept and exemplary in aspects of identity safety. And yet, addressing all the components and principles of identity safety invites a wealth of creativity and unique expressions for the way they overlap, interact, and connect with students, curriculum, and the school community. In the spirit of a growth mindset, every one of us can increase our knowledge and capacity to apply the principles. It helps to remember, too, that many positive identity safe strategies can be undermined by a lack of awareness for all the ways a student's sense of belonging can be harmed by thoughtlessly spoken words.

In professional learning settings where emotional safety has been created, educators can examine situations where acceptance is undermined and consider how to do better the next time. In one workshop, Sally, a teacher from a rural school, reflected on her own actions and how she could improve. She explained,

> I taught at a small school in Kansas. We had only three Black students in our seventh-grade class. I noticed that Ronald, who was Black, had been getting good grades but had stopped turning in work and was failing my class. I approached him and Ronald explained that his best friend, Jim, kept saying to him, "You're not Black—you're the whitest Black kid I ever saw."

> I responded with, "Just ignore it. He doesn't mean anything by it. After all, he still is your friend, isn't he?" When I now consider my response through an identity safety lens, I see that I should have done more. Without acknowledging his rightful identity and status as a young Black male, I had effectively disparaged him by silently agreeing with Jim's unintended yet injurious assumption that white must be better. Now, I would first have more conversations with Ronald about his identity and probably find him a Black mentor or ally for additional support. I also would get his permission to talk to his friend, Jim, about how such a comment can hurt. I would do that in a delicate way, knowing that boys that age are very sensitive. Then I would try to bring the two together, again with Ronald's permission.

Inquiry processes, interactive workshops, collaborative professional dialogue, study groups, coaching, and peer observation models all can deepen the work. This book as well as the books *Identity Safe Classrooms, Grades K–5* (D. M. Steele & Cohn-Vargas, 2013) and *Identity Safe Classrooms, Grades 6–12* (Cohn-Vargas et al., 2020) were written with the intent to be used in flexible ways by teams of educators. Activities at the end of each chapter can be used in this process. In this section, we highlight some of these processes and indicate advantages of the different ones.

When designing dedicated time for professional learning, staff can negotiate how to structure it. Models of delivery for adult learning include study groups, professional learning communities (PLCs), participatory action research, lesson study, coaching, and workshops, which all promote shared practice and collaborative growth. Asking the faculty to share their preferences for models that suit them increases their commitment.

Different groupings enhance and deepen sharing: teacher grade-level groups, cross-grade teams, race or gender identity-based affinity groups, subject matter groups, and others. Leaders can create affinity groups where participants select the one they feel most comfortable attending, ensuring no staff members are put on the spot to self-identify or are involuntarily placed in an identity group for which they do not ascribe, such as assigning mixed-race persons to a group of a particular race.

Formats: Built-in Routines, Rituals, and Listening Protocols

Particular structures maximize the way we absorb and retain knowledge, facilitate interaction, and support reflection.

Setting an Intention: After attending an Art of Coaching workshop, I (Alex) learned the power of setting intentions and anchoring yourself in the learning of the day. Now, I open every professional learning experience by welcoming participants and asking them to set a specific intention for what they hope to gain from the session. At the end of the session, I give them a few more minutes to reflect and write on how they actualized their intention. By asking individuals to set their personal growth target and reflect on it, they exercise their commitment to personally own their learning.

Reflection and Listening: In the busy life of a teacher, often there is little time for reflection to process new ideas, feelings, and experiences. A few minutes of reflection can serve as a breath of fresh air and calm the spirit. Activities that cater to these self-motivating qualities include visualization, meditations, and quick-writes. The reflections can be as brief as a few minutes and incorporated at the start of a meeting or workshop, in the middle or at the conclusion. I (Kathe) attended to the well-being of the teachers in front of me at the outset for every workshop I led, understanding that without their willingness, we would not enjoy much progress. As a teacher, I understood all too well the unique demands upon them and opened every workshop with an acknowledgment for their hard work and genuine efforts. I also tapped into their general well-being by asking them about their current concerns and their feelings. This allowed me to determine their receptivity and pivot toward a tailored approach. If needed, I would spend more time on the healing aspect and listening to gain their trust. Expression can refresh the soul, and a refreshed group is ready to lean in with great ideas. Opening a workshop session, for this reason, holds import and consideration for special treatment. It will set the tone.

Storytelling Protocols: Listening to and Elevating Voice

Most of us have been educated from birth to assume we know how to listen—simply because our ears are functional. Listening, however, is not the same as hearing. It is an essential skill that can be developed and honed. Educators can practice the skill when sharing their social identities and their ideas and perspectives on controversial topics. Teams can also adopt listening skills for problem-solving by paraphrasing what they hear, posing questions, offering useful feedback, and sharing solutions, always in the spirit of active listening. As an integral part of staff meetings, these skills can empower participants to speak and listen purposefully, avoid misunderstandings and further the momentum of their shared goals.

Leaders can highlight what these conversations mean on a metacognitive level, explaining how important listening and communication skills are when applied to student voices. This is described in detail in the identity safe component "listening for student voices." When staff engage in equitable participation and listening strategies, they will in turn be able to mirror these skills to their students. Here are some examples of participatory protocols that can be used in staff meetings and professional learning sessions:

- Check-ins in a circle format, where each person shares

- Fishbowls, where people are sitting in a circle within a larger circle of people. The inside circle engages in a discussion or debate in response to a prompt, while the outer circle listens without intervening. Later, the outer circle reflects on what they heard, with the inner circle listening.

- Small-group listening protocols ask participants to listen to one individual without interruption, and later paraphrase what they heard, asking clarifying questions.

- Storytelling protocols that allow educators to dive into their own personal experiences and share them with others. Stories hook the mind as listeners link them to their own prior experiences. Sharing stories also fosters empathy and understanding. Time is managed carefully to allow each participant equal time to share without interruption.

Closing Routines

Retention of new content is enhanced by routines that allow our brains to summarize or lock in what has been learned. Closing routines can incorporate these elements by asking participants to highlight new learnings, express appreciations, or set intentions for the future. The mere act of forming a circle and asking each person for a word to summarize feelings or what they will take from the session provides a sense of closure and unity.

Introducing Identity Safety

We suggest that identity safe practices can be initially introduced through an interactive workshop that includes an overview of the concepts and a presentation of research on stereotype threat and identity safety. Once the components and the principles are shared, participants can discuss which ones they may have already adopted and consider others where they feel they still can learn and grow. This gives the group a platform for basic understandings, which can then be extended through other models of professional learning.

Study Groups and PLCs

I (Becki) have supported several schools and districts with identity safety study groups. The first was my dissertation study, where I brought together a small group of elementary teachers from the district where I had previously served as curriculum director. We called ourselves ISPART (Identity Safety Participatory Action Research Team). We worked together to discuss, define, describe, and implement strategies that addressed each of the factors that emerged in the SISP identity safe research. The same year, Dorothy Steele held a voluntary study group in the district where the SISP research took place. She invited teachers who had been observed in the SISP study schools and other interested educators to deeply explore identity safety components. She used a teacher observation form for visiting each other's classrooms. What we learned from both groups became the basis for the book *Identity Safe Classrooms, Grades K–5* (D. M. Steele & Cohn-Vargas, 2013).

I have continued to lead in-person and online study groups. Study group members work diligently through the book chapters, develop action research projects, and/or select a specific area of practice (e.g., curriculum design, student discipline systems, assessment) to deepen the use of identity safe principles.

A Multiyear Pilot Process

We (Amy, Alex, and Becki) introduced identity safety to one district by inviting staff volunteers to attend a series of four full-day inquiry sessions and launch the process of implementing identity safety in their classrooms. In the first year, we proposed a model of teacher action research where each participant individually, and again with a partner, chose an area of identity safety to study, implement, and gather data. Results were then shared with the group. In retrospect, we learned that four sessions over a two-month period were too short a time to make action research conclusions or observe meaningful change in student achievement. The second year, we invited another group of volunteers, but we changed our model. Each session focused on one of the domains and its respective identity safety components. Participants identified strategies that they took back to their classrooms, practiced, and returned to share what they learned. Many strategies included in *Identity Safe Classrooms, Grades 6–12* (Cohn-Vargas et al., 2020) emerged from these pilots. We created a data bank of strategies, the Identity Safe Signature Strategies Spreadsheet (Appendix K), that is included on the Corwin Belonging and Inclusion in Identity Safe Schools resource page found at https://resources.corwin.com/BelongingandInclusionISS.

Coupled with the pilot, Amy and Alex introduced identity safety to site administrators and in districtwide professional learning meetings. Sessions were also held for groups with differing roles, including campus security who said it resonated with their efforts to connect with and build relationships among students.

Also, during years three and four, a grant was obtained to target identity safe formative assessment as part of Assessment for Learning Project (ALP) (https://www.assessmentforlearningproject.org/), a national network focused on formative and performance assessment (see Chapter 4). This led to a deeper exploration of how identity safety can be integrated into assessment practices. Amy and Alex worked with staff teams inside the district. They videotaped students sharing their formative assessment experiences and how it impacted their academic identity and shared them at ALP conferences.

Coaching Models

Coaching is a powerful tool to support practice as teachers and school leaders grow and learn about identity safety. Elena Aguilar (2013) describes coaching as one of the most impactful models of professional learning. It increases knowledge, builds capacity, and fuels motivation. Coaching incorporates trust-building through deep listening, thoughtful questions, and a means for continually refining practice. Aguilar points out that coaching skills are not only the purview of instructional coaches, but they can also be used by site leaders, mentors, and peers.

She reminds us that transformation takes time. Her book includes a strategic and high-leverage action rubric to help coaches select focal points that will yield high-impact results.

Identity safe coaches listen for patterns as well as what is left unsaid, refraining from telling their own stories. Then they paraphrase to ensure they've understood, asking clarifying questions. Coaches use probing questions that allow the participants to deepen understanding of their own beliefs, thoughts, and emotions. Lastly, they invite reflection and analysis, helping teachers transform individual practice, which can eventually even extend across the faculty (Aguilar, 2013). Coaching honors each teacher's expertise, choices, and needs while simultaneously drawing from shared identity safe school goals in a top-down and bottom-up process.

The Power of Coaching

As a career-long believer in the power of coaching, I (Alex) never actually had a dedicated coach until I began my work with Elena Aguilar. I met her at a time when I was new to my demanding role as a senior district leader and encountering significant life changes (having my first and then second child). Our work together gave me a space to bring forward all of my identities as I grappled with challenging and important decisions and to determine potential paths forward. One particular day, I was completely stuck, leading me to list all of the barriers and or deficiencies I thought I had; Elena took the unconventional approach of simply asking, "What if those things are true, what would you do?" Her question stunned me for a moment but then encouraged me to challenge my negative narrative and to be forward-thinking. I could not have done that if I had not trusted that she actually did not believe those things to be true about me. Great coaches believe in potential and possibility in the people they are working with. This is never truer than in an educational context. They create spaces of deep relational trust in which you can bring your full self to use as a resource in exploring your professional experiences and challenges.

On-the-Spot Teachable Moments

Often leaders may find themselves with a teachable moment for deepening cultural awareness and understanding differences. Louise Waters describes an on-the-spot opportunity for learning that became a multiyear journey toward identity safety.

> As a long-time parent at the elementary school where I became principal, I knew the cherished nature of the school's Christmas celebrations.

This included many immigrant students and families who felt that being part of Santa Claus, Christmas trees, stockings, and Christmas music made them feel like true Americans. However, I also knew Sikh, Muslim, and Buddhist families who were very ambivalent about the holiday. My first Christmas as principal, I listened and observed, knowing we needed to change but deciding to take it a step at a time. In early December I invited Indian staff and parents to set up Diwali displays in the library—and highlighted the nods to Kwanzaa and Hanukkah that had already taken place. Staff from these cultures shared their meanings and suggested ways to include them in holiday activities, just-in-time professional development on cultural diversity without directly challenging the Christmas tradition.

I also looked and listened. I talked with Muslim students as they crumpled up handmade Christmas cards at the first garbage can they passed, not wanting to show their parents but anxious to be part of the festivities. I visited classes where students made calendar chains of 24 red and green links with a recycled Christmas card, sometimes with religious images, for the 25th day. And I talked with non-Christian staff about their experiences.

By year two, I was ready for a second step. This time, the staff meeting started with everyone sharing favorite holiday traditions and the meaning these evoked. Cross-cutting themes like family, hope, peace, tradition, foods, and giving emerged. Then a panel of non-Christian staff shared stories about the pain of being outsiders, hiding their otherness as children at Christmas or as parents trying to honor their own religions traditions while helping their children navigate the holidays. And I shared what I had learned in my observations the year before, wondering how the 25% of our students who were not Christian experienced school in December. The professional development (PD) ended by brainstorming ways to keep the spirit of the season but make it more inclusive. Rather than assignments about Christmas, writing assignments began featuring favorite holidays, favorite foods, and descriptions of family celebrations— which might or might not be Christmas. Ornaments were decorations that could be for a tree or a wall, and cards could be for any reason, including a coming new year. Step two for creating an identity safe school was not abstract, but built on the need of the moment in that community. Not everyone changed and not everyone was happy, but over time, the themes and stars, candles, and the spirit of giving and peace replaced Christmas trees as markers for the season.

NAVIGATING THE COMPLEXITIES OF STAFF PERSONALITIES AND GROUP DYNAMICS

A "one size fits all" approach in the context of adult learning is destined to leave some educators out in the cold feeling unsupported. Every staff is made up of a mixture of personality types, backgrounds, and life experiences. When these variations are viewed as opportunities to receive a rich range of voices, adding layers of ideas, understanding, and inspiration to staff meetings, curriculum, school plans, and policies—as well as relationships—we can enjoy increased momentum for identity safety. Different people also bring many different attitudes to the change process. Some teachers thrive on innovation and become early adopters, ready to soar with new ideas. Others consider themselves "old school," preferring to stick to the tried and true. Some are new to the field, grappling with day-to-day survival. Possibly the most difficult group to facilitate are educators who feel burned out. They may harbor a perception of a constant bombardment of new curricula and programs. Identity safe modalities for adult learning can encompass and include every member of the teaching community, including the more challenging members. Even those who feel discouraged can benefit from the right approach. Sharing their vulnerabilities in a safe environment, for example, offers opportunities for others to step up and offer help. We can hold high expectations for staff when they respond to different approaches that will motivate and activate them to work together for a better school.

Anthony Mohammed and Sharroky Hollie (2011) make important suggestions for navigating transformation, considering the complexity of a school staff. They suggest leaders articulate a clear case for the changes they hope to make, all the while developing individual relationships with each member of staff, ostracizing no one. Just as with students, leaders offer support to each person, practicing and modeling inclusivity. Once teachers have been introduced to the concept and research on identity safety, we can support their implementation and practice in the following ways:

- For highly motivated teachers, invite them to do action research on identity safe topics.

- For seasoned teachers, highlight identity safe strategies that they do well and ask them to share with other staff.

- For new teachers struggling with behavior management, set them up to initiate relationship-building and belonging activities that build a classroom community with respectful interactions.

- For those who are burned out, cynical, or slow to change, encourage them to share their hesitations and address them with compassion and support.

- For paraprofessionals and others who often feel they are not a part of school transformation efforts, express the importance of their role for creating an identity safe campus and collaborate with them to identify an area of focus.

- For master teachers who incorporate identity safe practices, provide opportunities for them to mentor and support their peers, developing pathways toward greater leadership.

A collaborative culture where educators support each other is one of the best ways to motivate individuals and lift the entire staff to their highest level of practice. When staff members feel seen and heard individually and as a group, they will respond with trust, openness, and a willingness to collaborate and try new things. Leaders can structure time for team collaborations with professional learning opportunities targeted to their particular roles as teachers, counselors, and reading support personnel, helping each group apply identity safe practices. And when different members of the school community confer in their separate roles to serve the school and the students, we often realize some of the best results.

When we consider the different views that staff members may hold for a single student—such as a student's teacher, football coach, and a paraprofessional—each can broaden their understanding of that student with the input from the others and provide more meaningful service.

Validating both autonomy and cooperation and support teams to work together on their own sets the pace for collaboration. Setting up models to work regularly in small and large groups and providing methods for sharing information, insights, obstacles, and solutions will sustain momentum and inspiration. Delegating tasks and spreading leadership and responsibilities across many people highlights your trust in them and models equity as it increases capacity. New teacher leaders emerge, and a wide range of expertise expands what a school community can accomplish.

Rising to Challenges/Avoiding Pitfalls

In this section, we highlight ways to avoid two challenges or pitfalls that may befall a leader trying to introduce identity safety to staff.

INVOLVING THE FULL STAFF IN COLLABORATIVE DECISIONS

Eva, an elementary school principal, encountered resistance when she tried to bring the full staff together in a meeting that would include everyone: teachers, campus supervisors, school counselors, administrative assistants, and custodians. She was very enthusiastic about inclusion, and her purpose was to create a unified staff stance. However, once she set up the meeting, she heard rumblings that more than a few of the classified staff did not consider such a meeting to be part of their job description. They were even more surprised when she announced that we would be selecting representatives for the leadership team. In response to the complaints, she switched gears and slowed down, holding smaller meetings for job-alike groups. There, she asked them to share any concerns about their jobs while communicating that their roles were vital. Those brief encounters unified them, and they came to appreciate being represented on the leadership team.

GIVING DIFFICULT NEWS ABOUT THE RESULTS OF STANDARDIZED TESTS

An honest accounting of student achievement sometimes puts leaders in the position of walking a tightrope. On one hand, sobering news can serve as a wakeup call that moves staff into action to generate needed programmatic and curricular changes. On the other hand, when educators have been working hard to improve achievement, the news can deflate spirits or arouse defensiveness. The important item is to present news honestly and forthrightly, with acknowledgment and praise for genuine efforts. Noting that they made a difference with their students in ways unseen by the data can also assuage disappointment. If they feel honored in spite of discouraging results, they are more likely to hop back on board to explore solutions. Identity safe leaders can also deter staff from the temptation to blame their predecessors, which is an easy trap: "My students arrived in my classroom far below grade level, so it is not my fault." Much in the way we support our students, we can also provide similar feedback for staff.

- Express your high standards and acknowledge the efforts that teachers have made to support student achievement.

- Express your belief in their capacity to meet student needs and improve performance.

- Identify specific areas of improvement and progress to date.

- Ask them to identify solutions and tools to use to monitor progress.

When staff feel safe in our appraisal of the situation and our belief in their commitment and skill, they are more empowered to share impressions and solutions.

Closing the Gap Between Ideas and Action

Planning professional learning for an identity safe school involves applying the principles of adult learning to each of the levels: intrapersonal, interpersonal, and institutional:

- Offer choice in the format and content of personalized learning experiences that fit with the different needs of your staff.

- Combine opportunities for collaboration and autonomy in your options.

- Make time spent together vibrant, interactive, and meaningful.

- Vary activities to address different learning modalities that capture interest and spark enthusiasm.

Intrapersonal—Engage in professional growth for staff that fosters self-reflection:

- Provide for sharing of personal experiences that forged their social identities, values, and beliefs, including those personal experiences that shaped their views on and feelings about race and ethnicity. Allow for safe, personal exploration of implicit biases.

- Offer short activities that lend themselves to reflective conversations or quickwrites during meetings.

- Furnish time for longer activities that give them space to deeply interrogate their personal mission as educators and ways to put it into practice.

Interpersonal—Design professional learning opportunities that strengthen communication and positive interactions among staff with their students and their families. Incorporate activities that strengthen relationships:

- Set norms and agreements for meetings, data analysis, and team planning.

- Focus on trust-building and equal status.

- Raise awareness and open dialogue on equity issues, race, gender, and other differences.

- Prepare faculty to facilitate discussions on sensitive topics.

- Foster care, compassion, and a culture of support.

- Make space for connecting and getting to know each other through icebreakers, brain breaks, and more extended sharing opportunities.

Institutional—Frequently analyze data, revisit, and improve practices and policies that impact student achievement, identity safety, and equity. Build skill sets and staff capacity:

- Recognize, understand, and respond to biases and inequities.

- Work together to examine the unintended consequences of many regularly used practices and make changes.

- Review curricular and instructional decisions with an equity lens and monitor progress.

- Motivate and enlist all staff in transformation to an identity safe school.

Engage in a variety of formats and structures that facilitate staff collaboration and growth:

- Develop a shared language and understanding of identity safety principles, research, and effective strategies.

- Set aside time for study groups and professional learning communities.

- Arrange for peer observations, coaching, and other mentoring activities.

- Encourage teacher action research to hone identity safe practices.

Prepare to face the challenges of school transformation with awareness:

- Acknowledge and mitigate the many stressors impacting staff and protect their time.

- Start with the early adopters and be ready to draw in resistant teachers.

- Phase in identity safety and integrate it into existing focal areas.

Your staff are the most important purveyors of identity safety in its spread across your campus. You cannot do this work without them. Identity safe values will not convey through a single articulated message or handbook, nor can the scope of identity safety be covered in one training session. They take root in the personal leadership stances, skills, and actions outlined in this section, which can be obtained through reflection, ongoing and monitored staff conversations, and gains in cultural awareness. Once teachers understand identity safe teaching, their leaders can loop back on all instructional experiences to ensure they incorporate diversity, equity, and inclusion. Careful planning and taking time to develop a deep understanding of identity safety by all members of your adult community will yield a sustained commitment to bring an identity safe school to life.

Check Yourself

- What staff dialogue and training have our staff done in the area of diversity, anti-racism, and equity? How can I build on the work that has been done already?

- How am I modeling and facilitating courageous conversations to promote diversity, equity, and inclusion?

- What professional learning opportunities exist for certificated and classified staff? What adult learning principles have been incorporated?

- What coaching and mentoring opportunities are happening? How can coaches, administrators, and others who support classroom teachers increase their awareness of identity safety and equity?

- What are the curricular and other pedagogical initiatives staff are participating in currently? How are they responding? How can identity safe practices be integrated into those initiatives?

Using the Tools

Staff Support for Identity Safety

1. List the areas of identity safety that you plan to introduce (e.g., introduction to identity safety, creating belonging, identity safe assessments).

2. Consider the different staff roles and members of staff. What are their strengths and areas of interest? What identity safe practices are they already doing? What kinds of professional learning activities will strengthen their use of identity safe practices?

STAFF ROLE/ NAME	AREAS OF INTEREST	CURRENT IDENTITY SAFE PRACTICES	POTENTIAL PERSONALIZED PROFESSIONAL LEARNING ACTIVITIES

3. What professional dialogue and diversity activities have your staff participated in?

ACTIVITY	WHAT WAS DONE? FREQUENCY?	HOW WAS IT RECEIVED?
Dialogue about race		
Dialogue about gender		
Support for EL students		
Reducing stereotype threat		
Implicit bias reduction		
Anti-racist education		

4. Identify three goals for adult learning for the coming year. What are your next steps to achieve the goals?

GOAL	ACTIVITIES	TIMELINE

CHAPTER 4

Data and Assessment for an Identity Safe School

Introduction

Data and assessment are essential components of equitable schools. Information about student mastery and progress is part and parcel of teaching and learning. Information about school outcomes writ larger—related to access, discipline, staffing, and more—is a prerequisite for identifying and overcoming inequities linked to race, gender, and other demographic factors. But historically, data and assessment have too often resulted in harm rather than good, particularly for economically disadvantaged communities and communities of color. This chapter shares principles, systems, and practices for identity safe data and assessment. It offers strategies for disarming pitfalls by which data and assessment can work against rather than for equity.

Identity safe data and assessment relate to all identity safety principles.

- Stepping beyond *colorblindness* enables us to be clear-eyed and specific about differences and samenesses in experiences and outcomes among students, staff, and families of all backgrounds.

- *Fostering positive, equal status relationships* and *social and emotional safety* provide conditions in which all feel seen and valued and feedback is trusted, driving the most powerful collective learning possible.

- *Expressing high expectations* involves high standards that matter to those involved, the ongoing shaping and communication of those standards, and a durable faith in each and all's capacity to meet these standards.

- *Educators examining their own social identities* builds readiness to explore and address issues related to social differences that arise through data review and inquiry.

- Formative assessment is a core component for *student learning and teaching for understanding*.

- *Schoolwide equity* requires reliable data and trusted feedback loops to give leaders and stakeholders a clear view of how school is working for all groups of students, staff, and families.

Why It Matters

There are three key dimensions to why identity safe data and assessment matter for schools. The first is the well-documented power of collaborative, data-driven inquiry to inform school policies, structures, practices, and routines. This means including and going beyond student learning data to understand and improve how all aspects of the school benefit all groups of students, staff, and families. The most useful information is specific enough to be actionable, and disaggregated by race, gender, and other salient demographic factors to ensure a full picture of actions and outcomes. Access to these data, along with time and support for team-based inquiry, is crucial for deepening and sustaining equity in schools. But without identity safety, data-driven inquiry can be experienced as ascribing gaps to students and families. Bias and cultural blindness can threaten every step: from the questions we ask, the goals we set, the data we collect and report, how we think and dialogue together, the meaning we make, the stories we tell, and the actions we take with the information we gain.

The second is the imperative to hear and be guided by all voices, particularly those that have historically been excluded or silenced as shapers and decision makers in schools. This requires consideration of voices representative of the community by race, gender, and other important aspects of identity. Beyond being the "right" thing to do and a powerful strategy for trust-building, this provides knowledge and perspective dearly needed to inform improvement. But without identity safety, stakeholders may not trust or value these efforts. It takes sustained work at individual, team, and community levels to create a culture of equal and respected status for all voices (see Chapters 5 and 7).

The third is formative assessment and feedback, shown by a rich body of research as one of the most impactful instructional factors for student learning (Marzano, 2008; Paddington Teaching and Learning, 2013; Without identity safety, feedback may be experienced as confirming a stereotype or attributing inferiority rather than supporting learning. Under these conditions, feedback may advance inequity rather than fuel learning, particularly for students facing societally entrenched negative stereotypes and narratives.

Making It Happen

COLLABORATIVE DATA-DRIVEN INQUIRY

> *Not everything that is faced can be changed, but nothing can be changed until it is faced.*
>
> —*James Baldwin*

Despite decades of education reform efforts, inequities persist in almost every aspect of public education. Educators of color are vastly underrepresented in the classroom and as school leaders: in 2016, 22% of public school principals and 20% of teachers were people of color, compared to 51% of students. Students of color and students from economically disadvantaged communities experience large gaps in access to high-quality curriculum and instruction, and higher rates of suspension, special education identification, and dropping out of high school or college.

An *identity safe culture of data and assessment* first and foremost commits us to seeing and addressing inequities linked to race, gender, and other demographic factors. It asks us to embrace mistakes as learning moments; to be asset- rather than deficit-based in our thinking, language, and storytelling; to value many types of knowledge and wisdom; and to commit to a vision of equal status for community members of all types, roles, and backgrounds. It calls on us to understand and interrupt implicit and explicit racist practices in assessment.

Cycles of inquiry have been a feature in education in the United States for the last 70 years, influenced by thinkers such as William Edwards Deming (*Plan-Do-Study-Act*) (W. Edwards Deming Institute, n.d.), Paulo Freire (the *Praxis* action-reflection cycle) (1972), and Mike Schmoker (*short-term cycles* of improvement) (2011). The cycle starts with centering on current goals and naming sources of information to track progress on goals. Relevant data are gathered and presented in ways that aid in analysis and reflection. Reflection includes attention to illuminating and addressing root causes. This informs plans for new actions which in turn suggests new inquiry into the results; and the cycle begins again (Cushman, 1999). Assessment and data without cycles of inquiry is like a boat without a navigational system or clear roles for the crew, and cycles of inquiry without assessment and data is like a boat with a ready crew and navigational system, but no power or fuel. Cycles of inquiry are as foundational for equitable schools as are rigorous curriculum, cultural responsiveness, and progressive discipline.

Inclusive collaboration enables school communities to make well-informed, evidence-based decisions to improve student outcomes. Just as classroom formative assessment positions students as leaders of their own learning, collaborative inquiry empowers participants as producers and disseminators of knowledge geared to helping the school achieve its goals. Research on collaborative inquiry demonstrates its tremendous power for school improvement as well as for activating stakeholder engagement and leadership. An *inquiry habit of mind, team structures,* and *data use* stand out as key factors (Amels, et al., 2019).

Inquiry Habit of Mind

A well-developed inquiry habit of mind implies curiosity, asking questions, the capacity to switch perspectives, and the willingness to let go of existing routines to try out and adopt ways of doing things (Uiterwijk-Luijk et al., 2017). The first unit of change is at the individual level, as each member of the school community takes personal responsibility for how to be our best selves and bring our best effort in the service of students. In order for individuals to take risks to examine our practice, identify what is not yet working well, and try new routines and practices, we see our own and each other's "not yet" areas as opportunities for growth rather than markers of failure. We trust the inquiry process—the cycles of inquiry described below—as a sincere investment in ourselves and our teams as learners, thinkers, and doers.

Direct teaching of growth mindset and neuroplasticity builds faith and excitement about our capacity to grow and achieve our goals. One simple routine for supporting an inquiry habit of mind is to begin each meeting by setting an intention and/ or inquiry question, returning to them at the close of the session for reflection. (Aguilar 2014) (see Chapter 3).

Inquiry Calendars show how the inquiry will progress throughout the year, connected to a clear set of goals. The start of this calendar is a "looking back" view of prior year outcomes to celebrate successes; identify assets, barriers, and priorities; and to establish goals and the data that will be used to assess progress. Next comes a "looking forward" view focused on the upcoming school year. Then throughout the year, each team meets frequently to review and reflect on data, assess and discuss progress, and adjust actions as needed. Ideally, teams meet quarterly for more comprehensive data review and planning, and weekly or biweekly for more just-in-time data review and response. Sticking to the calendar and utilizing a common set of routines creates a strong through-line and sense of momentum in the work. An Inquiry Calendar Planner is provided in "Using the Tools" near the close of this chapter and in Appendix E.

Team Structures: Learning Communities

Learning communities provide a space and a structure for people to align around a shared goal and are the best home base for collaborative inquiry (Harvard Center on the Developing Child, n.d.). A learning community meets on a predictable cycle, whether daily, weekly, monthly, or quarterly. In addition to classrooms, key structures include teacher and staff role-alike teams, parent/caregiver and student leadership groups, schoolwide councils, and more. Collaborative inquiry will be strongest when *every* member of the school community—students, educators, and parents/caregivers—have a learning community home base. Practices (described in Chapter 3) such as group agreements, intention setting, reflection, community-building, cultural sharing, storytelling, and constructive listening help make space for all voices and honor diverse cultural norms and ways. These practices assist teams to maintain a growth mindset and to hear, learn from and apply divergent experiences and ideas.

Data Use: Purpose, Collection, Analysis, and Application

Clear and consistent process and routines for using data strengthen access for all participants. There are many models and routines to choose from; a Carnegie Institute's Continuous Improvement in Education white paper (Park, et al., 2013) and the Education Development Center Primer (Shakman et al., 2017) cited in the reference section are great places to start. Leaders can support space for all voices by utilizing individual reflection, round-robins and pair-shares alongside full group discussion.

These recommended data use steps may unfold in one or multiple sessions:

- Center on purpose and goals

- Prepare emotionally/affectively to work with the data (discussed further below)

- Orient to the data at hand and address clarifying questions

- Identify key data points (89% of parents stated . . . 92% of students grew . . .)

- Highlight data points that are strengths, growth areas, and areas for further study

- Share and build understanding of the *root causes* of outcomes, their reasons and origins

- Identify priorities for change as well as for celebration and further study

- Plan what to stop, start, and continue to do to achieve priorities
  - IF we . . . (stop, start, continue to do _____), THEN this will be true (we will achieve the priority of _____)

- Update the team inquiry calendar as needed to reflect the process and outcome data you'll need for upcoming sessions to track progress on any new IF . . . THEN plans

It is best to limit the amount of data to be reviewed each time so that meaning-making is center stage, rather than the numbers. When a lot of data are on the table, a "jigsaw" approach can be used by which smaller teams take on subsets of the data and share back data findings, interpretations, and questions with the whole group.

Centering on Goals

Effective inquiry is anchored in a clear set of goals. The purpose of the inquiry is to achieve the goals, and engaging with data is a means to that end and benefits from using SMART goals: **s**pecific, **m**easurable, **a**ttainable, **r**elevant, and **t**ime-bound (University of California, 2016). In an identity safe school, goal-setting happens through an inclusive process to surface diverse perspectives on the outcomes that most matter, on the barriers and challenges getting in the way, and on the strengths to leverage for change.

Teaching and utilizing *root cause analysis* illuminates and addresses underlying reasons for current outcomes. A root cause analysis asks us to investigate and understand why and how a problem is happening so that our solutions address these causes rather than just focusing on the symptoms they bring about. For example, causes for low attendance could be lack of transportation, morning responsibilities at home, a sense of not belonging or failing as a student, or difficult relationships with the educator and/or peers. When we get clear about the reasons or causes of a problem, we can set and pursue both *impact and process outcomes* to provide an actionable, specific path to improvement. For example, to achieve an impact outcome goal of increased attendance, we might also set and track progress on universal process outcome goals such as greeting 100% of students at the classroom door, recognizing students for excellent and improved attendance, and calling parents/

caregivers for every absence. We might set and pursue individualized process outcomes with students with persistent high absences, such as connecting them with a carpool, getting them an alarm clock or helping them set up alarms on their phone, strengthening relationships with educators and/or peers, and/or providing additional academic support.

In an identity safe school, *diversity, equity, and inclusion* form the centerpoint for goal-setting. (Beloved Community, n.d.):

- **Diversity:** To what extent is our community proportionally represented?

- **Equity:** To what extent do our diverse populations feel comfortable, respected, and powerful within our organization?

- **Inclusion:** To what extent are any demographics disproportionately represented in our programs? To what extent are the outcomes from our program predictable by participants' demographics?

A starting point is to comprehensively disaggregate data so that these guiding questions can be explored.

We-Why: Goal-Setting Centered in Relationships and Context

Hā is the Hawaiian word for breath. Through its Office of Hawaiian Education, the Hawaii Department of Education (HIDOE) has adopted the Nā Hopena Aʻo or HĀ Systems Outcomes framework. The framework provides guideposts for employees, students, families, and communities who want to develop and strengthen skills, behaviors, and dispositions reminiscent of Hawaiʻi's unique context and to honor the qualities and values of the Indigenous language and culture of Hawaiʻi (HIDOE, n.d.). This framework is defined by the community through a highly collaborative process and is strengthened for those who also adopt the processes and practices of HĀ work. HĀ Community Days is an example of a practice used to empower and engage a broad array of stakeholders through experiential learning and leading to connect and build understanding and trust through storytelling and story-catching, reflection and dialogue, and by working together on community projects. The Community Day is designed by an intentionally diverse team

(Continued)

(Continued)

including at least one school staff, community organization representative, and student. Participants begin by sharing the stories of their names to connect to "who we are and where we come from to help guide us in where we need to go" (HIDOE, n.d.). They share what is known about HĀ from their personal stories to inform the iterative process and greater narrative of the framework. The focus then shifts from the individual to the collective: Who are we as a community? What gifts, hopes, and dreams do we bring? What actions or work do we want to undertake? The individuals become a *We* united by a *Why*, a shared purpose. The We-Why is interactive and dynamic in response to ongoing community input and feedback.

See Appendix F for a We-Why Reflection Tool.

Preparing to Work With Data

Compassionate attention to social identity is required to build a culture of inquiry and trust. We can anticipate—without expecting or stereotyping that it will be the same for everyone!—potential reactions to working with data showing persistent equity gaps. Those with social identities bearing the brunt of inequities may especially feel anger, grief, or hopelessness. They may experience stereotype threat, the worry that the outcomes confirm a negative idea or story about an identity group. Staff with white or class privilege may feel grief, shame, or defensiveness. They may resist facing up to the role racism and other forms of oppression play in these inequitable outcomes. Staff may blame results on students, families, or communities rather than looking to professional practice as the focus for change. Alex and Amy created a tool (Kahn & Epstein, 2019) to help teams prepare to look at data, to make space for participants to work with such reactions that may arise before jumping into the inquiry work. Feedback showed increased engagement, clarity, and productivity in the data review, reflection, and planning sessions that followed (see Appendix A).

Data

Consider the list of data types below. Take note of which data are currently accessible with disaggregation for all relevant demographic subgroups.

- Student grades

- Student test scores (including standards level achievement)

- Attendance

- Behavior referrals

- Suspensions

- Expulsions

- Positive recognition (student/staff/family of the week, caught being good, etc.)

- Parent/caregiver involvement

- Staffing demographics by role

- Program participation (special education, English language development, advanced placement, etc.)

- Graduation and college-ready graduation

- Participation in tiered supports

- Participation in extracurricular activities

- Stakeholder perceptions (students, parents/caregivers, staff, community partners)

For grades, test scores, attendance, behavior, suspension, position recognition, and stakeholder perceptions: note whether you are able to disaggregate by teacher alongside demographics. Being able to provide teachers with their own data in these areas—*how many students have I positively recognized, and what is their racial and gender makeup?*—is a powerful lever for change.

Working with so many types of data is powerful, but we run the risk of data overload. We do need these data, but we don't all need all of it, and certainly not all at one time. Educators Debbie Clark and Stephanie Williamson (2018) of Buena Park School District share three strategies for avoiding data overload:

1. Collect data in one place.

2. Make the information easy to read and understand.

3. Give each team only the information they need to improve.

These three strategies will guide the consideration of potential data technology and platforms. Before selecting a platform, a school sketches out: (1) the data to be included and how it is currently collected and entered; and (2) the questions each team wants to be able to explore and answer. This will clarify the data that are needed and the formats that will make data most useful for ongoing improvement.

Data Management

To track goals requires a plan for collecting and managing the involved data. The more this can be accomplished through the data systems already in use, the better. For example, attendance outcomes, attendance phone calls home, and student recognition for excellent and improved attendance can typically be tracked through the main student information system. Data on something like greeting 100% of students at the door may require a tool for self-reporting. There is a balance to strike between data access and the extra burden data collection can place on staff. A tool for mapping out how data will be collected and managed is included in the final section of this chapter.

Data Analysis

White cultural assumptions about what constitutes knowledge dominate prevalent data analysis methods. It is a useful generalization to say that Western science favors data that are objective and quantitative. It values simplified, controllable study environments that isolate subjects from, and pays little attention to, context. In contrast, traditional knowledge always depends on context and an understanding of local conditions. It values subjective and qualitative information alongside that which is objective and quantitative (Nakashima & Roué, 2002). Identity safe data analysis asks us to ensure that both traditional and Western forms of knowledge are included and valued. It directs us to provide significant time and support for sharing, reflection, and dialogue to generate contextually rich knowledge. It invites us to each consider our assumptions about what constitutes knowledge. Numeric data on hiring, test performance, grades, and other quantifiable metrics are essential for tracking equity and disparity on those outcomes; but without a richer investigation of the ecosystem producing these outcomes, change will not come. Change is served by proactive, sustained focus to share and hear the voices of the community, to witness and understand each other's experiences, and to gather the fullest possible range of our knowledge of what is happening and why.

Andrew Knips (2019) offers six components of equitable data analysis. First, the data we consider can include the voices and stories of the community, rather than consisting solely of information about the community. Second, we can preempt implicit bias by naming it and inviting reflection and preparation to overcome it.

Engaging with positive text and images about people for whom we may hold bias has been shown to reduce that bias. Third, we can set ground rules to help us speak from a respectful, compassionate place, for example, an invitation to talk about students as if they were our own children. Fourth, we can invite participants to set a positive intention as an anchor for data analysis, for example, "seeing and building on students' strengths." Fifth, we can ensure that we look at multiple measures that collectively provide a richer, less biased view. And sixth, we can commit to disaggregating all data by race, ethnicity, gender, special education status, multilingual status, and other relevant aspects of identity or experience.

Systems to Support Collaborative Inquiry

In addition to the processes and habits of mind that are critical to supporting data-based collaboration, there are deeper systemic structures that need to be in place. The first is a set of common curricula and assessments that allow collaboration to even happen. These need to be tight enough that teachers can learn from each other and steadily improve their practice. This is critical in order to break through assumptions about the learning potential of historically underserved students. But they also need enough looseness to allow for innovation, since there is much we have to learn to have truly equitable teaching and learning. In one San Francisco Bay Area district this was called *collaborative innovation*. In this case, innovation contributed to, and was accelerated by, collaboration—the opposite of many schools where the most innovative teachers are islands of excitement sought after by parents/caregivers with access while the school as a whole continues to replicate marginal, inequitable practice.

The second underlying system involves data management itself. In order to support collaboration, the system needs to be nimble enough to provide data that address the probing questions sparked by staff inquiry. Standard disaggregation may say which students are being over-referred, but staff may want to know what time of day, where on campus, or in which teacher's classes. Having the flexibility to support this kind of inquiry is important in disrupting stereotypes and constructing solutions. For instance, addressing the over-referral of special education students is radically different if this is occurring at lunchtime or in a core class. Similarly, disrupting stereotypes of African American male students is much more likely when teachers realize that some staff members have no issues of disparate "willful defiance"—or of defiance with certain students who others habitually refer.

Community Voices

In an identity safe school, everyone's voice is valued and heard. Stakeholder leadership groups, surveys, focus groups, and listening tours are key resources. It's essential that all stakeholders have a say in the questions that are asked, the data that are collected, the meaning that is made from the data, the planning that flows from the meaning-making, and the structures and routines that hold and shape the work.

Stakeholder Leadership Groups

Stakeholder leadership structures like student government or the school site council serve as excellent home bases for soliciting, hearing, learning from, and being guided by community voices. These groups can also anchor ad hoc structures such as a design team convened to co-create a new program, or a professional development (PD) advisory committee to shape the adult learning plan. With support from school leaders, groups develop community agreements, a clear and shared sense of purpose (We-Why), and routines and protocols that fit the business at hand, make space for all voices, and build deepened connections and community over time.

Chapter 7 outlines a schoolwide process for an identity safe school plan.

Gathering Stakeholder Voices

Which stakeholder voices are important to hear, and at which time-points through the year? To begin, draft a timeline of the points in the year at which feedback and/or input from students, parents/caregivers, staff, or other stakeholders are needed to inform action and improvement. This can be a component of the broader inquiry calendar recommended earlier in this chapter. Consider gathering perspectives twice per year from all stakeholders: perhaps in mid-fall to inform current year improvements, and in late spring to inform planning for the next year. For middle and high school students, consider gathering their perspectives about both the school overall and their individual classrooms and teachers. It can also be very helpful to solicit ongoing or more frequent input, through a tool like a short monthly or always-available "pulse check" survey. Leverage the stakeholder leadership groups to co-develop and/or give feedback on the timeline and plan. Take note of the types of information you hope to gain, and which will be best served by a survey as compared to the richer but more time and energy intensive work of focus groups or interviews.

Surveys

Surveys are an efficient and familiar method for soliciting community voice. They are invaluable for gathering feedback, surfacing ideas, informing priorities, measuring satisfaction, and evaluating programs and activities.

Many excellent surveys are available open-source to adopt or adapt. The great resources listed below are included with links:

- RE-Center Equity-Informed School Climate Assessment (E.I.S.C.A.) (https://re-center.org/what-we-do/programs/eisca/)

- Tripod 7 Cs Framework for Effective Teaching (https://tripoded .com/wp-content/uploads/2017/01/Guide-to-Tripods-7Cs-Framework-of-Effective-Teaching.pdf)

- YouthTruth Survey (https://youthtruthsurvey.org/)

- National Teacher and Principal Survey (NTPS) (https://education .mn.gov/mde/dse/health/mss/)

- NYC School Survey (https://www.schools.nyc.gov/about-us/reports/ school-quality/nyc-school-survey)

- ChallengeSuccess.org

- California School Climate, Health and Learning Surveys (CalSCHLS) (https://calschls.org/)

Working with the relevant stakeholder leadership groups or teams, begin survey design by outlining what you want to ask about and learn. Then research available surveys and compile a draft set of items aligned to your purpose. Lead a team of stakeholders to review and reflect on the items and to identify which to keep as is, keep with edits, or omit. This process seeks to make the language used in the survey as accessible, clear, and asset-based as possible. Have at least five stakeholders take the survey and provide feedback. Taking a survey surfaces an opportunity for its improvement that can otherwise go unseen.

Draft a framing message for what the survey is about and why you are giving it. It's important to communicate the belief that our diverse perspectives and knowledge make our community strong, and to express gratitude for respondents' input, time, energy, and honesty. Consider whether the survey should be given confidentially or anonymously, depending on the content, context, and school culture. Be explicit about this choice in the survey introduction and framing so that takers know from the get-go.

It is important to be able to disaggregate results by race, gender, and other salient demographic factors, but the presence of demographic items has been shown to trigger stereotype threat. Place these items at the end rather than the beginning of the survey and make them optional. If you are able to give the survey confidentially rather than anonymously, you may be able to eliminate demographic questions from the survey itself and instead bring in those descriptors from your main data platform(s) by unique student or staff ID.

I (Amy) recommend scoring Likert scale survey items based on the percent of respondents who chose the top most favorable responses, rather than based on the average numeric response. For example, if using a 5-point agreement scale, *5=Strongly Agree, 4=Agree, 3=Somewhat Agree/Somewhat Disagree, 2=Disagree, 1=Strongly Disagree*, calculate the percent who responded 4–5 rather than the average of all responses. Numeric items using a 0–10 or 0–100 scale can appropriately be scored using both the average response and the percent choosing the top most favorable response(s).

Free response questions capture more nuanced and specific input and feedback. Consider organizing the survey by topic and offering an optional free response item at the close of each section. It's also important to offer space for "anything else a respondent wants to share" to capture unprompted input or feedback on the survey itself. Free response data can be analyzed by tagging individual responses as representing key themes or topics. A first read of the responses and analysis of available survey data or other input can help generate the topics. Tagging can be done lower-tech in Excel or a Google Sheet (comments vertical in the first column, with columns to the right named for the topics and ready for tagging with an X, Y, or checkmark). More sophisticated analysis can be done using a tool like NVivo (n.d.), enabling tagging along with highlighting and collating of key quotes. A great hands-on activity for making meaning and identifying themes from free responses is to annotate posters of key quotes and then discuss the quotes and annotations in a gallery walk format. This can also be done with quantitative data or other artifacts.

There are many excellent platforms for giving, analyzing, and reporting survey data. Some great options include Google Forms and Analytics (https://edu.google.com/products/gsuite-for-education/), SurveyMonkey (https://www.surveymonkey.com), Alchemer (https://www.alchemer.com), and Panorama (https://www.panoramaed.com). Panorama in particular offers strong content, accommodation of fully customized content, excellent data integration, and stellar online reporting of disaggregated results. Many learning management systems also now include surveying functionality. As surveying has become highly accessible technologically, there is also a risk of over-surveying. The annual inquiry calendar can assist by clarifying which information you hope to gain, and in some cases, streamlining the instruments used to produce that information. It's also useful to leverage available state- or national-level survey data such as the California School Climate, Health and Learning Surveys (https://calschls.org/), the Minnesota Student Survey (https://education.mn.gov/mde/dse/health/mss/), and many more.

Focus Groups

Focus groups are an opportunity to go deeper to surface and build stakeholder perspective and understanding. As with surveys, it is essential that stakeholders' voices inform the questions or prompts to be used so that the language is accessible, and the content is aligned with stakeholders' goals and concerns. Surveys and focus groups work especially well in tandem or sequence. For example, I (Amy) worked with a network of high schools to survey students about mental health experiences and needs. A Student Research Team analyzed the results and discussed themes and priorities, and then designed and led student focus groups for more students to go through the same process. This led to a second survey focused on what was already working well and what could be improved to support positive mental health for students, parents/caregivers, and staff. These results were then studied by student government and School Site Council teams, shared in community forums, and applied to the creation of a new social-emotional wellness initiative.

Listening Tours

A listening tour is a powerful tool for leaders to connect with stakeholders and learn from their experiences, perspectives, and insights. The core purpose is . . . to listen! Listening tours may have a more general focus, for example, to deepen understanding of what is working well and what most needs to improve. They can also serve a more targeted purpose, for example, to gather input on a curriculum framework or to inform the selection of a new school facility. It is best to offer a streamlined protocol and allow ample space for the interviewee to guide the flow of the conversation. For instance, in gathering family input, Bay Area educator Louise Waters recommends asking a few broad, open-ended questions like "What about this school works best for your student or family?" "How could the school better support your student or family? Is there anything else you would like to share with me as principal?" If these are designed to focus on identity safety, belonging, or access and nothing in this area has been forthcoming, you could change the last question to "Is there anything else you would like to share with me as the parent of an x (African American, Asian, special education, etc.) student?" The idea is to provide as few restrictions as possible on the conversation in order to gather authentic input.

Participatory Action Research

Participatory Action Research (PAR) centers the voices and leadership of those with the most at stake in a venture, context, or environment. PAR works best in a community or group with a shared or emerging sense of shared identity and purpose. The full inclusion of, and equal status for, all voices is a core principle. Participants explore and make meaning from their experiences and analyze and discuss data and input from other sources. PAR is an iterative process of research, action, and reflection to identify, understand, and achieve community or group goals. PAR has been associated with gains in self-efficacy as participants recognize the power and value of their knowledge about their own experience and context. PAR affirms that experience can be a basis of knowing and that experiential learning can lead to a legitimate form of knowledge that influences practice (Baum et al., 2006).

Formative Assessment and Feedback

Formative assessment is an ongoing feedback loop, organized around three guiding questions: *Where am I going? Where am I now? Where to next?* It's a process embedded in teaching and learning that provides teachers and students with the information and meaning-making space they need to keep learning moving forward: minute-by-minute, day-by-day, and unit-by-unit.

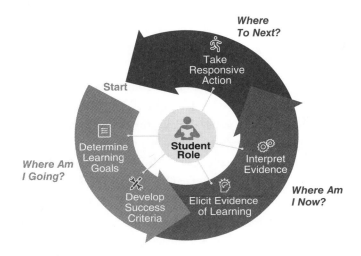

Source: Created by WestEd, wested.org. Reprinted with permission.
Assessment for Learning (n.d.). https://www.assessmentforlearningproject.org/

In multiple studies, *feedback* (delivered through a robust formative process) and *educator belief in student capacity* stand out as the two most impactful instructional factors for student mastery (Hattie, 2017). Educators and students engage with learning goals and success criteria, generate and work with evidence of student learning, and take leadership through reflection, planning, and action to strengthen learning outcomes. But without identity safety, feedback can wind up reproducing rather than disrupting stereotype threat, bias, internalized oppression, and other aspects of inequity. A teacher may provide feedback with a sincere belief and investment in a student's capacity to succeed. But for a student facing a trust gap, uncertainty about whether the teacher believes in them gets in the way. Research by Dave Yeager and colleagues (2013) shows the presence of a significant, pernicious racial-divide trust gap negatively impacting learning for Brown and Black high school students. When trust is low, feedback may be experienced as confirming a stereotype or attributing inferiority rather than supporting learning. We discuss ways to build trust in Chapter 5.

See Appendix G for an Identity Safe Formative Assessment Feedback Loop Reflection Questions & Planner.

The Learning Zone

In his TED Talk *How to Get Better at the Things You Care About,* Eduardo Briceño (2017) discusses the importance of deliberately alternating between the *learning zone* and the *performance zone.* In the learning zone, we expect to make mistakes we can learn from as we concentrate on what we have not yet mastered. In the performance zone, we concentrate on what we have already mastered and aim to minimize or eradicate mistakes. Formative assessment is the enactment of the learning zone. By actively teaching and modeling a growth mindset (Dweck, 2006), we prepare students and ourselves to approach formative assessment with confidence and excitement rather than fear or defensiveness. Formative assessment becomes a means to practice our deep belief in students' capabilities as thinkers and doers (Zambo & Zambo, 2008).

Phase One: Where Am I Going?

The formative assessment cycle begins by getting clear on *learning goals* and what the work looks like when done well. In this phase, a stance of exploration, curiosity, and even playfulness can avoid the trap of students judging themselves for not yet knowing what they have not yet learned. When students have the opportunity to explore and inform the learning goals, they are more likely to understand and value them. A *visible thinking tool* like *See-Think-Wonder* (Project Zero, https://pz.harvard.edu/thinking-routines) can be used to put the focus on exploring rather than mastering the learning goals during this first phase. Visible thinking tools graphically organize information in ways that support meaning-making. (Using a set through the year for multiple types of purposes builds familiarity and flow. Project Zero's Thinking Routines Toolbox is a great resource.

This phase also introduces *success or growth criteria* for what the work looks like when done well and as skills progress. It is helpful to use rubrics or checklists that describe qualities and components of the work across a developmental continuum. Tools like iRubric (www.irubric.com), Rubistar (http://rubistar.4teachers.org/index.php), Quick Rubric (https://www.quickrubric.com/), and others can streamline the rubric creation process. Providing students an opportunity to score a sample or anchor piece of work using the rubric can deepen their understanding of what the qualities look like in action. It can also assist educators to further shape the language of the criteria to make sense to students.

In this phase we can engage these steps to ensure we hold open the learning zone:

- Pre-teach *neuroplasticity*, the understanding that our brain is a muscle that grows over time through our efforts, and that where we start out does not define or limit us.

- Share examples of learning from our own mistakes to promote the power of embracing mistakes as an important tool for learning throughout life.

- Help students connect new learning to prior knowledge and skills.

- Pre-advertise the support that will be available to make sure all students succeed (in class check-ins, office hours, etc.).

- Assure students of our confidence that they will succeed with this new learning.

- Notice and connect individually with students who may need more support to trust and engage with the formative assessment cycle.

These guiding questions can assist educators to make this phase identity safe:

- How do we build trust with and among students in the feedback loop?

- To what degree do both educators and students understand and value the knowledge and skills that will be taught?

- How do we express our excitement about the knowledge and skills being taught and their relevance for students' lives?

- How do we express and model a growth mindset and faith in students' capacity to succeed at the task?

- How do we provide opportunities for students to explore, discuss, and give feedback on the learning goals and growth criteria?

- For students seeing less value in the knowledge and skills, how will we hear and respond to their experience and concerns?

- How do we use rubrics, course syllabi, and other formats to communicate learning goals and growth criteria?

- Are students clear about instructions, and do they have access to examples of what the task looks like when done well?

Phase Two: Where Am I Now?

In phase two of the feedback loop, students produce evidence of learning by engaging with a task, and receive feedback that references the preset learning goals and growth criteria. Since students all learn differently, it is very useful to provide a range of types of tasks through the year that leverage writing, presenting, drawing, and more.

Providing a structured opportunity for students to first explore a task before jumping in to completing it can assist them to identify prior and new knowledge, ask clarifying questions, and offer input into aspects of the task. Using a visible thinking routine (such as See-Think-Wonder [https://pz.harvard.edu/thinking-routines] or Think-Puzzle-Explore can deepen students' understanding and valuing of the task at hand).

Feedback can be provided by the educator, by peers, and through self-reflection. The use of a common rubric enhances the learner's access to organized, specific, and actionable feedback. Feedback can be provided on paper by highlighting or circling text on a rubric, or by using digital tools such as Goobric or iRubric.

Actively teaching and using a set of routines for giving and receiving feedback will boost student agency and confidence working with evidence. Ongoing promotion of growth mindset will assist students to stay in the *learning zone* both as givers and receivers of feedback. *Wise feedback* strategies (see Chapter 2) are at the heart of these routines. We can model and teach how to stay anchored in our belief in each student's competence as a learner, and to give feedback from that stance.

As a high school student shared, "Feedback is everywhere. Feedback is universal. It's not only in school; it's with a whole person, a job, just day to day with your family. Feedback is a tool used for growing" (LPS Student Interviews, 2018).

Phase Three: Where to Next?

In this phase, students make meaning of the feedback received, reflect on progress, and identify goals and next steps. Formative assessment (FA) is sometimes seen as a means for educators to gather information about student learning. This is certainly useful, but FA's greatest power lies with situating students as leaders of their own learning. In this way, formative assessment facilitates learning how to learn as well as advancing content mastery.

Phase three benefits from active teaching and repeated use of a set of routines. These routines can assist students to notice strengths and areas for growth, set growth goals, and identify learning next steps. Developmentally appropriate protocols and templates can structure students' movement through these steps. Routines can leverage individual, small group, and whole class components.

Educators can launch phase three by sharing their own meaning-making to strengthen their teaching using class-wide results. They can speak to what they see as strengths, growth areas, goals, and next steps in their roles as teachers, and in doing so continue to model growth mindset and the learning zone. This sets the stage for students to then look at their own results and to assist one another with next steps for growth.

The most critical aspect of phase three is to provide a pathway to improvement. Assessment of all kinds can be demotivating if it illuminates gaps without also providing a roadmap for growth. Eduardo Briceño (2018) names four aspects for learners to improve:

1. Believe and understand that we can improve.

2. Want to improve, for a purpose we care about.

3. Understand *how* to improve through *deliberate practice.*

4. Experience the process as *low-stakes* since mistakes are expected and should not merit negative consequences.

Research on *deliberate practice* shows the power of identifying and targeting practice toward specific aspects of performance (Briceño, 2018). For example, a singer might work to improve their tone or rhythm in one section of a song by repeatedly listening to and learning from recordings of themselves singing that one section rather than the whole song. A writer might work to improve how they are using evidence by reading and revising an essay with that one goal in mind and a detailed evidence rubric in hand. Although deliberate practice is a well-documented strategy for growth, it is rarely taught or focused on in school. We can significantly accelerate growth by teaching students about deliberate practice and providing routines and protocols that support focused attention to specific growth areas.

Along with deliberate practice, the success of phase three depends on two additional factors: (1) access to appropriate curricular resources, and (2) teacher time and space for differentiated support for learners. A student who has identified an area of focus will often need additional curricular resources for their pursuit, as well as some personalized time with the teacher for support with their self-directed learning plan. For the former, there are increasingly resources available through digital learning platforms tied to standards. It can also be very helpful for educators by subject or grade level to collaborate to share and strengthen a library of standards-based resources. Educators can provide personalized time by setting up short check-ins with students during class independent learning time, or by setting up office hours or other structures for additional support.

Standardized Testing

Bias significantly impacts how standardized tests are created, developed, implemented, experienced, and used. Students of color, students with less economic access, female students, students with learning differences, and students who face negative stereotypes or narratives bear the brunt of this inequity.

Many of today's standardized assessments were initially developed and tested with predominantly White, middle-class students and may feature items more suited to these students' language and cultural experiences. If the development of an assessment does not include representative samples of a group of students, that group could be scored to potential disadvantage (Test Bias, 2015). Existing assessments are a reference for new assessments in development, and in this way bias can be reproduced in the next generation of tests as test-makers align to expected performance for particular groups.

Standardized testing brings great risk of *stereotype threat*. A fear of confirming a negative stereotype can create stress and distraction that hinder test performance (see Chapter 1). Stereotype threat can be triggered by being asked to identify one's race or gender, so it is advisable to exclude demographic questions from tests. Educators can weaken stereotype threat by

- Engaging students just prior to testing with their values, heroes, or strengths.

- Taking time before testing to affirm your care and your belief in students' capacity and emphasizing the growth mindset by affirming that we can grow our abilities over time.

- Communicating that the test is designed for all students to do well and that it tests skills we've been learning together in class all year rather than how smart anybody is.

- Ensuring all students have access to high-quality preparation so that we can truly say to them: "You are ready for this. You got this!" Students from higher-income families often benefit from test prep programs as well as greater access to rigorous curriculum and expectations.

Assessment-makers are increasingly applying *universal design* to reduce bias and strengthen equity in testing. The seven elements of universal design in assessment include (NCEO, 2016)

- Inclusive assessment population

- Precisely defined constructs

- Accessible, non-biased items

- Amenable to accommodations

- Simple, clear, and intuitive instructions and procedures

- Maximum readability and comprehensibility

- Maximum legibility

This work continues to grow, but research continues to show unexplained differences in standardized test results among test-takers who have similar ability levels and only differ by socio-demographic grounds (Gierl & Khaliq, 2001; Kruse, 2016). These unexplained differences have been attributed to problems in the design and interpretation of tests (Brown et al., 1999; Kruse, 2016). A loosening of focus and reliance on standardized testing may be one of the silver linings of the COVID-19 pandemic impacting us all at this time of writing. As of November 2020, more than 1,665 colleges and universities have made college entrance exams like the SAT or ACT optional. Standardized testing paused in most states in 2020 and is likely to do so again in 2021. Ultimately, an identity safe approach to summative assessment would advance performance assessment tools like portfolios, public exhibitions, and capstone projects that foster a positive exploration of identity and experience as well as provide rigorous opportunities to demonstrate standards-based knowledge and skills (Choi, 2020).

Grading for Equity

Illinois English teacher Scott Filkins writes that grading formative assessment "is akin to ranking basketball teams based on how they do in practice" (Heitlin

Loewus, 2015). Options for how to handle grading for formative assessment include entering an "as-of" grade that gets overwritten as the work progresses through multiple drafts or retakes (not an average, but the most current score), entering a rubric score that does not count toward the grade, or leaving it out of the gradebook entirely.

Grading is broadly a critical area for improvement in the service of equity. Joe Feldman (2018), author of *Grading for Equity*, writes of three pillars for equitable grading: accuracy, bias resistance, and intrinsic motivation. To be equitable, grades

- Accurately reflect only academic performance rather than including non-academic criteria

- Use mathematically sound calculations and scales, such as 0–4 rather than 0–100

- Protect student grades from educator implicit biases

- Cease the use of points to reward or punish and instead teach the connection between the means and ends of learning (i.e., homework is valuable not because it earns points but because doing it improves learning)

Four practices in particular to be avoided:

- Assigning zeros for missing work

- Assigning scores for non-academic factors such as homework completion or behavior

- If using a 100-point scale, assigning any score below 50 or 55.

- Averaging scores per standard rather than the most current score in a grading period

Grading that is mastery or standards based helps students focus on "learning rather than earning" (Sackstein, 2018), because it provides more specific, actionable feedback for growth. At one school where I (Amy) worked, in a focus group students report that mastery grading helps clarify what they are learning and how they are progressing. Student Saida (pseudonym) shared: "The rubrics help me stay clear about what I'm learning and trying to do in my writing. I get feedback that helps me notice and use my strengths, and also helps me notice and work on areas of the rubric where I most need to grow" (LPS Student Interviews, 2018).

Changing grading practices touches on deeply held beliefs for teachers, students, and parents/caregivers and requires a thoughtful and collaborative process. A first step some high schools have taken is the elimination of credit for Ds. In traditional grading practices an F can stretch from 0 to 55 points and can include penalties not related to mastery such as missing assignments. In effect, most students with Ds are much closer to a C- than to most of the F range. Often the difference between a D+ and a C- is one or two missing assignments that could easily be remedied. However, the consequences for these missteps are huge since most four-year colleges do not accept D grades in required courses and stipulate a 2.0 GPA. Senior year, countless first-generation college students who meet their high school graduation requirements after having completed a full college prep schedule find themselves ineligible for a four-year college.

To disrupt this systemic inequity, in 2010, former superintendent Louise Waters worked with district and site leaders to eliminate D grades. Many teachers and counselors worried that this would push students out and increase drop-out rates, especially for Black and Brown students. However, according to Louise, the opposite happened. As part of the transition to no Ds, the schools put in place more transparent ongoing grade reporting to families and students, and more interventions like tutoring, and Saturday and intersession catch-ups. Rather than pushing students out, students rose to the occasion. Dropout rates declined significantly, and college-ready graduation rates climbed. Having started challenging conventional wisdom by eliminating Ds, schools began exploring master grading and other grading reforms.

Changing Elementary Report Cards

Early in her tenure, when she was an elementary principal, Louise Waters realized that their traditional grading system created a counterproductive learning environment for the sizable numbers of English learners, struggling readers, and students with Individualized Education Plans (IEPs). This was reinforced by her experience as a parent of a child with severe dyslexia. Whether through traditional or standards-based grading, he always fell far below grade level. Any kind of grading was completely demoralizing for mother and son and provided no actionable data to the teacher—for according to the report card he was unable to do anything. She was used to finding crumpled up papers with "unhappy face" grades dropped along the three blocks from school to home. Wanting to create identity safe assessment, grading, and data practices, she partnered with me (Amy) to design a standards-based developmental report card and comprehensive assessment and data management system for the 1,000 students in her school.

Over a few years, teachers collaboratively identified grade-level power standards with exemplars in reading, writing, and math. These were arranged into a K-5 nested continuum of Emerging, Beginning, Developing, Achieving, and Exceeding grade-level standard. Developing at fifth grade was Achieving at fourth and Exceeding at third and so forth. Teachers were committed to the fairness of the concept, but initially the transparency and accountability for the range of student needs was daunting. One teacher commented, "You mean I have to teach at all of these levels in every class?" Of course, that was the point. Those students had always been there. Armed with the knowledge of exactly where students were performing, teachers could no longer justify simply teaching to the middle. Gradually we built up assessment, instructional, and grading strategies that made this possible. Students were able to see their growth and knew what their next steps were. Even kindergarteners proudly explained this during student-led parent conferences twice a year. Wall charts and parent handbooks sharing the standards and mastery exemplars supported parents/caregivers to see their child's progress and be clear about where they were in relation to grade-level expectations. Students, parents, and educators gained very specific information about learning that they applied in ways that accelerated growth. That in turn created motivation, which increased effort, which further increased growth, and onward.

The data system was instrumental in supporting these practices to become embedded in wider school structures. By creating a continuum of levels K-5 and tying these to grade-level standards, it was possible to create the kind of data that allowed the Student Study Team to look for patterns across the 1,000-student school. With these data, they found that most English Learners were on or approaching grade level (Developing or Achieving) in English reading after four years. This was particularly true if they had a well-developed primary language. By identifying English Learner students who did not meet this growth marker and then looking at their primary language assessments, it was possible to find previously overlooked students who might have language processing issues independent of being ELs. This became particularly clear in cases where siblings were making the expected rate of progress while one child in the family was not growing. What the school found was that ELs were being under-identified for special education and intervention support as staff ascribed their academic struggles to being new to the country.

Rising to Challenges/Avoiding Pitfalls

Data intended to spotlight inequities can reinforce deficit-based narratives about students, educators, parents/caregivers, schools, and communities. Working to overcome implicit and explicit biases builds our trustworthiness to provide the right conditions for learning. We can be conscious and intentional about the language we use to describe performance and groups. We can use more developmental rather than norm-referenced language, for example, "Developing" or "Emerging" rather than "Below or Far Below Standard." We can avoid color-coding that may inadvertently bring a deficit lens. For example, in one district, students who were not yet approaching mastery reported a big increase in using a provided feedback report when the display changed to show shades of green rather than green-yellow-red. Students got the same information about strengths and growth areas, but it did not trigger stereotype threat or sense of failure.

Engaging all stakeholders as partners in improvement can be challenging, particularly if they have past experiences of unequal status or exclusion. The path is to listen to stakeholders (through surveys or discussion), feed back what you've heard, and listen again, with an open and humble heart. Involve many types of voices in shaping data and assessment activities so that they reflect the diversity of the school community. Build connection and trust by offering a steady thread of opportunities to build communities by sharing and hearing each other's stories. Teach storytelling and constructive listening with all stakeholders to strengthen the readiness to share and hear.

Many educators have experienced a pitfall of "too much data but too little information." Encourage the targeted use of data to explore key themes and topics in any one sitting, rather than a broad-stroke view of the school's entire world of data. Feature data that provide actionable information in areas that matter. For example, a list of students' letter grades is less actionable academically than a list of their rubric levels and feedback in five essay-writing skill areas. Statistics about the number of behavior referrals per student and subgroup is more actionable when it enables analysis by time of day, educator, and location.

Closing the Gap Between Ideas and Actions

THE WE-WHY: IDENTITY AND PURPOSE

There is tremendous power in coming together as a community for a common purpose. The status quo of inequities in the education system and broader society create disparate access and opportunity based on race, gender, immigration status, and other demographic factors. Privilege can blind us to inequity we are not ourselves facing. Most humans carry some forms of implicit and/or internalized biases. These dynamics interfere with building the shared understanding and purpose needed to transform schools. A first step toward common purpose is to hear and share stories about our experiences and perspectives. This informs a shared understanding of what matters for the community and why, and is the base for shared goals and collaborative action.

As a next step, take stock of your school's *We-Why*. Who is your school's We? What stories, identities, and gifts stand out? What shared and divergent purposes are present? Which leaders, teams, and groups do or will you call into this conversation? Which voices may have preferential status, and which if any may be facing barriers to inclusion or trust? We've provided a template to use or adapt for exploring the We-Why, shared in the references at the close of this chapter and in Appendix F.

Data Management

The data analysis and reporting functionality of many student information systems (SIS) and learning management systems (LMS) has steadily improved over the past decade. There is often much more that can be accomplished by further maximizing these tools to provide accurate, timely, and valued information. Almost all high-quality systems enable disaggregation by race, gender, and other factors, albeit sometimes with more or less steps involved. Many enable in-system surveys.

As a next step, draft or revisit your *inquiry calendar* that outlines when teams and stakeholders will come together and the data they will use. Sharing the inquiry calendar up front (well before the year starts) with data providers and collaborators will enable them to best align their support to meet your data needs and timeline. A template for an Inquiry Calendar Planner is shared and discussed at the end of the chapter in "Using the Tools".

Boosting the Learning Zone

In the learning zone, we expect to make mistakes and learn from them to grow. When stereotype threat is present, we may feel that making a mistake will confirm to others a negative stereotype about a group we represent. When implicit bias is present, we may not see another clearly but instead project limiting assumptions or see that person through a deficit lens. We may fail to hold or communicate a belief in learners' capacity to grow. When explicit bias is also present, access to the learning zone is in very deep peril. This bias may be interpersonal, such as name-calling or harassment; or it may be structural, such as White-dominated representation in curriculum and assessment content. When explicit bias is not actively and effectively interrupted, the learning zone completely breaks down.

A next step is to reflect on your school's learning zones. What learning zone opportunities are provided for students, staff, and parents/caregivers? What is working well? What barriers do you notice, and for whom? What do you see as most important to change or improve, and for whom? We have found Eduardo Briceño's TED Talk video (2017) to be a great learning zone conversation anchor for students, parents/caregivers, and educators. A link to the video is shared in the references.

Alex and I (Amy) developed two tools for supporting the learning zone in classroom assessment. The first is the Identity Safe Feedback Loop Planner (see Appendix G), providing guiding questions and recommended strategies to strengthen identity safety through each phase of the feedback loop. The second is a tool to prepare educators for equitable, asset-based dialogue, analysis, reflection, and planning with student data/student work: *Appendix A: Preparing for Equitable Data Inquiry*.

Check Yourself

- What am I doing to build an inclusive, authentic We-Why, and what are my next steps?

- Do teams and stakeholder groups at our school develop and center on clear goals? Describe.

- Do teams and stakeholder groups have access to valued data for assessing progress on those goals? Explain.

- Are data disaggregated by race and ethnicity, gender, and other salient factors to enable attention to equity successes and gaps? What changes are needed?

- In what ways are our language and thinking about assessment asset-based, and how can it be further improved?

- What is our school's level of understanding of how stereotype threat, implicit bias, and structural bias impact data and assessment; and how can it be further developed?

Using the Tools

Establishing an inquiry calendar makes visible the essential questions, goals, and timelines for informing progress with the best data available. Using a common template can aid in growing a schoolwide inquiry plan from the bottom up.

It can assist leaders to quickly step into each team's reflection and improvement process.

Our Inquiry Calendar Planner first invites a team or person to center on their purpose and goals, including both *impact* goals and *process* goals. *Impact* goals address the desired outcomes key to a role, for example, high performance and growth in student academic mastery, student attendance, parent engagement, stakeholder sense of belonging, student graduation rate, diverse hiring, staff satisfaction, etc. *Process* goals address the degree to which activities are implemented, for example, recognizing students for growth and excellence each week, making 10 positive phone calls home each week, providing two formative assessment opportunities each week, etc.

The next step is to draft a calendar of inquiry sessions and to specify the data and guiding questions/ideas to explore for each session.

Inquiry Calendar Planner (Use With Appendix E)

SESSION NAME/ DATE(S)	IMPACT GOALS		PROCESS GOALS	
	DATA TO EXPLORE	GUIDING QUESTIONS	DATA TO EXPLORE	GUIDING QUESTIONS

1. What are any next steps to get access to these data, including results for race, gender, and subgroups of focus?

2. How and when will you hear the voices of those closest to the action and with the most at stake? (Using, for example surveys, focus groups, and the like)?

 online resources | Available for download as a full-page form at
https://resources.corwin.com/BelongingandInclusionISS

CHAPTER 5

Identity Safe Partnerships With Families and the Community

Introduction

As principal, I (Becki) loved to head over to buy a cup of hazelnut coffee at the fruit stand on Fruitvale Avenue that bordered our school. On my way, I would greet parents with their babies in strollers, and other parents working in local shops. I could check in with the local parish priest to see if we could use their social hall for our holiday assembly. I could find out about upcoming programs from the librarian at the Cesar Chavez Branch of the Oakland Library, known as the first Spanish library in the United States. It always felt good to meet friendly neighbors in the community.

This chapter will address those indispensable relationships that emerge when you invest in the talents of parents/caregivers and interested organizations and individuals willing to contribute to the success of the school. Gathering input and participation of community stakeholders contributes greatly to equitable results for students. Educational leaders who extend their reach into students' neighborhoods, homes, and communities find many helping hands. The parent/caregiver talent pool is a power source like none other when the intimate connection between students and their families is recognized and honored. And it doesn't stop there. Community organizations and civic leaders, resources that support the schools, are also integral parts of a wider network.

Launching a culture of authentic partnership involves three essential qualities: *knowing your community*, *listening to all voices*, and *building trust*. We will expand upon these qualities further in this chapter. We can apply these qualities in the following ways as we establish and strengthen identity safety:

1. Supporting parents/caregivers in meeting the academic, social, and emotional needs of their children.

2. Empowering families as partners and active participants in decisions and life of the school.

3. Engaging and drawing the larger community into the school and connecting the school with the community.

This synergy between students of diverse backgrounds flows both in and out of the classroom to touch upon all members of the community. The Learning Policy Institute (LPI) highlights the power of a team approach to support a child's academic achievement and healthy development stating,

> Research and the wisdom of practice offer significant insights for policymakers and educators about how to develop such environments. The challenge ahead is to assemble the whole village—schools, health care organizations, youth and family serving agencies, state and local governments, philanthropists, and families—to work together to ensure that every young person receives the benefit of what is known about how to support his or her healthy path to a productive future. (Darling Hammond & Cook-Harvey, 2018, para. 39)

Through identity safe practices and partnerships, leaders can transform their schools into "communities of courage," promoting safe, supportive learning environments where all members, including students, their families, teachers, and staff, as well as the wider community, support each other (Villenas & Zelinski, 2018). The ethnicity, religion, language, gender, and other traits that make up a sense of self become a vehicle for mutual enrichment that will drive productive connections between individuals and groups. Involving students and families as well as local organizations, churches, mosques, synagogues, and youth organizations turns our schools into a central hub for the community.

Why It Matters

Imagine how it feels for a student to spot their parent/caregiver crossing the yard on their way to volunteer in the school or the classroom, or when a grandparent shows up to tell a story of immigration to the class. It can be a source of great pride for the children to have their family members helping at school. More classroom visits from other parents/caregivers or grandparents can naturally follow. The message spreads: "This school is a safe place for us." Engagement with students' families and the community imparts a direct message of identity safety to all members, which includes not only who you are, but also your family, your culture and background, where you come from, and where you live. When families are valued, students feel valued.

The welfare and education of children cannot be served without attending to the welfare of the entire community. Students are not islands, isolated in their ideas about who they are, their ethnicity, gender, religion, or their culture. Their identities are intimately connected to all those around them, including their peers, their teachers, families, and social groups.

In the late 1960s, Yale professor James Comer (2005) developed a model that drew upon child development and the involvement of the community in school governance. The Comer model, still in use today, incorporates a deep understanding of student growth, engagement of families, and partnerships that bring in an array of resources to support student and family well-being. In the model, a management team, composed of administrators, teachers, staff, and parents/caregivers, collaborate to oversee the planning and implementation of school efforts. The team includes representatives from two other teams: a student–staff support team that coordinates a range of academic and social support services, and a parent/caregiver team that organizes parent/caregiver activities and involvement in the school. The model has been well researched for five decades and has been found to positively impact school performance and healthy child development. One school initiated the Comer model when only 42% of students were performing at grade level. Seventy percent of the students were African American and 85% were low income. The main intervention involved the focus on child development and the inclusion of families and the community in decision-making. No significant curricular changes were made at the time. By the fifth year of ongoing implementation, 98% of students were performing at or above grade level (Comer, 2005).

Leaders who reach out to families and enlist the community are quick to experience rewarding outcomes. When students of color and their families feel more included, they engage and achieve at higher levels. A welcoming climate where one child's differences are openly accepted allows other students to feel more free to be themselves. Researchers have found that students of all races, including White students, report greater feelings of safety in diverse schools where acknowledgment and acceptance of differences are the norm (Juvonen, Kogachi, & Graham, 2017). These partnerships lead to a positive school climate that feeds into improved academic student progress across all socioeconomic and educational levels, and ethnic and racial groups. Parents/caregivers volunteer on many levels, including participation in school governance and policy development (Epstein, Simon, & Salinas, 1997; Henderson & Mapp, 2002). Parents/caregivers and the greater community will all take up the reins for compelling collaborations when they believe they can make a difference and when they know their unique identities are valued.

Involving the community in school affairs offers a direct contrast to a deficit model, which aims to "fix" children who come from "broken" families and communities. No child benefits from an assumption that something is fundamentally wrong with them solely because of their background, whether they are a racial or ethnic minority, or their family is poor, or they belong to a family of immigrants (Dudley-Marling & Dudley-Marling, 2015). Deficit thinking is characterized by attitudes that assume students of color and low-income students show up with huge learning gaps. By extension, their families are also considered deficient. Stereotyped beliefs and biased attitudes lead to assumptions that these families do not value education, have little to offer their children, and worse yet, do not even care about their kids. These beliefs harm students and lead directly to stereotype threat, internalized feelings of inferiority, and shame about their parents/caregivers. When parents/caregivers feel judged, they shrink from coming to school for any reason. Then, in a vicious cycle, some educators make excuses for not reaching out, labeling it as a lost cause. Or they lament the lack of family involvement and create a false rationale for not forging relationships to involve them. They may claim that families do not have time to connect with school due to overwork and poverty. The time issues are real, but that is not a valid excuse for not reaching out. Educators can find ways to make a concerted effort to ensure that all parents can be involved and work to eliminate deficit mindsets among staff members.

Tara Yosso's model (2005) speaks to the individual cultural capital of students and their families, each lending to the cultural wealth within the community. Yosso defined community cultural wealth as "an array of knowledge, skills, abilities and contacts possessed and used by communities of color to survive and resist macro and micro forms of oppression" (p. 77, para 3). Leaders can acknowledge cultural wealth contributed by communities of color as "holders and creators of knowledge" (Delgado Bernal, 2002, p. 106). Schools can invite and receive families with honor and appreciation for their cultures and points of view. In the process of seeing their communities and families as assets, educators begin to shift from a deficit-based to an asset-based mindset (Simmons, in Gonzalez, 2017).

Interpersonal interactions that motivate families to engage in school projects together can affect all aspects of performance in the school. By bridging communication between groups and individuals, educational leaders can enjoy a school where community resources are recruited to enhance and support the school experience, where parents/caregivers step up willingly to lend their experience and expertise, where teachers work together with families to enrich the curriculum with cultural diversity, and where students can realize their highest potential.

Making It Happen

Several important qualities generate identity safe connections with families and communities. The journey begins with an accounting of our own beliefs while supporting staff to do the same. Individually and as a group, we can take the time to investigate our attitudes concerning our families and school community.

This can be part of the process of examining our biases that we outlined in Chapter 3. This process will strengthen our commitment to invest in our community with open hearts and minds. The following questions can help you launch into your inquiry:

- How is your own social identity a factor or asset for building trusted partnerships with parents?

- What assumptions do you hold about parents/caregivers? Are you operating on the belief that all parents/caregivers want the best for their children and hope that the school can help them learn and grow? Why or why not?

- What can you learn from parents/caregivers of all backgrounds about their child's needs? How do their children learn, and what is important to them?

- How can you educate parents/caregivers about the academic goals of the school, the methods for teaching and learning, and the assessment systems?

- How can parents/caregivers contribute and offer ideas for improving the school?

- How can you access cultural capital in the community to add resources for the school?

These attitudes are fundamental to your success in creating identity safety, especially in multicultural partnerships and cross-cultural relationships. Even if you or your staff have kind intentions, your behavior can be perceived as condescending. If individuals think you feel sorry for them—or worse, are trying to fix them—they will withdraw and hesitate to return. If this is the case, be prepared to work on your explicit and implicit biases and support your staff team to deeply explore these issues as discussed in Chapter 3.

LAUNCHING AUTHENTIC PARTNERSHIPS

To launch authentic partnerships, identity safe leaders perform three tasks simultaneously: (1) knowing the community, the students, families, and the neighborhood; (2) listening to all voices; and (3) building trust. In writing this section, it was difficult to decide which of the three actions need to happen first. They are truly reciprocal. We cannot know how to invite the many voices of the community without understanding them. People will not feel safe to speak up without feeling trust. And, we cannot build trust without understanding the community. Consider your strengths, and your school's strengths as well, as you move forward through these three key areas. You may realize that you have accomplished a good measure of these goals already.

Ask yourself several questions as you proceed. Have you taken the time to get to know your community in a meaningful way? If not, find ways to reach out. Which voices are the loudest? Do some dominate, demanding center stage? Which voices are absent? How can you build trust with those who are not usually heard? Identity safe leaders understand that all of us are works in progress, and it's okay. By allowing our vulnerabilities to show and accepting our own imperfections at times, we can help others understand that none of us need to be perfect in order to stand up and be counted. We can each find strength in supporting ourselves and others to do our best.

1. Knowing the Community

Once, while visiting a high school, Clara spoke with several students who were failing and on the edge of dropping out. She wanted to understand how they felt about school and whether they believed their teachers and school leaders cared about their futures. One boy was quick to answer back: "Our principal does not care about us. He leaves every day and drives out of our neighborhood and back to the suburbs. He does not know that I go home to a mom who is zoned out on drugs. Does he care about me? I doubt it; he does not even know me."

The boy's stark honesty, while disturbing, was no surprise. It clearly shows how unspoken or ignored lifestyle disparities can lead students to feeling disconnected from their teachers and administrators. Many educators do not live in the neighborhoods where their students attend school, and the majority of educators in this country are White. While those realities may be slow to change, culturally responsive leaders can communicate to students that they are willing to take time to learn about them and their lives off campus. Educators who are from their communities bring a foundation of cultural awareness and understanding that builds trust with students and parents/caregivers. Educators of all backgrounds can work to forge strong relationships with parents/caregivers across gender, economic, geographic, and other differences.

Knowing a community starts with your students, but it doesn't end there. In the article "Confronting Inequity/Building Community Knowledge," author H. Richard Milner states,

> Even when they are not able to live in the same neighborhood as their school, educators can build knowledge about the community by reading and talking about the events in students' lives, and by immersing themselves in the fabric of the community. They can attend community meetings, council meetings, religious ceremonies, and community events and reflect on their own lived experiences as educators in relation to those of their students. Engagement in the life of a community, as opposed to observing at a distance is the key. (Milner, 2017, para. 4)

For students, knowing that we are interested in their welfare and we care about their families and neighborhoods can make a huge difference. When students believe we respect and enjoy the people in their communities, and that we are doing everything in our power to work with them to make a positive difference in the lives of their families and themselves, trust and optimism grows.

Take the time to learn about the groups who live in your community and their history. Learn the demographics of the families and discover the major political and social groups and events that have bearing within the community. That can include the election of new politicians, a major religious celebration, the shutting down of a large industry in the town, or the opening of a new center. Find out, as well, if any harmful events have occurred in the area. Observe these events carefully and determine how they affect different groups within the community.

It pays to keep in mind that your identity, if different from the groups or individuals you approach, may not be embraced right away. You can attempt to overcome this by getting to know and working closely with community leaders who represent these groups. Then, take time to understand the social networking in these different groups, including their personal identities and how they share power.

To get started, you can be proactive in the following ways:

- **Start with your students.** From elementary to high school, students can be enlisted to draw pictures of important landmarks in the community. Older students can help with the research. This can expand into an illustrated map (see "Using the Tools" at the end of this chapter).

- **Invite neighbors and local leaders into the school for coffee.** Ask them to share the history of the area, tell their stories, and show pictures. This can turn into a hallway exhibit.

- **Take a stroll around the area.** Have students or parents/caregivers introduce you to people in the neighborhood; visit the taqueria, meet the local barber, and introduce yourself to the pet groomer.

- **Discover the local assets.** community service organizations, businesses, churches, mosques, gurdwaras, and synagogues. Learn about their services and seek commonalities.

By knowing and valuing the cultural capital of people in the local community, you are fostering identity safety for everyone and can incorporate it into the fabric of school life. Drawing on community wisdom enhances your school's identity safe practices.

2. Listening to All Voices

The path toward involving the community in an identity safe school includes listening to the many voices and discovering their preferences, skills, strengths, concerns, and needs. We initiate our conversations with safe questions that draw upon their values and expertise, allowing them to open up as they choose.

Engaging Questions to Get to Know Parents/Caregivers

- How does your child and family describe themselves and their social identities?

- What are your hopes and dreams for your child? For older students add: What are their hopes for themselves? How would you like the school to support your children with their social-emotional and academic needs?

- Who do you want your children to be by the time they leave this school?

- What motivates your child and gets them excited at school and at home? What calms them when they are upset?

- Who are their friends? Is anyone making your child feel unsafe through teasing, bullying, or exclusion?

- What are some family cultural practices and traditions? Would you like to share them at school?

- How can the school support you?

Providing safe spaces for people to speak up allows them to participate in self-affirming ways. This can include arranging for language interpreters, working with them in smaller groups, and/or meeting on a one-to-one basis.

Tips for Initiating Conversations With Parents/Caregivers

- **Prepare.** But do not overprepare—leave room for spontaneity. Find out what you can about the culture of the individual and the nature of the meeting, if they asked for it.

- **Be proactive.** Find out if they speak English or if a translator or sign-language interpreter is needed. Find out the correct pronunciation of their names and preferred pronouns. Greet the individual when you see them, introduce yourself, ask for a meeting, send a goodwill text or e-mail or phone message, and so on.

- **Listen with an intent to learn.** Ask questions to prompt engagement. Be aware of their cultural and social norms. Notice their strengths as well as vulnerabilities or areas where they may feel stereotype threat. Show your intent to understand by paraphrasing what you think they are trying to say and have them confirm that you understood.

- **Honor their communication style.** Take note of their mood, and do your best to honor it. If they are nervous, be patient; if they show anger, express concern; if they seem happy, mirror their enthusiasm.

- **Be kind, honest, and humble.** These are strengths, not weaknesses. Your audience will sense your willingness to support them when you don't condescend, when you acknowledge your mistakes openly, and when you show understanding for their admissions.

- **Refrain from demonstrating cultural insensitivity.** Inappropriate comments—"I have so many Black friends," "I own a lovely photo of a Mexican village," or "I know just how you feel"—even when well intended, hide a host of assumptions that claim cultural competence without an ounce of inquiry or self-examination. They are usually both apparent and insulting to those on the receiving end.

- **Keep a flexible mindset for a desired outcome.** You want the parents/caregivers to feel welcomed and safe, to discover their talents, gifts, connections, and to assure them that you care and will investigate a problem, seeking mutual agreement on solutions, soothe them and calm their worries, and so on. Allow conversations to flow and be willing to change your tack if needed.

When Conversations Get Difficult or Conflict Erupts

Inevitably, circumstances will require you to engage in sensitive conversations with parents/caregivers—situations that have the potential to either blossom into a bonding experience or erupt into defensiveness (or worse, an adversarial exchange with a loss of trust). Educators can build skills to handle a delicate situation that breaks out in the principal's office, on campus, in a parent/caregiver meeting, or following a racist incident, or a hate event, which has rocked the school.

For some incidents, parties can be brought together; at other times, it is preferable to initially meet with and listen to each party separately. Allow each party to tell their version of what happened, letting them speak without interruption. Give room for their anger, fear, or frustration to be expressed until it subsides enough to address the situation and possibly frame it in a different light. Build empathy and ask them what they think is needed to restore justice or solve the problem. Asking them what they feel the other party may be experiencing can promote empathy. Acknowledge their feelings, which is not the same as agreement but rather encourages understanding. Consider the root of the conflict. Do they feel they were treated unfairly or disrespected? Was there a prior conflict between these people or their children?

Do not rush into solutions. A cool-down period can take place over a few days. That gives you time to investigate further. After listening fully to all parties—and only when they seem ready to hear each other—move from confrontation to problem-solving using a restorative approach with a goal of understanding what occurred and allowing harm to be repaired.

Compassion as a Navigation Tool for Difficult Conversations

I (Kathe) recall a difficult conversation with the parent of a girl in my class. Her daughter had been feuding with another girl. I received a note from the mom, Emma (pseudonym), one morning asking to talk. She rushed into my classroom after school, claiming that the other girl had excluded her daughter from a game they had been playing several days ago. She had confronted the other girl's mom, Katie (pseudonym), in front of the campus after school, and thought she had been "very fair" in giving her a chance to discipline her daughter so that she would apologize. She claimed that Katie had listened, then climbed into her car and drove off with her daughter. I had already talked to Katie, who explained that she felt disrespected when Emma had demanded that her daughter apologize without greeting her and hearing her daughter's side of the story. She said that she was embarrassed that it happened in front of other parents.

Using compassion as my lead, I remembered when my own daughter had been teased by a friend in school. I shared it with Emma. "It was hard to see her get hurt. It felt like it was happening to me," I told her. Emma agreed, then surprised me, sharing a time when she had been hurt herself as a child in school. We chatted along these lines, and I noticed her entire demeanor changing. The tension was gone. She confessed to me that she had been a little hard on Katie, but she didn't think she deserved to have been completely ignored by her. This gave me an opportunity to share what I had come to understand from Katie, and I offered Emma a different lens for viewing the event. In the end, Emma expressed a desire to make amends with Katie, and I saw the two women chatting later with their girls playing together nearby.

Compassion, as opposed to blame or judgment, is a wonderfully advantageous tool for de-escalating a situation. It creates an identity safe space for injured individuals, leading to a successful processing of events. Conflicts can become opportunities to grow when we respect differences and arrive at mutual understandings.

When Tension Erupts Into Conflict in a Meeting

Even experienced leaders may find themselves mediating a conflict or major disagreement that erupted, steering the meeting off course. Here are a few reminders:

Be Prepared

- Know your group, their perspectives, and their potential areas of tension.

- Plan by setting goals for the dialogue and gain familiarity with the discussion topic.

- Consider the different paths or detours the discussion might take ahead of time.

Create a Welcoming and Inclusive Space

- Invite everyone to join in the conversation. Explain the purpose of the dialogue, set ground rules and basic discussion guidelines (see community agreements in Chapter 3).

- Ask participants to add their own ideas and sum up important points.

- Notice who has spoken and who hasn't. Allow for wait time.

- Resist the urge to speak after each comment or answer every question. Let participants respond directly to each other.

- Stay neutral and promote an atmosphere of respect.

Intercultural Sensitivity

- Gain an awareness of cross-cultural dynamics to support meaningful dialogue.

- Remind participants that no one can represent their entire culture nor can they represent another person's experience. Each individual and member of a group is unique.

- Encourage group members to empathize with others without stereotyping or speaking for other cultures.

- Avoid making assumptions about individuals based on a stereotype of their culture. Cultural traits are not monolithic. All members of cultural groups are unique individuals.

- Be careful not to equate or compare different people's experiences.

- Keep in mind that approaches to time differ. Some groups tend to be more flexible with time while others are sticklers for punctuality.

- In some cultures, more value is placed on getting down to work first and building relationships along the way. Other cultures start by building relationships, and then people begin to work together and complete the tasks.

- People in some cultures learn by measuring and quantifying information. In other cultures, experience and intuitive reasoning are trusted processing qualities.

When Tension Manifests

- Help those in conflict with each other by considering their different perspectives and outlining the pros and cons of each. Guide them to see the values they have in common.

- If the conversation is scattered, invite everyone back to the same page with the question, "What seems to be the key point here?"

- During meetings, have a blank poster labeled Parking Lot, where you list ideas that are off topic or not on the agenda that can be addressed at a future meeting.

- When different opinions are expressed, ask for clarification: "Why is that important?" or "What experiences have you had with this?" or "Could you help us understand the reasons behind your opinion?"

- Check in with the other participants: "Do you agree? Why or why not?" Then ask, "What could be another perspective on what has been said?" or "How might others see this issue?"

With hard conversations, you can never eliminate all the difficulties, but with practice, you will guide members into more meaningful interactions and enjoy both learning and growth. Your job is to help the group members have a rich conversation that leads to new understandings (Everyday Democracy, 2008).

Entry Points for Connecting With the Community

Surveys are a quick and easy way to take the pulse of your community. They need to be available in a variety of formats (paper and online) and in the languages of the school community. Also, you can gather small focus groups, by language group, to discuss particular suggestions, issues, and responses. With focus groups you can discover the nuances that a survey will not reveal. It will also allow you to develop relationships. Be sure to report findings to the school community and act on what you have learned (see Chapter 4).

Home visits help you get to know students and their families. Visiting a student's home can be very valuable in building relationships and offers opportunities to learn much about the child's world. Be sure to call ahead if you are planning a home visit. Some families love having school leaders and teachers visit their homes. Others prefer not to have visitors.

Open the door to involvement in the school in meaningful ways, including the school decision-making processes. Parents/caregivers can contribute in a myriad of ways as volunteers or committee chairs, as we outline later in this chapter. The deepest trust builds as people work together for their children and the greater good of the school.

Building Trust

Trust, the third element in the triad of *knowing the community* and *listening to all voices*, carries the glue that bonds the other two, providing the safety net they both need to flourish. Trust is a central theme throughout this book, and it is an enduring ingredient for creating identity safety across the school community. It is the basis for meaningful collaborations and can determine the difference between a mediocre school and one that excels. Building trust with the families and the community sends a message to students that we are not interested in giving mere lip service to the values of acceptance, anti-racism, and compassion but rather we are willing to work with them to make these elements a living reality.

Trust does not manifest without inclusivity. For an entire community to feel safe, every group within it must feel safe. When race is a forbidden or scary topic, fear and exclusion can result. The best approach for dispelling fear is to acknowledge it. Engaging in conversations about race with people of different races plays an important part of building trust with families in the school community. Goodwill can lead to disclosures that open hearts and minds. In Chapters 1 and 3, we shared that in 2020, a Black parent group in San Diego, who call themselves "Small and Mighty" given their small representation within a school of predominantly White and Asian families, held a Town Hall Zoom meeting, "From Allies to Action," whose purpose was to discuss race and the experiences of their Black children as a minority group within the school. The group had formed after one of their members approached the principal, Joe Erpelding, to share some of the racist incidents experienced by their children.

Roxanne Macray Gordon was one of those members. She revealed her son Wyatt's experiences at the school to Joe. In first grade, Wyatt was told by a White student that she didn't want to touch him because she was afraid that her skin would turn "black" like his. Gordon also informed Joe that a student in Wyatt's class was told by her older brother to approach Wyatt and call him the N-word. "I did not learn of this incident until a week later," she shared. "One day, Wyatt and I were driving home from baseball practice when he began to cry. I asked him what was wrong. He then proceeded to tell me that story of being called the N-word by a classmate. Wyatt clearly did not know how to process being called the N-word, and it took him a week to feel comfortable enough to share what had happened to him at school on the playground. . . . My husband and my heart broke for our child, when he shared the hurtful things he had suffered through in the classroom and on the playground." Joe listened, and together with the "Small and Mighty" group, arranged an online Town Hall meeting with the school's parent community.

In that online meeting, the "Small and Mighty" members shared their personal stories and addressed the issue of white privilege in an effort to create understanding for conditions that confront them in their daily lives. It was a courageous first step. They subsequently held a second Town Hall meeting, and their efforts contributed to influencing positive changes in the school and the district: The "Small and Mighty" parents were engaged in two teacher training sessions where they led staff in small groups. Joe also arranged for them to address a meeting of principals as well—the first time Black parents had ever addressed administrators as a group in the history of the district. Groups of Black parents in other schools also banded together, forming their own Small and Mighty groups. The district's Racial Equity and Improvement Plan has been approved by the school board, and an ethnic studies course and ethnic literature course will be available for students in the following year. Twelve new Black teachers and one assistant Black principal have been hired. Small can definitely be mighty. (More details about the journey for Erpelding, their principal, during this process can be found in Chapter 2.)

In Chapter 3, we offered ideas for staff dialogue about race that also apply to community conversations. In the article "Critical Community Conversations: Cultivating the Elusive Dialogue About Racism With Parents, Community Members, and Teachers," Bettina Love and Gholnecsar Mohammed (2017) offer additional guidelines for dialogue about race and racism, stating that "creating a safe sharing environment is crucial to the progress of community building for a better and just tomorrow" (para 2). They encourage facilitators to situate these conversations in the context of the history of race as a social construct and the prevalence of racism today. They suggest that participants share stories about local issues that directly impact their families such as gentrification. They propose that the ultimate goal of these critical conversations is to take action for social justice. Learning to navigate these waters requires courage and sensitivity, yet advances on this front will create important strides toward achieving trust and community-wide identity safety. There is no shortcut to the process of building trust. It is earned as you consistently stand up for students and their families. It is demonstrated when you protect the most vulnerable students and speak up to change unfair situations. It is evident as you "walk your talk."

Finding the Courage to Speak Up

When I (Becki) was working as curriculum director, I attended a districtwide parent/caregiver education meeting featuring an author known as an expert on gifted education. At one point, the speaker made the following comment: "Gifted people often get the short end of the stick. They really should have separate classes to maximize their potential. Unfortunately, the civil rights movement worked against them, throwing them into classrooms with students who were not of their caliber." I was aghast. Not only had this comment blamed Black students for causing an unwanted and harmful effect on the

(Continued)

(Continued)

"gifted students," but she was indulging in a white supremacist assumption that Black students are not among the gifted. What would the few Black parents/caregivers in attendance be feeling? I jumped up and walked out of the room. I'd participated with district teachers and administrators to ensure equitable conditions for students of color, and this talk was undermining those efforts.

Just outside the door, I saw a friend and colleague, Jennifer. "Can you believe that comment? It flies in the face of everything we are trying to do in our district." We commiserated, and halfway down the path, I stopped. In our Equity Team, we'd discussed speaking truth to power, of standing up for what is right . . . and here I was leaving the scene. "Jennifer," I said, "I am going back in there."

Once inside, I interrupted the speaker. "Excuse me. I want to respond to your comment about the civil rights movement harming gifted students. I am not sure what you meant to say, but I want to assure you that as a district administrator, together with my colleagues and community leaders, we are all working very hard to ensure equity for students of all races, and ethnicities, including those who are gifted. I just needed to make sure that you and everyone here understands this."

The speaker said nothing and eventually continued with her presentation. I felt that it was a moment when I was able to use my white privilege and speak up. Years later, I was sitting with a school board member and a Black woman entered the room. She greeted me warmly and told me that she knew who I was. She had been present that night and spoke of the humiliation she felt when the comment was made. She was grateful that I spoke up. It was a lesson that I never forgot. Speaking up in a difficult situation is never easy, but the experience had a transformative quality for me as an educational leader to take a stand and support all students and families in feeling valued and counted.

Communities will take note of our behavior, our positions, opinions, and biases. Are we there for them or not? It is a question families of color and others must deal with on a daily basis as they navigate through a dominant culture that often excludes them. For White leaders, cultural humility and an unassuming attitude is an essential part of extending support. It's an easy mistake to extend a helping hand without first checking to see if it is wanted or even needed. Open-ended questions, like asking "How are you doing?," can help you avoid falling into the "white savior" trap.

When we stand up for our families, they will be more trusting and willing to enter our open doors. And if we hear them sharing openly with us, we know that we are building trust. It becomes incumbent upon us not to break it.

Welcoming Diverse Students and Their Families

Families come in all shapes and sizes with multiple aspects of family identity, which can include children raised by one or two parents, grandparents, and foster or adoptive parents. Families can be blended or shared custody families. They may include LGBTQIA+ parents or siblings, first-generation immigrants, mixed heritages or ethnicities and religions, or any combination of the characterizations above. Welcoming all families into the school and valuing their diversity is a powerful contributor to identity safety.

Diverse families can participate in the school experience in a variety of non-colorblind ways that allow them to share cultural traditions and practices. Sharing their traditions and their careers, playing music, cooking, and teaching a craft connects parents/caregivers to the school and offers a familial and comfortable environment for students. Parents of older students can help with special clubs like the Gay Straight Alliance, the Black Student Union, the Korean Club, and sports teams. Multicultural influences, however, do not end with one-stop be-all celebrations. When we absorb the idea of belonging for diverse students and families, our daily attitudes will, of their own accord, spawn a wealth of ideas and opportunities for contributing. It will come to us naturally.

Trust and Building Family Connections

Communication Methods

- Use a variety of ongoing communication tools: newsletters, blogs (with translations), online, calendars, and alternate ways to share information that can be used for regular contact. Take care to ensure that all families have access.

- Try not to rely too much on remote access. Calling families and meeting in person with them is the best way to build relationships and foster communication.

Translation and American Sign Language (ASL) Interpretation

- Ensure your meetings have translators even if the number of people who need it is small. Translation can be done through simultaneous translation, using earphones, and also having a translator sit with a small group of parents/caregivers.

- Obtain ASL (American Sign Language) interpreters if the school has deaf parents/caregivers.

- Privately approach parents/caregivers who might need translation to avoid embarrassment for them in having to publicly claim they need support.

(Continued)

(Continued)

Facilitating Parent/Caregiver Access

- Build direct relationships with parents/caregivers and give them your contact information early. Encourage them to contact you via text, phone, or e-mail with concerns or needs.

- Schedule meetings at times they are available and adjust as needed.

- Provide childcare for meetings.

- Parents/caregivers sometimes need help with carpools to attend meetings. Posting a public board for rideshares can be helpful.

- Provide substantial snacks at meetings, especially for parents/caregivers who arrive directly from work.

- Avoid placing low-income parents/caregivers on the spot by constantly asking for donations.

- During the coronavirus pandemic, many schools have been forced to move PTA and other parent/caregiver meetings online, and providing homes with technology and connectivity has made this possible. Unexpectedly, without childcare and transportation issues, attendance has often increased significantly.

SUPPORTING PARENTS/CAREGIVERS IN MEETING THE ACADEMIC, SOCIAL, AND EMOTIONAL NEEDS OF THEIR CHILDREN

Parents/caregivers are children's first teachers, guiding them through all phases in the journey of growing up. This can be overwhelming, especially if the children have mental or physical challenges, if parents/caregivers are immigrants, or if they struggle to keep their families afloat financially. Schools can be lifelines for parents/caregivers, especially during hard times. I (Becki) know this from firsthand experience. I met Kathe when my daughter, Melania, was a student in her third-grade class. Melania was new in the school and Kathe went above and beyond to ensure that Melania made new friends. Since I was a teacher in another town at the time, Kathe called me at home to check in. When she discovered that due to illness my husband could not drive Melania to school for several weeks, she offered to pick her up every morning and drive her to school. That is something I will never forget.

Parents/caregivers often seek advice on how to help their children, and at times, they can be demanding. Many of these interactions happen on a one-to-one basis. It is important not to act as if we know the "right" way, implying that their parenting skills are misguided or wrong. This is especially relevant in regard to parenting styles and modes of discipline. Addressing these sensitivities requires a nuanced approach. It is best treated as a give and take, with everyone sharing what has worked for them and exploring their questions together.

Even when conversations within the office grow uncomfortable, recourse is always available. After Jay, a junior, was caught pulling the fire alarm, the dean, Mr. Garcia, called Jay's mom, Anna, in. When Jay passionately denied it, his mom declared that he would never lie to her. Mr. Garcia tried a compassionate tack. "Jay," he began. "Last week, Ari told me that an older classmate, Derek, was bullying him. He said you stood up to Derek and told him to stop. Derek heard you and left. Thank you for being so kind." Jay leaned forward in his chair, looking less defiant. A few minutes later, he admitted to pulling the alarm. After a stunned look at her son, Anna apologized sheepishly to Mr. Garcia, who reassured her that he understood her desire to support her son. Anna admitted that if she had thought about it, she would have realized that Mr. Garcia had no reason to make it up. In the end, Anna understood that Mr. Garcia empathized with her desire to stand by her son, but she also came to realize that she was not helping him by blindly defending him.

Parents/Caregivers as Partners in Academic Achievement

For parents/caregivers to partner with us in supporting student learning, we aim to ensure that they understand the school's vision, goals, and methods. In Chapter 4, we explain the importance of including parents/caregivers as partners in the understanding of our vision for teaching and learning, assessment, and data collection. During the pandemic, the importance of understanding the curriculum became paramount as teachers were training parents/caregivers to assist with student learning at both the elementary and secondary levels. This understanding and capacity to encourage their children and support learning produces highly successful results, both for distance and in-person learning.

Bringing parents/caregivers up to speed on the school's approach to identity safety, student-centered teaching, social and emotional learning, and use of data to drive instruction helps them better understand how the school operates and facilitates supporting their kids at home. There are many ways to do this that are both fun and instructional. I (Kathe) organized math nights at my school. The activities were interactive and designed to engage multiple language levels for parents and multiple skill levels for students. Eighteen different languages were spoken at the school, and it was fun to watch the diverse mix of families and their children interact and connect over the activities. The math served as a universal language, bridging them together with lots of interaction and laughter.

A Partnership for Literacy

As principal, my staff and I (Becki) wanted to find a way to communicate how we taught reading to the parents/caregivers. In addition to English-speaking families, we had large numbers of families who spoke Spanish, Cambodian, Lau, Mien, and Vietnamese. A teacher came up with the idea of making short videotapes of children reading in English at grade level. Six hundred parents/caregivers attended our meeting that began with a student performance. Afterwards, they divided into separate rooms for sessions in their primary languages where they viewed the videos and discussed how reading was taught. Parents shared that they were glad to learn about how their children were learning to read and said they felt more prepared to help them (Cohn-Vargas & Gross, 1998).

Supporting Families in Promoting Student Identity Safety

As the primary role models for their children, parents/caregivers are the ones who communicate an appreciation for their values, backgrounds, family histories, and social identities. Starting from a young age, children absorb many positive as well as negative unspoken messages about their identities from other adults, their peers, and the media. Race has no meaning to babies; yet researchers Katz and Kofkin (1997) found that infants already note differences. The manner that adults around them react to these differences influences the meaning that young children attribute to these categories. Researchers have discovered that—whether or not people are consciously aware—middle-class white culture is treated as the standard for normality and values in the United States. This includes everything from appearance, to beauty, language, food, and cultural practices (Winkler, 2009).

Many avenues exist for educators to support families as they strengthen their children's identities, bring out the joy and pride in their families and cultures, and counteract negative narratives based in stereotypes or in the privileging of white culture.

Using Counter-Narratives With Families

The Journey Project draws on traditions from African rites of passage, particularly the Kwanzaa principle of Kujichagulia (self-determination). The model is being implemented in Baltimore and East Cleveland, schools serving a majority of Black students. Project leaders identify central "guardians," advisors who offer guidance, foster trust, and use counter-narratives to help families distance themselves from the disempowering stories of dominant narratives. Another aspect involves engaging families in a process to develop *cultural armor*, which Fanon Hill describes as a "protection garnered from knowing the strength of one's cultural heritage" (Wasserman, Sabater, & Hill, 2017, p. 12; see Figure 2). Cultural armor helps children of color cultivate pride in their background but also counteracts negative stereotypes, stereotype threat, and white supremacist culture. Participants describe feeling accepted and valued, where their stories are shared without judgment. Researchers found that the Journey Project's use of counter-narratives led to community bonding and individual self-determination, which in turn created authentic family engagement in their children's education. Parents/caregivers increased volunteering and meeting attendance, confidently expressing ideas and concerns (Wasserman et al., 2017; Wasserman & Sabater, 2018).

Another important avenue to help children develop positive identities, sustain cultural armor, and take an anti-racist stance involves giving parents/caregivers tools for introducing and discussing race with their children.

Supporting Parents in Talking About Race With Their Children

Many parents wonder how to best talk to their children about race. Caron Jackson-Harrigan, a Black mother of two in New Jersey, explains that while mistakes may be inevitable when discussing race with children, it is an ongoing process that goes beyond one conversation. Parents/caregivers can ask their children about what they have seen or experienced and hurtful comments or racist language they have heard or viewed. They also can teach their children not to spread or follow hateful social media posts (Russell, 2020).

One study of 17,000 families with kindergartners determined that 75% of the White parents interviewed almost never talk about race with children (T. Brown, et al., 2007). Sociologist Margaret Hagerman (2018) studied 30 affluent, White families in the Midwest, pointing out that White kids draw from many sources to learn about race. They learn from conversations as well as what they witness and hear from people around them. They observe their parents' everyday behaviors. Hageman explains they learn "when to lock the car doors, what conversations to have at the dinner table . . . when to roll one's eyes, what media to consume, how to respond to overtly racist remarks made by Grandpa at a family dinner . . . and where to spend leisure time. (Restaurants, vacation destinations and community events can be deliberately and by-default mostly white—or purposefully not.) These small actions send subtle yet powerful messages. Parents may not even be aware that they are conveying ideas about race through these behaviors, but children learn from them all the time" (Hagerman, 2018, paras. 7–8). Children believe what we do over what we say.

When initiating conversations about race with White children, listening is a vital and initial key toward unpacking their sentiments about race. If parents hear a child making a comment with racial undertones, it is important to probe further. Listening is a powerful start, but in light of the responsibility for raising a conscionable and socially aware generation, these conversations require much guidance and information about oppression and white supremacy, and they need to continue throughout their childhood.

The luxury of not engaging in conversations about race is a choice most families of color do not have. They know that their children, at some point, will experience bias and racial discrimination, and in order to prepare them for these probable events, they must open the topic of race and expose their children to some very difficult ideas about the way the world works and provide them with strategies for how to navigate safely. Kenya Young, NPR journalist and a Black mother, reflects on giving her three sons "the talk," referring to conversations that Black parents feel compelled to have with their children, particularly their sons. This includes how they should deal with the police should they encounter them. Young shares, "I remember the kids asking to go to the park and the laundry list of what I had to tell them: 'Don't wear your hood. Don't put your hands in your pocket. If you get stopped, don't run. Put your hands up. Don't make a lot of moves. Tell them your mother works for NPR.' I mean, it just went on and on" (Young, 2020, para. 8).

As school leaders, we can support our parent/caregiver groups in engaging and facilitating these important conversations about race with their children. The goal is to lead them into embracing positive aspects about race, perspectives that will inform interactions within culturally diverse groups at school and in the world.

See Appendix H: Developmentally Appropriate Conversations About Race and Gender With Children and Youth: Tips for Educators and Parents/Caregivers.

EMPOWERING AND ENGAGING PARENTS/CAREGIVERS AT SCHOOL

An identity safe school invites parents/caregivers to actively engage with their children's education and participate in school decisions that affect their children. Multiple points of access allow each family to become involved in ways that work with their personal schedules and comfort levels. This can include everything from an informal weekly coffee with the principal after dropping off their children at school, to innovative volunteer opportunities and leadership and advisory roles in school governance.

Authentic engagement for parents/caregivers includes a sense of self-determination as we described in the Journey Project earlier, and as they come to view themselves as true partners in the enterprise of educating their children. Researchers found that when parents/caregivers felt efficacious, they are more likely to see the school as competent. Their motivation to participate also has been correlated to student achievement (Gordon & Louis, 2009; Grolnick, 2015).

Parent/Caregiver Volunteers: Role Models That Support Student Identity Safety

Students of all backgrounds feel pride when they spot their parents or caregivers on campus participating in valued activities. Opening the door to parents/caregivers allows the school to greatly extend its capacity to meet student needs. Parents/caregivers can help in classrooms, the office, the library, and the schoolyard. Here are some possibilities:

- **In the classroom:** Share their professions and personal stories, edit newsletters, help the teacher

- **In the parent/caregiver community:** Lead workshops; teach sewing, cooking, or carpentry; reach out to other parents/caregivers

- **In the schoolwide community:** Organize events, translate, serve on committees

- **In the wider community:** Obtain donations, extend school partnerships to organizations

In each case, their status and value are elevated in identity safe ways.

Bringing Immigrant Parents Into the School

Louise Waters shares,

Through ongoing parent conversations, I discovered a sadness among many immigrant parents. They were proud of their children's growing English but alarmed at the loss of their native language. They worried that without the ability to communicate, they

(Continued)

(Continued)

could not support their children academically. But their deepest fear was losing their authority. How could they ensure their children respected the teacher? How could they protect them from drugs or gang activity if the children no longer respected them, their culture, or their language? Building on these conversations, we started early-morning language academies in Spanish, Tagalog, Farsi, Vietnamese, Punjabi, and Spanish for English speakers. Two hundred and fifty students attended. Previously almost none of the parents participated in school activities and most were reticent to interact with the school at all. Now, many stayed, socializing around the flagpole after bringing their children to language class. At our fall festival, language academy parents ran food booths to fund academy activities—biryani, pansit, and imperial rolls sold fast. The classes participated in the spring talent show and their families attended. Now teachers were able to find translators and easily connect with parents/caregivers. And I was able to build strong relationships with this quarter of our families, ones previously invisible in our school. The insights I gained through these interactions were invaluable in building a cohesive school community.

PARENTS/CAREGIVERS AS PARTNERS IN GOVERNANCE AND PROBLEM-SOLVING

Parents/caregivers can play an important role in school governance. Most schools have official advisory committees that incorporate parent/caregiver's input into the school plan, including English-language development programs and funding decisions. Often these committees are operated in a perfunctory way. Identity safe leaders take the time to provide skill-building for parent/caregiver members of these committees. Meaningful participation can strengthen leadership skills as they advise on school issues and resource allocation, and address concerns. Parents/caregivers are watching to ensure that their suggestions are taken seriously and put into practice.

Skill-building for meaningful participation includes working with parent/caregiver leaders on setting agendas, learning how to facilitate and run effective meetings, and employing tools for consensus and decision-making and data analysis procedures. When schools have a majority of one ethnic group, a useful practice that supports identity safety involves forming smaller groups of parents/caregivers of a particular ethnic group to give them a chance to voice their concerns. The group "Small and Mighty," described earlier in the chapter, is one such group who meets regularly with the principal to support the small percentage of Black students at the school.

PARTNERSHIPS WITH THE GREATER COMMUNITY

While no school can meet all student needs, community partnerships offer more than merely filling the gaps for areas where school services fall short. Community connections can broaden your influence to the extent that your school transforms into a community hub. You will enjoy resources and help at every turn. Partnering enables wraparound services that provide families with access to resources to meet basic needs: food, health care, housing, mental health, and counseling support.

Schools have limited funding and these outside community relationships can greatly extend the capacity to serve students. For example, community organizations can be particularly beneficial to students with special needs, providing resources to meet a variety of challenges faced by these students and their families. These partnerships increase academic achievement, improve staff performance, and create a positive and identity safe school climate for everyone. Researchers have demonstrated that high-performing schools greatly benefit from broad-based community support (Ubben, et al., 2011, p. 302).

When Arlene served as principal, she was a pioneer among the early schools to offer wraparound services to extend our capacity to meet students' emotional and physical needs. She helped set up a school-based clinic, services by volunteer dentists, adult education, and a robust free after-school program. An out-stationed county mental health counselor performed her regular duties on the school campus. The proximity was convenient for students and their families. In addition, they had case managers from the Family Preservation Unit of Child Protective Services, a county program that helped families at risk of having their children removed from their homes. The case manager did everything from providing respite care services to purchasing a washing machine for a family.

An Array of Local and National Organizations Support Schools

Gender Identity and Sexual Orientation Support: Gender Spectrum (https://www.genderspectrum.org/) provides guidance to schools across the United States on how to understand and support students with a range of gender identities.

Gang Prevention: San Jose, California, schools partnered with a local gang prevention organization where former gang members led a motivational assembly and worked with small groups of middle school students on an ongoing basis to provide alternatives to gang membership.

(Continued)

(Continued)

Climate Surveys: Center City Public Charter Schools in Washington, D.C., implemented school climate surveys and partnered with a local organization to support parents/caregivers in interpreting achievement data (Villenas & Zelinski, 2018).

College Prep: In Simpson County Schools, in Kentucky, five community organizations each donated $10,000 for a fund to ensure that each student in their school district could have access to dual-enrollment college classes (Villenas & Zelinski, 2018).

Partnerships Strengthen Cultural Connections

Community partnerships are invaluable in offering authentic cultural experiences within the school. Leaders can reach out to organizations, from Black churches to local Native American community organizations. Colleges have an array of cultural student clubs that can be invited to make presentations, mentor, or support identity safety. Following is a small sampling of college clubs from many ethnicities: the Black Women's Collective (https://brc.ucsd.edu/programs/collectives/), the Women in Engineering club (https://www.sjsu.edu/getinvolved/student-orgs/index.php), Hindu Yuva (https://hinduyuva.org/), Filipino Student Association (University of Michigan, https://maizepages.umich.edu/organization/FASA), and the Native American and Indigenous Student Association (University of Illinois, https://oiir.illinois.edu/native-american-house/get-involved/affiliated-student-organizations). In another example, the Confederation of Somali Community in Minnesota (https://www.mnopedia.org/place/confederation-somali-community-minnesota) supports schools in serving the refugee community in their state.

Community groups provide enrichment through the arts and music, cultural, and linguistic services that greatly enhance students' sense of cultural pride. Partnering with museums and zoos, colleges, libraries, the media, business, industry, and youth organizations also bring added dimensions to the school experience. Local Rotary, Lions, Optimist, Kiwanis, and fraternal groups often provide funding for school activities and sponsor events.

Community Partnerships During Times of Crisis

Brockton Public Schools in Massachusetts was greatly impacted by COVID-19. Some families suffered illness and deaths while others faced tremendous economic hardships. Fortunately, they had previously built strong partnerships with organizations in their community. They assembled a team of bilingual–bicultural community relations facilitators who worked together with school counselors, parent/caregiver advocates, and paraprofessionals, all of whom reached out to the families.

The team provided information and connected families to health resources, as well as food and job assistance. They formed a multilingual call center staffed with volunteers, including nurses, crisis counselors, and others to provide more support (Cohn-Vargas & Zacarian, 2020).

Educational leaders routinely deal with daily problems and some experience major crises from student suicides to natural disasters, to hate incidents where a gay teacher or Muslim student is targeted. Here are a few tips for handling crises (Cohn-Vargas, 2017):

- **Carefully investigate:** Take time to find out what happened before making any big decisions. Investigate before drawing conclusions.

- **Transparency and communication:** Immediately share information with staff, and next with the student and parent/caregiver community. Offer as much information as you can without breaking confidentiality or legal restrictions. Develop clear talking points to share with staff to communicate consistent messages when members of the school community speak with the media. Dispel misinformation and take down harmful social media posts.

- **Allies:** Find allies, mentors, confidants, and trusted colleagues to assist you in gaining support from various sectors of the community.

- **Stand strong:** The willingness to take bold stands and challenge dominant narratives will lead to a safer cultural environment. As you work to form interpersonal as well as group partnerships to challenge the status quo and radically change old paradigms, your commitment to develop and sustain an identity safe school will propel your efforts.

- **When a crisis appears to subside, don't stop working to address the causes:** Crises often result from underlying issues that cannot be resolved quickly. After taking immediate action, work with your colleagues and the community to enact longer-term changes and monitor progress.

Rising to Challenges/Avoiding Pitfalls

Working with a diverse community and forging new pathways of equal status has its share of challenges and pitfalls. We addressed some of them earlier in this chapter. Here we discuss unintended consequences of calculated risks, responding to criticism and controversy, and what to do after the faux pas.

FACING UNINTENDED CONSEQUENCES

Often you find yourself taking a calculated risk—even if you are uncertain it will be effective. In some instances, you will be pleasantly surprised, at other times, you'll experience unanticipated failures. When things work out well, be sure to acknowledge the people who contributed ideas. When things fail, try not to point fingers, blame, or say, "I knew it." By adopting a learning approach with a growth mindset and avoiding defensiveness, you can remain centered on the principles of identity safety and continue the path forward.

HANDLING CRITICISM AND CONTROVERSY

As leaders, we often find ourselves in the hot seat. When inviting many voices into the planning and decisions at school, it is likely your ideas will be critiqued. After listening with an open mind, proposed alternatives may be unrealistic or incongruous with school goals or essentially unworkable. You also may hear criticism that change is moving too slowly, or that results have fallen short. Sometimes parent/caregiver communities are politically divided about controversial topics, like sex education. At other times, individuals and groups vie for power and may attempt to win you over in ways that make you uncomfortable. These situations call upon your personal leadership skills to communicate that you are listening while also standing up for your beliefs. By drawing on your social and emotional intelligence (see Chapter 2), you can avoid falling into traps or getting baited with petty problems. You can rise to the challenge by adhering to your moral compass, to the values of identity safety, and to your commitment to keep students at the heart of all decisions.

RESPONDING AFTER YOU MAKE A FAUX PAS

When working with people, it is inevitable that you will stumble with a faux pas. It can be a relatively insignificant remark or omission, like forgetting to thank one of the parents when announcing the names of everyone who organized an event. Other times, it may involve a potentially harmful situation, such as disciplining a student and later discovering that they had been falsely accused. People are often quite willing to forgive you, even for bigger mistakes, if you express remorse, take accountability for your errors, and demonstrate that you learned from it by doing what you can to repair the harm.

Closing the Gap Between Ideas and Action

As you reflect on community involvement at your site and choose areas to build upon further, consider the following:

Learn about and build trust with all sectors of your community:

- Make an effort to meet the many groups that make up your school community on campus and in the neighborhood (e.g., attend a service at a Black church, a Catholic mass in Spanish, visit the karate studio where many students go for lessons).

- Identify where trust is lacking and make a plan to connect with the community; listen to their thoughts and feelings.

- Invite members of the community who have not usually been involved in the school affairs to meet with you in small groups. Ask them how you can help them feel a sense of belonging.

- Meet with parents/caregivers of students served by special education and ask them to help with efforts to make the school more inclusive for their children.

- Find new ways for community members to contribute and equalize status in the school.

- Reach out to gay parents/caregivers; meet with them to learn directly how their kids are feeling at school.

Support parents/caregivers with their children's identity safety:

- Educate parents/caregivers on how to understand and meet academic and social and emotional needs of their children.

- Provide and support counter-narratives to help families build cultural armor, cultivate pride in their backgrounds, and counteract negative stereotyping and white supremacist attitudes and structures.

- Engage in dialogue about race with parents/caregivers to increase their awareness of ways to support their children in similar dialogues and contribute to identity safety and acceptance on campus.

Increase parent/caregiver involvement in contributing to the school and in decision-making:

- Invite parents to share expertise and volunteer in classrooms, committees, and leadership positions.

- Utilize innovative strategies, translators, and community organizations to reach immigrant parents/caregivers.

- Develop service-learning projects with parents/caregivers in different careers, especially those in nontraditional jobs.

- Provide skill-building for parents to participate, help make decisions, and lead efforts to improve the school.

Involve the greater community:

- Invite members of local organizations to meet together at the school to discuss partnering opportunities.

- Reach out to representatives from the city council, religious institutions, businesses, community and campus cultural organizations, nonprofits, and service clubs in your community (Rotary, Lions). Invite them to contribute to the school.

Respond to crises and conflicts:

- Be a compassionate listener and avoid rushing to solutions when a concern or conflict is brought to you.

- Use community agreements to ensure decorum and respect in meetings. When tension does build up, guide group members by calmly inviting everyone to listen to the differing perspectives and seek commonalities.

- When community members criticize you, try to remain open to hear them and avoid becoming defensive.

- In the event of a schoolwide crisis, aim to be transparent and inform the community as much as possible to avoid rumors.

- Consider bringing in an outside facilitator for some contentious issues.

Check Yourself

- How are you listening to and addressing the varying needs of different families, including those whose ethnicities are represented in smaller numbers?

- How can you draw on the parent/caregiver community to involve role models from all ethnic groups and gender identities in your school?

- How do you accept accountability for things that go wrong in ways without eroding trust? How can you acknowledge a mistake and communicate your vulnerability while also maintaining your dignity?

- Do you have any critics in the greater community? What concerns have they expressed? How can you be open to their concerns while standing up for your beliefs?

Using the Tools

Community Time-Lapse Mapping Activity

Take a stroll around the school and neighborhood with a few parents/caregivers and/or students and have them show you around and introduce you to their favorite places and people, including barber shops, convenience stores, restaurants, and parks. Do the following when you return:

1. Draw a map and highlight the places and people you met. Include addresses and contact information.

2. Make a list of the local cultural organizations—for example, Asian Law Caucus (https://www.advancingjustice-alc.org/), Native American Health Center (https://www.nativehealth.org/), Filipino Cultural Foundation (http://www.pcfitampa.org/), and local NAACP (https://www.naacp.org/). Arrange meetings with some of the community leaders. Add the information to the map.

3. At another time, go to the places of worship where your students attend. Find out the schedules of services; their Sunday School and after-school Hebrew, Muslim, Hindu, Buddhist or catechism classes; and other extracurricular activities they operate. Add that information to your map.

4. Next, check out community organizations. Locate the farmers markets, food banks, libraries, YMCAs, Boys and Girls Clubs, and other after-school programs. Add those to the map.

5. Find out which local businesses could help your school with funding and resources (e.g., banks, insurance agencies, real estate offices). Add them to your map.

6. Share your map with your community and make a plan for reaching out together.

 Available for download as a full-page form at
https://resources.corwin.com/BelongingandInclusionISS

CHAPTER 6

Coherence and Congruence

Schoolwide Systems and Activities to Support Identity Safety

Introduction

Identity safety is a gestalt that emerges as the components are enacted and consolidated into a way of being that becomes self-perpetuating. A school system, like a natural ecosystem, is more than the sum of its parts. All parts are interconnected and play upon each other. Plants require the nurturing of the sun with enough water and nutrients to thrive. In a school environment, the sun can be likened to the aspect of equity, shining its warmth and inclusion upon every member of the school community. Water can be seen as the flow of communication, the interactions that promote respect and understanding, while the teachers and staff are the ones who provide the nutrients through attention and learning, and all are enriched by the wisdom and support of the families and the greater community. The students are likened to the seeds that grow and thrive in such a community. If any of these elements are missing, the seeds will not sprout, and the plants will wither quickly or fail to thrive. In a natural environment with a healthy ecosystem, nature finds its balance. Congruence and harmony speak to the natural support between participants in these systems, allowing for their mutual beneficence. Coherence addresses the consistency between them, an implicit form of reliance upon their interdependence within the whole system to flourish. The regeneration of an ecosystem depends primarily upon this congruence and coherence of its diverse creatures and plants. The same is true for interconnected systems and people in a school environment.

In the first two chapters, we introduced identity safe research, the role of leadership, and the power of a systemic approach for implementing schoolwide identity safety. In subsequent chapters, we delved into the supporting systems for realizing schoolwide identity safety, which includes professional learning, data and assessment, and family and community engagement. In this chapter, we examine the importance of congruence and coherence for the entire system, which serves to connect our practices, behaviors, and attitudes with all other stakeholders in the community. To support this connection, we will present a few additional—yet no less important—supporting systems for sustaining a unified approach. They include classroom practices, prevention and intervention systems, discipline and behavior management, schoolwide activities, and the well-being of the adults in the community. Schoolwide identity safety cannot be successful—indeed we run the risk of undermining our very efforts—if we fail to take into account all these systems as they intersect with the lives of students in and outside the classroom. In Chapter 7 we will share ideas for developing a concrete plan to implement identity safety in systems across your school.

Why It Matters

To create an identity safe ecosystem throughout a school requires both *coherence* and *congruence* across the interconnected subsystems of curriculum, pedagogy, and behavior management, which are bridged with all the interlocking human relational systems of staff, students, families, and the larger community. When we speak of coherence, we refer to collective understanding of identity safety, ensuring that everybody "gets it" in order to enact the core values in a unified way. This invites the consistency needed to sustain it. The aspect of congruence for identity safety refers to the attitudes, behaviors, and practices that bind us together in shared values, visions, and goals for a safe and welcoming school. The fruit of this compatibility can be seen and felt throughout the school. Through a broad and unifying perspective, coherence and congruence offer the cement or glue that ensures that everyone communicates a shared message in a way that proclaims, "This is our school—we take care of it together!" Taken independently, each aspect of identity safety has the power to contribute to a student's sense of self and their capacity to achieve and grow. When all components are integrated together and applied with a long view for congruence and coherence, these experiences can impact a child into adulthood.

Cultivating a wider lens allows leaders to create connections across all the systems that operate in a school. We consider the classroom first, given the primary influence of teachers over the well-being of students and the responsibility of a leader to oversee implementation of identity safe practices. We hone our lens to spot and reinforce identity safe practices in classrooms. Leaders can encourage the propensity for teachers to share and effect change in each other's classrooms (see Chapter 3). We support them as they implement identity safety, and we connect them to practices in other classrooms. To this end, we become adept at observing teachers while using an appreciative inquiry approach. This allows us to recognize and target strengths in each classroom, leveraging them into greater gains for teachers to use with their students.

It is vital that we also maintain vigilance for spotting signs of racism, microaggressions, and bias in classrooms. We take action when we witness the subtle and not-so-subtle behaviors and attitudes that undermine identity safety for all students. This following example is sadly too common. A Native American student reports:

> I was placed in a GATE middle school class, since I had qualified for GATE in elementary school. When I walked into the room for the first time, my teacher said, "Are you sure you're in the right place? This class is for gifted students." In high school my other teachers also acted as if I didn't belong in AP or honors courses. Even my counselor doubted I could handle an advanced course.

As described in Chapter 3, you protect against microaggressions and racism by working with staff to examine their biases while sharpening your capacity to recognize bias in yourself and others. This will support you in developing the skills to take action to educate, prevent, and stop it.

Our responsibility does not end with promoting identity safety for students of different ethnicities and races. It is within our purview to attend to the needs of all students. This includes those with particular learning, social/emotional, and language challenges that impact their school experience. The way these students are identified, and the academic support that is provided for them, can make all the difference.

When all classrooms and the entire school engage in identity safe practices, the benefits are not simply extended from room to room but translate to exponential effects that resound across the campus. From the moment anyone sets foot on that campus, a feeling of warmth and acceptance can rise from the very floorboards before a word is spoken. As the effects are felt and the word gets out, identity safety will reach beyond the school into the community and to local organizations and businesses.

Making It Happen

HONING YOUR IDENTITY SAFE LENS: CONGRUENT CLASSROOM PRACTICES

Your lens for observing identity safe practices in the classroom can be honed by considering the four domains and 12 components that emerged from the Stanford Integrated Schools Project (SISP) research (D. M. Steele & Cohn-Vargas, 2013) (see Chapter 1). The entry points for identity safe practice can come through any of these doors, but as a leader you will want to consider the full meaning and impact for each of the components upon students as you choose the most appropriate ones to focus on at any given time. This enables you to move toward supporting teachers for fully implementing identity safe classrooms at your school.

Observation Ideas

When you mindfully observe in a classroom with an intent to understand what you are witnessing, you can take note of the different identity safe domains in the following ways:

- **Domain 1, Student-Centered Teaching:** You will notice the way students' lives connect to what they are studying, and how their agency and autonomy are fostered as they learn to get along and work together.

- **Domain 2, Cultivating Diversity as a Resource:** When teachers cultivate diversity as a resource, it will show up as they draw upon students' backgrounds and integrate the diversity into curricular content. You also notice whether and how they use culturally responsive pedagogy, communicate high expectations, and meet each student at their academic level.

- **Domain 3, Classroom Relationships:** The nature of relationships between teacher and student will reveal themselves through the quality of interaction and in the way feedback is given to help students grow. Observe whether students are interacting together in friendly and affirming ways.

- **Domain 4, Caring Classrooms:** You know you are witnessing a caring classroom when you see students who appear to be emotionally and physically comfortable, and when prosocial values are expressed in a calm, well-ordered, and affirming environment.

Please refer to two resources that will help you hone your identity safety lens. The Identity Safe Signature Strategies Spreadsheet (see Appendix K; the Belonging and Inclusion in Identity Safe Schools Resource site: https://resources.corwin.com/BelongingandInclusionISS) was developed with input from many educators. It has numerous examples of strategies in each of the domains of identity safety. The Identity Safe Classroom Observation Form (Appendix D) was designed for teachers and administrators to use to highlight the specific actions that can be observed in an identity safe classroom. For an in-depth exploration of each of the domains and components with many examples and strategies, refer to the books *Identity Safe Classrooms, Grades K–5* (D. M. Steele & Cohn-Vargas, 2013) and *Identity Safe Classrooms, Grades 6–12* (Cohn-Vargas, et al., 2020).

More Things to Look For

Identity: Consider the ways students express their unique social identities—from their family background (e.g., race, religion, ethnicity) to other different cultivated experiences (e.g., swimmer, soccer player). Researchers have found that when a person's identity is freely expressed and valued, prejudice is reduced and cooperative interdependence develops (Gaertner & Dovidio, 2000; D. M. Steele & Cohn-Vargas, 2013). These questions can help you integrate these key ideas for fostering identity safe practices during your classroom visits and observations:

- How does the teacher validate and acknowledge each student in the learning community?

- Do you see affirming gestures, words of encouragement, and wise feedback as the teacher engages with students individually and when they work together?

- How do students express aspects of their identities in unique ways through age-appropriate activities?

- Did they write and talk about their identities in safe and inviting ways?

- Do students see people who look like them respectfully represented in the literature they are reading, in the history they are studying, and on the walls of the classroom?

- Did they share artifacts from their cultures and social identities in the classroom?

- How are questions framed? How is feedback given? (Watch for hidden assumptions or stereotyping.)

How Matt Starts the Year

Matt, a social studies teacher in an ethnically diverse San Francisco classroom, helps students examine their identities from the start of the year. He begins the year by asking students to examine their lives and link to other biographical and autobiographical literature, laying a foundation for identity safety in the first month of school. To start the process, he works to build trust and break down stereotypes by allowing students to share hopes and dreams for their lives. They move on to interview their relatives, enriching their understanding about their identity, background, and family history.

The class proceeds to read short vignettes, from fiction (*There There* by Tommy Orange, 2018) and nonfiction sources (excerpt from *The Autobiography of Malcolm X*; X, et al., 2015), as well as a piece Matt found online about a transgender person selecting their new name. Matt holds discussions to find key ideas about identity in the different readings. He then guides the students to circle back toward an inward focus, asking them to write about their name (Do they like their name? Do others make assumptions about their name? If so, how?), Students in small groups reveal the story of their name and report out to the class. Matt explains that because everyone has a name, it is a great entry point for them all. Many have deep and complex stories. Even for students who have no story at all, each will at least have an opinion about their name. Sharing in this way helps break down stereotypes as they learn to respect others. As Matt says, "That is where it all begins."

Belonging: Notice how educators attend to each student and consider if all students participate and show a sense of belonging. When they are meaningfully engaged in the classroom activities, they will feel invested in their learning and thrive. Whether prosocial skills are being taught or a complicated math theorem is presented, sweep your eyes across the room and ask:

- Who is engaged and who isn't . . . and why?

- Does everyone behave like they belong here?

- Is there evidence of positive relationships among students of all ethnicities?

- Do they approach their teacher for help?

Creating Identity Safety During Circle Time

I (Kathe) initially used our third-grade classroom "Circle Time" to set up and discuss identity safe values regarding classroom and playground guidelines for helping everyone feel safe and included. At the beginning of the year, students mostly wanted to share about incidents where they felt violated or teased, but in time—once they came to trust the guidelines and realize that their voices would be heard—they found ways to support each other in feeling safe. Some went out of their way to spot others who looked like they might be lonely and invited them into their play. I specifically remember a nine-year-old girl who sat quietly without ever speaking up during the first couple weeks of school. Eventually, she had something to say throughout the day. When I complimented her on her participation, she volunteered the reason, stating matter-of-factly, "I fit in." She then shared with me her new friendships and how others in the classroom had reached out to her. She gained the confidence that launched an active, vibrant, and welcome young voice into our classroom.

Growth mindset: Nurturing a growth mindset will help everyone realize their own potential while dismantling negative stereotypes and weakening the grip of stereotype threat. By manifesting the attitude that mistakes are viewed as a way to learn and grow, a sense of safety and a willingness to take risks evolves. In a culture of acceptance, minds stretch, leading to creative thinking and innovation.

- What is being done in classrooms to teach students about the growth mindset?

- How does the teacher work to strengthen the growth mindsets of individual students?

- How is the students' effort being encouraged and validated?

- How does the teacher address academic mistakes and errors?

- How does the teacher work to incorporate the growth mindset in addressing behavioral issues?

Equal status: Efforts to equalize status will take root with committed efforts and consistency, and ultimately, they will make a big difference in the lives of the students. Ask:

- How does the teacher bring forward the gifts of each student as they explore and learn about themselves and each other?

- What activities help disrupt hierarchies of popularity where students rank each other's acceptability?

- What does the teacher do when students exclude or make fun of a student in the class?

Diversity and interdependence: Cooperation and getting along with others is one of the most important skill sets that students learn for their future lives. Ask:

- How does the teacher embody and practice interdependence while ascribing value to all identities?

- What kinds of cooperative activities are taking place?

- What strategies are being used to ensure all students are actively participating?

Attention to these key concepts offers amazing potential for rapid gains toward student identity, belonging with equal status, and interdependence. These concepts can be treated as doorways into every aspect of an educator's curriculum.

STARTING THE YEAR TOGETHER: A SCHOOLWIDE EFFORT

Guiding the faculty toward a congruent approach can be strengthened when they start the year together with a unified focus on identity safety. While identity safe practices can be initiated any time of the year, the first six weeks of school grant a significant and opportune slice of time to introduce identity safety and build an inclusive environment. Students are forming impressions that can last the entire school year, and it is beneficial to establish understandings and a sense of belonging early. While educators in each subject area and grade level open the school year a bit differently, they can apply a unified approach across all classrooms while adapting to their own styles. The following considerations apply to every grade and subject area as the school year begins.

Getting to Know the Students and Helping Them Get to Know Each Other

A single activity can be enough to initiate the process. For example, in an interview for the publication *My Jewish Learning* (Esensten, 2020), I (Alex) shared that

> simple acts like greeting students at the door can be enacted in ways that are identity safe and ways that are not. Being intentional about learning how to properly pronounce students' names, use appropriate pronouns,

and being aware of biased statements or comments (e.g., gendered norms around learning math and science, focusing on negative behaviors and not learning) create environments where students feel valued for who they are. While for many this seems like an easy thing to do, I am constantly humbled by the ways we can unintentionally cause a student to feel disconnected from their teachers and/or school. It is essential to know your students and use that knowledge to create a space of validation, support, and belonging.

I (Kathe) played a name game with my third-grade students on the first day of school. I knew how important it was for children to feel "seen," and knowing their names and how to say them was a powerful way to open the doors for recognition and sharing. To achieve this with dozens of children as soon as possible, I asked them to call out their names and add a little dance or phrase. The class and I would then repeat the name and the phrase, and we would follow the dance steps if they offered any. I videotaped the game, took it home, and memorized each face and name, ready for the next day. Marcelino, a high school teacher with 150 students over the course of a day, prompted students to introduce themselves. In his notebook, he would write a phonetic version of each pronunciation that was new to him. He also reviewed it at home.

The year can begin as students are welcomed and engage in activities to gain a deeper understanding of one another and their teachers. Students can meet briefly with partners or in trios to ask a few key getting-acquainted questions. They can then introduce one another to the class, featuring the information they've shared, which also serves in learning a valuable prosocial skill. This activity can also take the form of a longer interview with open-ended and nonthreatening questions.

TIPS FOR CONGRUENCE IN STARTING THE YEAR
Formulate community agreements together with students.
Teach the growth mindset.
Learn about the students and how to say their names.
Tell students about yourself. Model authentic and appropriate sharing.
Help students get to know each other.
Show them you care.
Make expectations clear.
Introduce and initiate formative assessments.
Introduce the concepts of identity and identity safety with discussions and activities.

Setting Expectations and Exploring Prosocial Values

Each year, educators have a renewed opportunity to build community in their classrooms. Taking time to discuss the agreed-upon school values can work in tandem with considering personal values and student preferences as they identify those that are meaningful to them. Teachers can ask students, "How do we want our class to feel?" and "How can we work together in ways that show we support everyone?" They can draw parallels between the expressed values and specific expectations of the course, enabling students to contribute ideas for creating community agreements and classroom norms. This is also a perfect opportunity to teach them about identity safety in age-appropriate ways (see Chapter 1). By starting the year together, the faculty can calibrate their initial activities, debrief with each other, and experience the fruit of their efforts throughout the year.

IDENTIFYING AND ADDRESSING STUDENTS' UNIQUE NEEDS

In our classrooms, we have children with a diverse set of social, emotional, behavioral, and academic needs, and we work to ensure they all thrive and none slip through the cracks. These may include children who have experienced trauma and have trouble focusing. Others are English learners, who are developing language skills while needing access to subject matter as they learn the language. And yet others have learning challenges that call for specific interventions (e.g., auditory processing issues, dyslexia, visual and hearing impairments). Some lack executive functioning skills and have trouble focusing or controlling their impulses. And some students have social and emotional challenges that impact their communication skills, sensory awareness, and the ability to get along with others. Many have a combination of these needs (e.g., learning and executive functioning challenges). How we address these needs will impact their identities. To create an identity safe environment, these students need to feel belonging and acceptance for who they are—and not in spite of their challenges. Belonging begins with feeling completely "seen" and accepted. In terms of the learning challenges they face, we can communicate our faith in their ability to improve and our intention to support them.

Identity safe leaders work to ensure their staff are knowledgeable about and committed to meeting the varying needs in their classrooms. They back the classroom teachers with a schoolwide support system and a continuum of services. It starts with a proactive approach for intervention before a student falls behind or disengages from school. This necessitates protocols for identifying, providing, and coordinating the services available to students.

Often, students with particular learning and academic needs are stigmatized. They may feel different because they are learning at a slower rate than their peers or their behavior interferes with others, causing them to feel like they are "bad" or "stupid." Before we examine a process for identifying and serving the specific academic and behavioral needs of students through a model known as Response to Intervention, we will consider some ways white supremacist attitudes and biases can play into educational decisions that also negatively impact students of color and English learners.

Disproportionality: The Over-Identification of Black, Latinx, and EL Students in Special Education

Researchers have demonstrated that Black, Native American, and Latinx students are regularly identified for special education at rates higher than White students (Grindal, et al., 2019). In addition, research has shown that Black students are pulled out of regular education classes for more hours than White students with a similar special education diagnosis. Latinx and Native American students with identified disabilities are taught in separate classrooms more frequently than White students with similar diagnoses. Harry and Anderson (1994) found that with some categories of special education, non-subjective tests are unavailable, so diagnoses rely on the judgment of the professionals (e.g., ID-intellectual disabilities, SLD-severe learning disabilities). All these factors create unfair conditions for students of color that impact not only their educational experience but their future.

The misplacement of students of color in special education can result in lower self-esteem, a weakened academic identity, and ultimately, it can lead down a path to dropping out of school. Data reveal that 80% of the prison population consists of individuals who have dropped out of school (Whaley & Smyer, 1998).

English learners are another group who need careful consideration to determine how to best serve them. Debbie Zacarian (2011), an author and expert in the field of advancing achievement for EL and special education students, points out that some schools with limited services for ELs—including those who have no bilingual staff in the child's home language—can mistake language needs for learning disabilities. In other cases, an EL student who is not progressing may be receiving EL services but not the kind of interventions that would target their specific learning challenges.

For these reasons, careful attention and professional development is needed throughout the process of identification, placement, and services. In addition, leaders can manage the entire process along with frequent monitoring to ensure students are progressing once services are provided.

Using Data to Analyze and Address Disparities

Solutions to the issues of disproportionality begin by collecting data to see if students of all racial and ethnic groups are referred to special education in equal proportions. If that is not the case, you can work with your teams to investigate classroom interventions, evaluation systems, and referral processes to make requisite changes. Providing professional development for all staff will help uncover and address attitudinal factors, or biases that negatively impact special education referral and service decisions.

RTI: An Intervention Model

The RTI (Response to Intervention) model of intervention can be applied to students with unique needs as well as students who need extra support to perform at grade level along with their peers. When the RTI model is used properly with identity safe practices, students will receive specific strategies that will allow them to progress. It will also prevent students from being placed into special education for biased reasons. RTI categorizes levels of support in three tiers. The first tier is universal, meaning the more obvious needs of some students help us to see how to strengthen the general educational environment and program for all students. Higher-tiered strategies are engaged only when lower-tiered ones have not yielded positive results. Educators can work to ensure that the tiers are approached in ways that do not humiliate or lower the status of students. Each tier can work to support identity safe practices.

Tier 1: All students in general education classrooms are taught together in both the whole group and mixed smaller groups with the following identity safe goals:

- Work to make the classroom activities accessible for all students at all times (e.g., provide vocabulary support for English learners).

- Use a variety of participation strategies to give all students opportunities to participate and be heard and feel that their ideas have value (see the Identity Safe Signature Strategies Spreadsheet, Appendix K, at https://resources.corwin.com/BelongingandInclusionISS).

- Teach about respectful interactions and acknowledge the many ways each student contributes to the class.

- Articulate the value of different learning styles and respectful interactions with those who learn in different ways. Teach that intelligence is expressed in many ways and encourage a growth mindset.

- Use trauma-informed practices (see Chapter 1).

- Intervene to stop all forms of exclusion, bullying, teasing, and harassment.

- Teach students to speak up and stand up for themselves and others.

- Form groups with careful attention to combinations of students who will work well together (e.g., try not to pair a student who gets frustrated easily and lashes out with another student who works more slowly).

Tier 2: For students who need additional support, scaffold their learning with small group lessons that are targeted to specific learning or behavioral needs in the following identity safe ways:

- Ensure that small group instruction is valued and described to students in asset-based language. Encourage them without making them feel inadequate.

- Provide scaffolds for executive functions (e.g., attention, memory, flexibility, impulse control).

- Ensure higher-level thinking skills are integrated with basic skills for students at all academic levels.

- Notice if students in targeted instruction feel stigmatized and take steps to safeguard against feelings of being singled out or humiliated.

Tier 3: For students who need more intensive interventions, longer-term targeted instruction can be offered inside or outside the classroom. This can include a wide range of services (see below). When providing these supports, consider the following identity safe practices:

- Be cognizant of language used to describe additional supports and stop others from making disparaging comments to students individually or in front of their peers.

- Pay attention to the emotional reaction of students who receive additional supports and work to ensure they are not alienated from the group if they are pulled out for any activities.

- If students are pulled out, work to ensure they can quickly step back into the classroom activities when they return.

- Watch how we speak to other adults (parents/caregivers or staff) about students who get additional services. Be careful not to label or stereotype them (e.g., calling them "my special needs kids"). Make an effort not to use deficit language when speaking to parents or other staff members. Asset-based language will promote trust.

Providing Support and Communicating Respect During Evaluation and Intervention Processes

We can intentionally consider how to ensure identity safety when engaging in Student Study Team and Individualized Education Plan meetings through approaches that offer confidence to students and their parents/caregivers. Inviting parents/caregivers to a preparatory meeting to explain and answer questions about all steps of the process invests their trust and alleviates fears. Engage a language interpreter as needed for parents/caregivers and/or students who will feel most comfortable speaking a language other than English. Prepare with staff prior to meetings, as needed, to check assumptions about students' families and backgrounds, such as presuming that a family lives in poverty because they drive an old car, or that all Latinx students are Mexican (see Chapter 3). A shared and congruent identity safe approach from all staff members who interact with the child (counselors, administrators, parents/caregivers, teachers) will translate into consistent communications of assurance and caring to the students.

In meetings about the students, including parent conferences, we present children in a positive light with asset-based language, highlighting their strengths as well as areas where they need support. We never talk down to parents/caregivers or make disparaging remarks about their children. For example, we avoid blanket statements and assumptions about the child's intelligence or potential, such as stating they won't graduate or go to college. Nor do we label energetic students as hyperactive, especially Black boys, who are disproportionately diagnosed with ADHD.

When working with students who are being evaluated, we need to remember to fully acquaint them with the testing processes and administering assessments in ways that build comfort. These processes can be stressful for students as well as for their parents/caregivers. We always seek to treat students and parents/caregivers with respect and create understanding. We use student, educator, and parent/caregiver surveys to learn from their observations and experiences, and we evaluate their impressions alongside academic assessment results. Surveys always ask about strengths and interests as well as surfacing areas that are not yet going as well. We define terminology and let students know that the goal is to find out how they learn best, as opposed to thinking the test will measure what they know and don't know. Then we can provide them with effective teaching methods to help them progress.

Schools can meet many student needs in innovative ways by offering a wide range of supports. Here are some examples:

- **Tutoring formats:** Individual tutors, mentor and peer-to-peer support, summer school, blended learning

- **Academic support groups:** Reading classes, English language development groups, primary language groups, math skills classes, school counselors, and advisory classes

- **Social and emotional learning supports:** Individual and group counseling, advisory classes, social skills groups, service learning, affinity groups (e.g., African American Male Achievement [Oakland Unified School District, n.d.-b], summer bridge programs)

- **Behavioral supports:** Conflict resolution training, restorative justice circles

A unified identity safe approach for meeting the unique needs of students, providing scaffolds and supports using asset-based language, and treating each child and family as valuable members of the school community makes a tremendous contribution to schoolwide identity safety.

EQUITABLE STUDENT BEHAVIOR DISCIPLINE POLICIES AND SYSTEMS

While students who feel a sense of belonging are more likely to embrace and meet behavior expectations, conflicts are bound to occur and are a natural part of growing up. Vibrant yet calm and well-ordered campuses and classrooms rely on systems where students learn to manage their behavior. Then, when they do misbehave, we can employ strategies that teach rather than punish.

Studies on punitive models of discipline, such as removal from class, suspensions, and expulsions, have found that these practices are disproportionately applied to Black and Latinx students when compared to White students who engage in similar behaviors. For those who are summarily dismissed for any infraction, and who must spend large amounts of time out of the classroom, absenteeism increases. Being excluded from the classroom harms students academically and does not help them learn new ways of behaving (Townsend, 2000). And for all students, when some among them are unfairly targeted for punishment, the climate can feel unsafe for everyone. The feeling of "Who's next?" can persist. All students benefit when students who misbehave are treated with compassion and understanding, which prevails when restorative and fair consequences are applied.

Anonymous Student Stories

One Latinx middle school student reports that at his school

the kids were openly racist, but when I reported it, the school did nothing about it. The other kids taunted me by telling me that they had "freedom of speech" and had a right to be racist toward me. They said I should be deported, and Mexicans like my family were taking their jobs. One kid said that they would call ICE on me. I wish schools would teach kids to respect each other. This country was founded on immigrants. Why is it that these schools are diverse, but people think it's okay to hate? Why do my teachers sit back and let it happen? This district failed me.

A Black middle school student wrote,

Once at school, a fellow POC (person of color) friend of mine was accused of selling drugs (which he was not doing). Our group of friends was all races, but I was the only Black one in the group. The administration brought me into the office, and had the police there to question me for having "ties to an alleged gang." None of this was true.

An Asian middle school student reports,

When I would not let a classmate copy my homework he blurted out "Maybe it's better because you probably have the 'rona' and would give me the China virus." The other kids started laughing at me. I reported it to the teacher who just said, "They were just kidding." It did not feel funny to me.

Unfortunately, these reports represent only the tip of the iceberg. Unfair disciplinary practices and harassment of students of color, gay students, those with disabilities, or those who are perceived as "different" create the effects of lifelong trauma for many. Identity safe leaders can draw upon research-based models for creating positive discipline systems. Studies of conflict resolution programs have demonstrated that students who are taught these methods in elementary school are able to avoid escalation and solve problems on their own, even as they move up in the grades (Johnson, et al., 1994). Conflict resolution skills particularly benefit students who engage in repeated acts of aggression, helping them learn self-control and improve peer relationships, ultimately improving their academic achievement (Deutsch, 1992). Restorative practices are also useful tools in preventing and resolving disciplinary incidents. Students learn to take responsibility for their behavior and repair harm. Conflict resolution, restorative practices, counseling, and support groups also reduce disciplinary referrals, suspensions, and expulsions (Fronius et al., 2019).

Student identity safety necessitates a consistent approach to disciplinary policies, procedures, and practices inside and outside classrooms. When teachers, administrators, yard supervisors, and counselors come to agreement on expected student behaviors and responses to disciplinary infractions, the consistency sends a reliable message to students about expectations. By analyzing practices in the context of the identity safe school principles, conflict resolution and restorative practices can replace punitive discipline, leading to a culture where students are supported in learning from their mistakes and repairing harm. This, in turn, fosters acceptance and belonging. Consistency, however, cannot take hold until all staff members are on the same page. Staff awareness is crucial for creating supportive discipline practices that carry a unified and clear message to the students. In the following example, a deeper look at the data on referrals exposed erroneous assumptions that led to unfair practices and differentiated staff treatment of a group of boys.

As principal, Louise Waters shared a process she used to challenge staff perceptions about student behavior. Some staff had consistently complained about a small group of African American boys who they felt "got away" with things. First, she shared data on the number of referrals the boys had amassed. It was clear there were many questions about that, as well as the consequences that had been exacted upon the boys, particularly if they had been suspended.

In response, she showed them data from her investigations of the incidents. Frequently, the causes of the infractions listed in the referrals did not accurately match the student's behavior and/or did not rise to the suspension level. Sometimes the staff member had reacted without seeing, or perhaps seeking out, a full picture of the incident. For example, a multiethnic group of boys had created an ongoing teasing game passing insulting notes in class. All were complicit, but only the two African American boys were given referrals. They challenged this as unfair, refusing to leave the room. In this instance, like many others, racially biased narratives, hyper-monitoring, and failure to listen to relatively minor incidents came to be labeled as defiance for authority, provoking the consequences of what was now a more serious offense.

Waters then shared data for each of the boys (leaving off their names). This included the number of referrals from specific staff members over the preceding two years. In every case at least one educator working with each boy had never given a referral. This was followed by quotes from the boys detailing why they seldom had problems in those classes.

During professional development, or in conversations held privately afterwards, some of the teachers expressed a new awareness of times they had jumped to erroneous conclusions. Many requested a follow-up staff meeting to explore readings on alternative discipline strategies. At the end, Waters invited them to connect with peers who had built strong relationships with the boys. Over time, a collective lens emerged about these specific boys, as well as steps for building consistency and a more restorative approach to school discipline in general.

Staff who engage in an exploration of implicit biases and self-reflection are better prepared to catch themselves before punishing students of color more hastily and harshly than their White peers. Dialogue as well as supervision can increase staff accountability for fair disciplinary practices, thereby strengthening schoolwide identity safety. Schools cannot become identity safe without careful attention to fair and nonpunitive discipline practices.

STRENGTHENING SCHOOLWIDE UNITY: EVENTS, CAMPAIGNS, CLUBS, AND CAMPS

What happens outside the classroom plays a role in enhancing or diminishing the impact of identity safe strategies inside classrooms. Identity exploration, dialogue, challenge, rigor, and cooperation can also be encouraged through schoolwide events and extracurricular experiences. Creating spaces where students can flourish culturally as part of whole school activities can be achieved by welcoming families into the school (see Chapter 5) and by offering opportunities for students to experience affinity groups and cross-cultural interactions. Below are some ideas for identity safe schoolwide events for elementary grades:

- **Student leadership groups:** student council, conflict manager club, bullying prevention club

- **Literacy/math/science:** author chairs, where students make, read, and share books; library events focused on books that promote identity safe practices, cross-grade activities, international science fairs

- **Assemblies:** upper-grade students leading assemblies to address bullying prevention, multicultural presentations with guest performers, or students giving musical and dance performances

- **Family events and celebrations:** cultural celebrations and theatrical plays that draw on all cultures and do not fall into stereotypes, family math and science nights, career days (featuring parents of all backgrounds in a range of careers)

Sharing Cultures Through Writers' Workshop

When I (Kathe) taught third and fourth grade, I trained parent/caregiver volunteers each year to work with the children at different stations for a Writers' Workshop, which included all stages of writing, from rough draft, to peer edit, a final edit, and the "publishing" of the book. Children were encouraged to write about their families, traditions, and cultures, and often parents/caregivers would assist them in the process. Parents participated in ways that highlighted their skills and comfort levels in the classroom, which included helping with the edits and fashioning the books. Every month, I held an "Author's Chair" mini-event, where students with finished books could read them aloud. Parents were also invited to enjoy and support their children as they read their books in the Author's Chair. The books then became available in the library for check-out by other students or families. The sharing of these stories allowed families to recognize the cultures and expressions of other children in the classroom and their families.

In middle and high schools, identity safe values are naturally realized when students have spaces to congregate through sports teams, theater, bands, orchestras, and clubs focused on areas of interest. In each case, the persons in charge of these activities will need to understand and engage in identity safe practices. This necessitates training targeted to their specific subject areas, with strategies that strengthen identity and belonging. Emphasis on practices that can undermine student identity safety hold equal import and require attention.

Student leaders can discuss and reimagine student government to embody identity safe school culture. Here are some additional ideas for identity safe secondary school clubs and activities:

- **Affinity groups and clubs:** Black Student Union, Gay Straight Alliances, Mandarin Club, La Raza Club, Autistic Self-Advocacy Groups

- **Social justice activities:** bullying prevention, student-led assemblies that highlight diversity, community service projects

- **Visual and performing arts:** poetry slams, theater, forensics, mural-making, African drumming

The different clubs can form coalitions to collaborate and organize activities for the entire student body (Cohn-Vargas, 2016). Coalitions can plan and participate in national campaigns and activities that open doors of understanding like "World

Hijab Day," "Transgender Day of Remembrance," "Bullying Prevention Month," "The Special Olympics," or "Black Lives Matter Week." Students themselves can guide the direction of change in their school as their club activities and principles spill over into shared student experiences.

A schoolwide student-led campaign to promote identity safety can bring an exciting and fun focus to change efforts. A club or coalition of clubs can launch identity safety efforts with an assembly, a school pledge, a video contest, a mural, and/or a half-time activity at a football game. NotInOurTown.org features a collection of videos with examples from across the United States (Cohn-Vargas, 2016).

Social Justice Virtual Camp Experience Raises Awareness of Anti-Racism

In late spring, 2020, diversity consultant Dhalia Balmir felt increasing frustration as racial unrest spread across the United States. She felt overwhelmed as a parent, considering the racist events happening in her own son's school district, as well. She explains,

> Children need to learn the truth of our history and how to navigate the social justice realities of the current day. Educators and parents often avoid these topics, leaving children who are inevitably exposed to them on their own to make sense of them. I turned my frustration into action and began creating a pilot virtual social justice camp curriculum for grades sixth-eighth and ninth-10th.

In summer 2020, Balmir and a fellow educator launched the Connected Conversations With Youth, a Virtual Social Justice Camp, and opened it to secondary students. Youth from many racial/ethnic backgrounds participated. "For two weeks, we ran two cohorts of experiential learning with active engagement, and discussion on the following topics: social justice, microaggressions, history of race and racism, school to prison profiling, privilege, and conflict resolution."

The experience of the camp was priceless. Many were experiencing or had witnessed some of these concepts in action but didn't have the words to name them. Below are some testimonials from the youth:

> I would say that it's important to be educated on topics such as racism, because sometimes you hear people saying ignorant things, and then you can educate them, and this camp helped us be more educated so that if we ever experience any of the situations we learned about, we know what we can do or say and how to react.

It helped me learn more about how it can feel to be different.

I learned on our talk on microaggressions, how even little things can make a big difference on others.

In summer 2021, Balmir plans to run the camp again and adapt another camp for younger children. She believes that the camp experience will help youth learn to be leaders and agents of change for social justice.

Special projects, clubs, community service, and schoolwide events can each contribute to a spirited identity safe school climate. Such resources go beyond establishing a culture of respect to ensure that students have equitable access to exploring and developing their interests and talents. Whether it is through visual arts, robotics, a mariachi group, African drumming, capoeira classes, or a biotech club, an array of extracurricular opportunities led by charismatic instructors who believe the students can foster creativity will fully engage students beyond their classroom hours.

RESILIENT ADULTS: ATTENTION TO EDUCATOR WELLNESS, SUSTAINABILITY, AND REDUCING STRESS

Given the impact educators have upon their students, attention to supporting them by creating a welcoming staff environment—ensuring they feel valued, healthy, and happy—goes a long way toward creating an identity safe school. Staff will experience success with students when they are committed—if their energy and vitality are strong and their physical and mental health balanced and stable. In a state of wellness, teachers are hopeful, acknowledging progress and expressing appreciation. They are honest about real issues and communicate problems with transparency. An identity safe environment is enhanced when a strong staff work together toward positive transformation under conditions that value individual and organizational resilience. Strengthening student resilience is difficult without resilient educators.

Staff wellness then becomes a critical contributor to an identity safe school. Leaders play an important role in supporting their staff in every aspect of wellness—from physical and mental health to getting enough sleep. This includes attending to staff workload and realistic expectations for change, including the pace for implementation of identity safety. In order to embrace the challenges associated with change and to persist through adversity, resilience is essential. And as wellness is strengthened by resilience, so too is resilience strengthened by wellness. These qualities grow in tandem in response to the degree and quality of support received.

Wellness is nurtured in a friendly environment that features positive staff relationships, where people step up to help one another, and where joys and sorrows are shared. Elena Aguilar's (2018) book *Onward* highlights the need for schools to build emotional resilience and wellness into the culture to foster a positive environment and the stamina for major transformations. Yet, this does not happen with depleted personal resources. Self-care can be facilitated through encouragement and modeling, and practiced in concrete ways:

- Staff meetings can begin with a few minutes of mindful meditation or a check-in moment to see how members are feeling.

- Compassion can be cultivated with simple activities where each person writes what they are grateful for on a sticky note and posts it on a wall or board.

- Opportunities for staff members to have fun together with light-hearted activities, games, or celebrations develop and further friendships (e.g., student–staff baseball games, lip-sync contests, secret gift exchanges).

- Attending to the ebb and flow of the workload, a principal creates schedules that are aligned with staff obligations. For example, they can cancel staff meetings during the week that report cards are due and offer refreshments for teachers for appreciation and sustenance.

Stress is an inevitable part of life, and for educational leaders, mitigating stressors for staff can alleviate those pressures that are negatively affecting their performance. School faculties look to their leaders to protect them from turbulence at the district level, to ease growing burdens, and to care for them as human beings. Addressing the "whole educator" makes a difference in the same manner that the "whole child" matters. Actively modeling, teaching, and supporting growth mindset and the learning zone (see Chapter 4) can help teachers and other staff members step away from unfounded expectations and embrace and share their learning as a developmental process. The leader's personal response to stress influences the staff, especially when the stressors are beyond their control, such as the coronavirus pandemic that forced many schools to go virtual overnight.

Staff, like students, are impacted by trauma, grief, and changing life circumstances. A leader who fosters caring and has strong relationships with individual staff members supports them through difficult times. Educators also experience secondary trauma stemming from feeling very connected to the personal struggles experienced by their students. Finding ways to release some of these intense emotions and detach somewhat—while still caring—is a way to stay resilient. Some leaders and their staff took the challenge of the pandemic as an opportunity to strengthen bonds of collaboration among themselves as they worked together, supporting each other in finding solutions. Don, who taught in the administrative credential program at Notre Dame de Namur University in Belmont, California, held a weekly open session to discuss issues and share solutions with his graduate students, many who held positions as new administrators. For this group, the sessions became a lifeline, and they in turn transmitted similar supports to their site staff and school communities.

Rising to Challenges/Avoiding Pitfalls

Taking the time to explore and consider our staff's thoughts, ideas, and hesitations about identity safety matter when enlisting their participation. Here are a few ideas for finding the right balance in your approach for them to accept the change process while avoiding pitfalls as you begin.

MOVING TOO FAST

Enthusiasm is an asset, and we can use it to run with a vision, and to a degree that is the magic that welcomes others on board. It can be contagious, and it pays to express it. However, it's also important to keep an eye open for its reception lest we charge into the process without considering the input of others. Nor does rushing allow you, as the leader, to set up the conditions for the change to be successful. Moving too quickly can backfire in the form of resistance, anger, and frustration from stakeholders, leading to a loss of trust. Sometimes, after traversing down the rapids, you may need to trek back upriver and start over. Taking the time to invite input is more likely to lead to changes that stick.

It's important to keep an eye open for how individuals are responding to the change process. Those who are adverse or slow to warm up to rapid changes may balk and stymie our efforts. When we take the time to invest in both the ideas and concerns of all members in the school community, we can proceed in accordance with their readiness. When we can offer new ideas and resources as enhancements for and integrations into what we already do, we avoid the perception that we are piling more work on educators' plates. When we (Alex and Amy) wanted to develop identity safety in our district culture, we knew that the district and schools already embraced many similar ideas and would resonate with the new ones. We decided to run a pilot series of workshops with voluntary participation in order to slowly usher in the new ideas and resources, show how they could improve our practices and outcomes, and gather support in a steady manner. In the second year, we felt prepared to introduce the changes to the entire staff. By the third year, identity safety was widely known and applied in many different and creative ways.

Brockton High School (Noguera, 2017), whose school improvement efforts were described in Chapter 2 and Chapter 5, began with a group that called themselves "The Willing." The efforts of this dynamic and enthusiastic group of educators embodied the willingness to take risks and do whatever was needed to achieve their goals. Over time, as others witnessed their successes, they too hopped on board. Often a steady and sustained approach will yield desired results.

NOT GETTING STARTED UNTIL EVERYTHING IS PERFECT

At the other end of the scale, some leaders and educators may feel that success is reliant on intense preparation, and they work beyond school hours studying, reading, and reflecting on everything about identity safety, inequity, systemic racism, and whatever else they can find. The intent is admirable, and while we recognize the significance for understanding the issues and developing nuanced and knowledge-based discretions, we can still assure ourselves and others that we move forward with implementation together, learning as we go while absorbing new knowledge. There is no meaningful reason to wait. With a growth mindset, we can allow the input and guidance of many voices to assist us in creating an inviting and identity safe school.

COMING ON TOO STRONG

Yet another challenge occurs as a leader with strong convictions seeks to make drastic changes with little input. A leader with forceful convictions might be exactly what is needed when a school is struggling and needs a jumpstart. However, if they exclaim, "This is how we are going to do it now. You will need to get on board or move to another school," they run the risk of alienating even the best-intentioned. It takes courage together with careful navigation to build the trust that you will need to address pressing conditions that are harming students.

Sometimes, a new leader, arriving as an outsider, may see more clearly than long-standing stakeholders whose vision may have grown myopic. These leaders who are aligned with identity safety principles can spot glaring disparities, noting that students are not well served and concluding that the entire school needs an overhaul. However, when an uncompromising new leader bursts in like a landmine, a major backlash will likely ensue. The veteran staff may rally against the new administrator, and the leader may be the one who moves on too soon.

ENSURING EVERYONE IS ON BOARD

In the same way that we allow students to grow at their own rate and level of comprehension, we can provide space for educators to do the same. When teachers are hesitant to embrace identity safe teaching, it can help them to see our commitment to their success by encouraging and supporting them consistently in ways that make their engagement irresistible. Pairing them with successful identity safe teachers who they like and respect can make the difference, too. However, in the end, their participation is requisite. Blunt force will not convince them, so give it time; yet if they remain stuck, you may need to counsel them to find more suitable employment. Some may choose to find other jobs rather than collaborate with the changes. Others may eventually see the value and join the team effort.

In each of these cases, be resolute and let your moral compass place the students at the heart of every decision you make, which includes your approaches to staff. We can prepare and fortify ourselves by developing facilitation skills for some of the hard conversations that emerge during a change process. However, we need not stop or slow the process. Students cannot afford to wait for the benefits. It is our hope that skeptical teachers will discover that the time taken to focus on identity safety will prove motivating and that student behavior and performance will improve so that ultimately everyone, including educators, will benefit from the process.

Closing the Gap Between Ideas and Action

Once identity safe concepts, research, and principles are introduced to the staff, integrating identity safe practices need not be a linear process. Taking the time to hone your understanding of all identity safety domains and components will provide the context for recognizing identity safe practices as you move from classroom to classroom to observe.

Drawing other educators together at the start of the year can lead to congruent implementation and developments. The start of the year is a perfect time to launch identity safety with staff and students. Opening with a focus on forming relationships and promoting prosocial skills will yield a strong sense of community. For students, this can ultimately save time later that might otherwise be used for conflict resolution and discipline. We receive students from the first day by

- welcoming them and getting to know them,

- setting expectations, and

- initiating identity exploration activities.

Setting up congruence in systems across the school can be summarized to include the following:

- Ensuring that all staff who lead the classroom as well as after-school and curricular systems understand and employ identity safe practices.

- Using intervention systems with careful attention to the identification of student needs, including supportive diagnostic processes and targeted interventions that build confidence, competence, and do not stigmatize students.

- Developing behavior management expectations, discipline systems, and response to conflicts that are fair and emphasize learning from mistakes and repairing harm.

- Attending to educator health, wellness, and stress reduction in ways that lead to their resilience and fulfillment, ultimately benefiting students.

Check Yourself

- How are you honing your identity safe lens through observations of the identity safe principles, domains, and components?

- How are teachers working together for a unified identity safe launch at the start of the year?

- How do you work with teachers to set expectations and promote pro-social values?

- What have teachers done to make their classrooms warm and welcoming? How can you support them to do this?

- What systems are in place to ensure that student needs are identified and assessed, and additional supports are offered without stigmatizing students?

- How do you work with students to resolve conflicts and help them take accountability and repair harm?

- What steps are you taking to promote educator resilience and well-ness?

- How have you informed adjunct staff who lead sports, bands, and other after-school activities about identity safe practices?

Using the Tools

Observation Planning Checklist

After staff have been introduced to identity safety, observing classroom practice will help lead to a congruent implementation. It is important to communicate with staff about how you plan to perform these observations. We recommend creating a plan for observations that is qualitatively different from evaluation observations. Also, ensure staff that as you work toward identity safe practices, you are learning along with them.

1. Explain your process for identity safe observations to the entire staff:
   a. What is your purpose?
   b. How will you carry out the observations? Will you hold preconference and debriefing sessions?
   c. Who will observe? Will you go alone? With other administrators? With coaches?
   d. How will feedback be given?

2. Identify an observation tool (see Appendix D: Identity Safe Classroom Observation Form).

3. How will you share some of your noticings anonymously with the full staff?

4. Will you follow your observations with peer observations? Explain your process:
   a. What tools will you use?
   b. What structure will you develop (e.g., rotating substitutes)?
   c. How will you teach feedback strategies?

 Available for download as a full-page form at
https://resources.corwin.com/BelongingandInclusionISS

CHAPTER 7

Planning and Implementing Schoolwide Identity Safety

Introduction

As we draw our journey together to a close, we hope you are inspired to take the ideas from this book and put identity safe principles into practice in your school. Identity safety is a way of thinking and acting that braids together many ideas, strategies, and practices. It may seem overwhelming to consider all of them at once, and it is not necessary to do so. Schoolwide planning initiatives bring the stakeholders into alignment. Developing a process and a plan solidifies your commitment to ensure that students are at the center of all decisions, that belonging and inclusion is paramount, and that resources are equitably allocated. A wide lens when planning also helps determine priorities and carries the vision into all school operations. Engaging the community together motivates everyone to set into motion actionable and achievable results.

In an *Ed Week* article, author Sarah Sparks (2020) reported that researchers found little benefit from educator anti-bias training that is not combined with a schoolwide effort to integrate the new awareness into concrete policies and practices to meet the needs of students. Sparks recommended integrating anti-bias training efforts into a comprehensive diversity plan with specific goals based on the analysis of disaggregated ethnic and racial student data.

As you determine the best path for your school, please consider these options that can be flexibly adapted to your school's unique culture. You may want to begin with the "willing" to seed your efforts and get them going or you may want to choose to work with teams that are already in existence. Eventually, you will want to form a Leadership Team and engage in a process to develop your Identity Safe School Plan. Making a plan for a sustainable system will allow you to maximize human and material resources at a rate that will lead to changes that endure and extend over time.

The overarching goal is to create a sustainable system of identity safe practice across the school, one that will continuously grow. In this concluding chapter, we give a general overview of preparation, planning, and managing a change process. This chapter offers concrete steps in the planning process to lead your team forward. We are not advocating for this sequence of steps to be set in stone; however, leaders will need an organized process for any chosen approach. The suggested activities can be adjusted to fit into existing structures and school processes, even incorporated into required school plans and improvement efforts. School teams seeking to create an equitable environment and close achievement and opportunity gaps will benefit from developing a coherent identity safe school plan.

Why It Matters

Most schools have embraced some of the aspects of identity safety. Many schools have instituted intervention courses and tutoring to improve outcomes for students who are not achieving at grade level. More than a few have organized diversity workshops for students or promoted cultural competencies through professional development for staff. Commonly, schools disaggregate and review academic achievement data to ensure the program is working for all students. Many have coordinated mentor programs, AVID classes, or academic advisories. Most schools have held bullying prevention assemblies and introduced reporting protocols. Yet, in many cases, these efforts are not coordinated, and in some schools, only a few of these aspects have been addressed, and still in other schools, a stark paucity of identity safety prevails.

In each example above, what might be missing is a schoolwide plan that systemically incorporates each component of identity safety and seeks to match school policies, practices, and approaches with those expressed goals to enact true cultural change. To fail at the level of schoolwide application can invite beneficial yet isolated results that likely will not stand the test of time. When we uphold identity safety by strengthening and coordinating our approach—including attitudes and behaviors, the classroom and curricula, faculty, staff, and community education, fair grading, and suspension policies—we can enjoy confidence in more lasting outcomes. For this, initial efforts are directed toward investigating the current school climate and culture, taking a deep look at prevailing attitudes and beliefs, and supporting the construction of a cohesive schoolwide action plan. We describe this in further detail later in this chapter under "Designing the Process".

Think about *your* school. Ask yourself some hard questions. What attitudes are conveyed to students so that every child is motivated to work to their potential and develop an academic identity? What structures are in place to ensure that a disproportionate number of students of color are not subject to suspension or other disciplinary responses or enrolled in special education classes? What policies are in place to prioritize funding for what matters most: student achievement, belonging, and wellbeing? These questions may not have yet been posed to or explored by staff, leaving the solutions out of sight.

Educators may be surprised to discover that even on a campus where achievement scores tend to be high and discipline problems generally low, a large number of students may feel disenfranchised. Educators may not have noticed that English language learners can spend an entire day sitting silent in all of their classes. The number of times the phrase "that's so gay" or the N-word are bandied about among students on a daily basis would probably astonish most leaders. Administrators may not realize that some students have been subject to negative stereotypes or judgmental comments in the presence of their teachers, yet nothing was done.

Making It Happen

An identity safe school planning process delineates specific action steps to meet the goals and address issues that emerge in the climate assessments and from other data sources. In some cases, new school policies, structures, and practices need to be created or adjusted to better align them with the goals of identity safety. Changing structures, traditions, and practices is no simple task. Some changes may require major adjustments to funding. Many complex issues and different points of view emerge. While not all problems can be solved at once, a planning process and realistic implementation timeline allows the school to prioritize solutions that involve everyone, including teachers, security guards and social workers, as well as unions or educators' associations.

TEAM MEMBERS

The Principal

The importance of a committed principal and administrative team, together with a good measure of shared tenacity fueled by motivation, embody key ingredients for actualizing real change. Positioned advantageously with a major role in overseeing school climate, administrators can inspire others and guide the journey. They can facilitate data gathering and analysis, provide time for professional development, and set in motion activities to transform the school culture. Administrators also hold the cards for enlisting support from district leaders to initiate policy changes, implement new schedules or bus routes, and eliminate other inequitable practices.

A highly involved principal who is willing to persevere and go the distance provides a needed model for others to follow. They set a high bar for the staff to design an equitable curriculum that meets all students' needs. Conversely, when a principal cheers others on without demonstrating their own commitment and deep involvement, staff members may feel that they, too, can remain disengaged. When enough key people are enrolled, administrators can formulate a leadership structure with them that maximizes effective involvement of all stakeholders (parents, staff, students), ensuring that their time is used wisely. Planning and implementation efforts can be assigned to this group of committed individuals in the form of a leadership team.

The Leadership Team

A leadership team, dedicated to guiding the different processes, works to formulate specific plans, oversee tasks, overcome obstacles, and assess growth. To begin, leaders cultivate the culture of identity safety *within* their team, building a microcosm for the larger school community to emulate. Developing trust with one another sets the stage for extending it to the rest of the staff, students, and parents. When the team's values for creating a safe and welcoming school are aligned, they will be ready and willing to ask hard questions, take risks, and determine when to bring the community together for dialogue, feedback, or input. This, then, becomes a vehicle for broadening identity safety to include the entire school.

Many schools already have a designated leadership body; however, that body may have multiple roles. While the larger team needs to understand and support identity safe school efforts, a smaller steering committee of leadership team members can be assigned to launch and exclusively shepherd specific identity safety efforts. This will allow sufficient time to devote toward examining equitable practices and school climate issues. Subsequently, they can submit recommendations to the larger Leadership Team.

The structure and membership of the Leadership Team and ancillary members are always based on the needs of the school as determined while designing the process.

Diverse Stakeholders

While a leadership body guides the processes, more voices are needed to represent the larger community in formulating the Identity Safe School Plan. Leaders can optimize the best moment for expanding to include additional stakeholders. The role of the stakeholders involves identifying concerns, reviewing data, providing input, generating solutions, and assisting in setting priorities. This can be accomplished through surveys, interviews, focus groups, listening tours, Town Halls, and other means of dialogue and feedback. For focus groups and interviews, thoughtful consideration of connection and culture will guide effective grouping of stakeholders. Accounting for interpersonal relationships, group dynamics, individual values, and fair representation of diverse cultures can help create balanced groups ready to forward an identity safe agenda.

Department, subject area, and grade level teams often operate as self-contained worlds of their own. An inclusive structure incorporates teacher representatives from these various departments and grade-level teams, and offers a means for the representatives to solicit input, present it to the Leadership Team, and later report back to their departments. Additionally, the Leadership Team will also benefit from the participation of classified and support staff (e.g., counselors, nurses, social workers). As we discussed in Chapter 5, a range of parent/caregiver voices will also advance an identity safe culture. Setting community agreements at the outset of each of these processes will allow for equitable participation and mutual respect.

Student Voices

As all identity safety efforts are geared toward providing the best possible experiences for students, hearing their voices forms an important part of the process. Whether we engage them in surveys or in-person interviews, their willingness to "tell it like it is" can be likened to the wind pushing the sails of a boat. Their feedback shows the current conditions, guides where we head up, and informs us how to adjust the sails to get there (see Appendix I: Grades 3–5 Student Identity Safe Classroom Survey and Appendix J: Grades 6–12 Student Identity Safe Classroom Survey). We also need to place them at the helm, and invite them to furnish solutions to their problems with their reliably fresh and relevant ideas. One group of Latinx high schoolers in Los Angeles complained that they were tired of their peers calling them "illegals." They organized a campaign on campus, which they labeled: "No Human Was Born Illegal" (Cohn-Vargas, 2016).

Students at all grade levels can contribute solutions to school problems. Fifth graders in a school in Union City, California, asked every child for the solution to bullying on campus (Not in Our Town, 2014). They were featured in a short film, *Leaving a Positive Footprint*, where each child wrote their proposed solution to bullying on a cutout of a footprint. They then taped the cutouts onto the floors throughout the hallways, creating a path of footprints to follow for a safer school. A group of middle school students in Carmel, California, went to every class in the school to find out where bullying was taking place on campus. From there they made a map of the places students felt most unsafe. They discovered that students were particularly vulnerable in one dark hallway, so they invited every student to dip their hand in different colors of paint and blanketed the wall with handprints. That hallway was dubbed the "high five hallway."

Older students can shine as members of the leadership team, representing agency for all students. When students witness their fellow classmates working with adults on matters that affect them, it strengthens their sense of voice and import. Educators can include student voices from the many different ethnic and social groups on campus, which can be drawn from student government, clubs, and by designating student representatives.

DESIGNING THE PROCESS

With the goal of designing a plan for schoolwide identity safety for students, staff, and parents, we suggest a process that include four main parts:

1. **Start with a deep look at identity safe principles, values, and beliefs:** Formulation of a schoolwide vision.

2. **Audit, assess, and analyze the climate and culture:** While analyzing the current state of identity safety in the school and looking through an equity lens, ask: What is working? Where is it not happening? How can we name and articulate what we want to make happen? Answer these questions in the context of analyzing the collected data.

3. **Develop goals and an action plan with concrete steps:** Information from data analysis becomes the basis for identifying root causes, setting goals, determining priorities, and defining the necessary steps, timelines, and tasks, with persons responsible for different aspects of the plan.

4. **Implement, monitor, and adjust the plan:** Once goals are determined, implementation begins. That process becomes iterative and includes continual monitoring and making minor and major changes along the way as new data become available.

A powerful way to launch the process can involve organizing several day-long community retreats with the goal to introduce participants to identity safety and engage in Steps 1–3 together. Including a range of voices in the shared experience will greatly enhance the richness of the dialogue and the resulting solutions. The Leadership Team or Steering Committee (a subset of the Leadership Team) can be responsible for overseeing implementation, and report back to the larger group to analyze the impact and determine next steps. The design developed by the team will ensure that a well-organized interactive approach is enacted to yield the desired results.

STEP ONE: A DEEP DIVE INTO VALUES AND BELIEFS OF IDENTITY SAFETY

A deep dive refers to dedicated time devoted to building an understanding of identity safety in the context of the values and culture of the school and considering what is needed.

Retreats provide an opportune and relaxing time for teams of stakeholders to unpack sentiments, ideas, and values. At an initial identity safety retreat, teams can assign the following items to their agenda for reflection, discussion, and sharing:

- Exploring identity safety principles and components to gain shared understanding.

- Examining values and beliefs in the context of identity safety.

- Discussing how to broadly engage stakeholders with shaping and ultimately buying into the shared values.

- Inaugurating a shared vision for identity safety.

- Exploring ways to integrate the values and the principles of identity safety into the school's operating systems and structure.

These ideas can be brought back to everyone in the school and incorporated into the school's existing vision or used to create a new vision and mission statement. The vision reflects the group's ideas for how they want their school to look and feel, while the mission statement addresses the plan to get there. Identity safe leaders work with their team to develop values and beliefs, which need to be simple yet meaningful and relevant, communicating clearly to both students and staff alike. Once finalized, depicting the values and beliefs in a graphic that can be posted in common areas and written into handbooks will solicit support and collaboration. Their visibility allows everyone to revisit these key attitudes and keep them alive.

The work, inspiration, and time dedicated to discovering shared values at the retreat extends to the students when we give them opportunities to create meaning from them. As they tap into the vision of a safe school where the well-being for themselves and their classmates is a priority, they can recognize the personal effects

A Values Process Sustained

During my (Alex) first year as principal, I undertook a process to create a collective identity with the school community to anchor our commitment to all for being seen and valued. When I began, both achievement and morale were low. I discussed the issues with my staff and in advisory classes, then worked with students to discuss, vote on, and select the following values, which were incorporated in a set of guiding values for the school:

- Hard work
- Caring
- Resiliency
- Integrity

Initially, staff selected the value of *respect*. As a community, we reflected around what we wanted to aspire to or reflect. In a meeting with the student leaders and staff I explained that *integrity* might be a more dynamic value to guide them. I shared how respect can sometimes refer to compliance while integrity is rooted in individual agency where students integrate positive values for themselves and each other into their decision-making processes. The message proved to resonate with all.

Even after several years when I no longer worked at the school, these guiding values continue to be a lived experience at the school. The school has spun them into the fabric of their daily activities. For example, the values are imparted to incoming 9th graders and new students at the beginning of each school year. They are honored on a weekly basis for practicing the values. At the end of the year, students reflect on the tenacity they've shown for exercising them, offering them opportunities to acknowledge and strengthen them.

and jump on board. Their participation is the indispensable element that breathes life and vitality into each and every value across the campus. You may need to change your school vision and mission to align it with identity safe practices, which will in turn guide your action plan.

The process of building schoolwide agreement around a set of values and beliefs is a powerful tool for shifting attitudes and promoting positive behavior. Negative behaviors will diminish as these values are affirmed and recognized through practice. This can take time as program and policy changes are initiated, but the pace will increase as rewards are seen and felt. This process necessitates the participation of students, and it is in part through their engagement that progress can be measured. We include familiarizing students with the concepts of identity safety as part of our launch for a schoolwide focus. When our attention is centered on the students, when we convey a solid bedrock of beliefs to them and the staff, they will eventually come to respect and understand the meaning of a true identity safe school.

STEP TWO: AUDIT, ASSESS, AND ANALYZE THE CLIMATE AND CULTURE, POLICIES, AND PRACTICES

An audit encompasses a comprehensive examination of school climate and all systems and practices, using data and input gathered from the many voices. The process involves acknowledging areas of strength and weakness. Each of these areas will contribute important information for tailoring identity safety efforts to specific site needs.

As described in Chapter 4, gathering data regarding feelings and attitudes together with additional data from multiple sources—including academic data and grades, behavior referrals, suspension, expulsion, and attendance records—expands the scope for understanding conditions at the school. In addition, other sources such as student and family surveys, parent involvement, or staffing demographics can augment efforts for informed choices. Data have the unique capacity to inform leaders when modifications are needed.

It is crucial to disaggregate all types of data and deepen the inquiry to validate a meaningful view. In addition, it is important to review the school's practices, policies, and resources for standards-based instruction, grading, retention, college preparation and counseling, the methods and effectiveness of academic remediation, and the strategies used to teach prosocial skills. A look at funding streams will allow you to identify the way resources are allocated and determine if resource distribution matches school values.

Reviewing disaggregated data by race and ethnic group and other key differences in the student population (e.g., gender, religion, disability) allows your team to dig deeper in order to ascertain whether the vision and school practices assign equal status and value to developing social, emotional, ethical, and intellectual skills for all. Also, triangulating the data by comparing the responses to surveys, focus groups, academic data, and funding expenditures will yield information on specific gaps in meeting student needs.

Data can inform school leaders about when and where bullying, cyberbullying, harassment, and teasing occur, and what groups (if any) are being targeted. Data are gathered to determine the presence of bias-based incidents, name-calling, and microaggressions. We follow up by asking students how they feel about the way these incidents were handled, and if they were resolved. Proaction will allow administrators to deal with the root of the problem before tensions explode into larger incidents. See Chapter 4 for information on how to develop surveys and focus groups to shed light on how students from diverse backgrounds feel in class, in the hallways, the cafeteria, the gym, or the schoolyard, as well as on school buses or walking to and from school.

A careful process for examining data with your team will yield valuable information that—once analyzed—can map a path toward an identity safe school. We provide sample data analysis questions in the section "Closing the Gap Between Ideas and Action".

STEP THREE: DEVELOP MEASURABLE GOALS AND AN ACTION PLAN FOR IDENTITY SAFETY

A successful identity safe school plan considers the specific needs of different sectors of the population, no matter how small, including English learners, special education students, and other traditionally underserved members of the school community. It includes effective instructional practices that lead to achievement and also identity safe student-centered teaching goals, which involves listening for student voices, teaching for understanding, and fostering cooperation and autonomy. Begin with five to seven measurable goals with clearly articulated targets and timelines. Eventually, more can be added. At the elementary level, a strong plan defines schoolwide goals as well as curricular and behavioral targets for grade levels. At the secondary level, the plan can include specific departmental objectives together with schoolwide behavioral expectations.

When identity safety principles and domains and core values are juxtaposed alongside data and assessments with an intent to detect the patterns and feedback that expose inequity, we are guided toward creating a blueprint for improvement in our school. The plan also includes goals for culturally responsive teaching, which is addressed with the identity safety domain and components of *cultivating diversity as a resource.*

In one high school, data analysis led to discovering that as a result of scheduling considerations, tracking by academic level in English and math led to placing all low performers together for all their classes, including art and physical education. This essentially created segregated tracks with students of color in the lower tracks. Unpacking student experiences allowed them to rethink and change their placement policies.

See "Using the Tools" at the end of this chapter for sample questions to use when selecting goals that address identity safety principles. Whether an Identity Safety

Plan is a stand-alone document or integrated into an existing school site plan, it needs clear and measurable goals that can translate into a living document that guides curricular and instructional decisions and schoolwide efforts.

STEP FOUR: IMPLEMENT, MONITOR, AND ADJUST THE PLAN

The Leadership Team can regularly take time to reflect on how the plan unfolds, make the necessary adjustments, and determine and celebrate what has been accomplished. Progress and impact data need to be regularly communicated to the larger school community.

As a change manager, your modeling and guidance can enlist all staff members to implement the plan and can shepherd staff toward flexibility, enabling them to pivot when necessary in alignment with their expressed goals for an identity safe school. Your knowledge of their particular strengths—as well as the subtleties of individual resistance—can direct your communication with them and between them. Your reassurance, approval, and guidance can keep everyone invested. By aligning roles with each educator's particular capacities boosts confidence and gives everyone a chance to contribute (e.g., skills of facilitation, editing, computer tech, outreach, public relations, organizing, public speaking, etc.). When you identify particular needs, you may be pleasantly surprised at who volunteers for the different tasks. By having your finger on the pulse of morale while nurturing strong relationships with individuals, you can navigate around the roadblocks.

This will empower you to adjust timelines when it becomes apparent that additional consideration is needed. Sometimes, you and your team may want to add a new goal when encountering a climate survey that presents unsafe feelings from a marginalized group. For example, a new survey may reveal that many LGBTQIA+ students do not feel they belong at school and that exclusionary tactics from other students, or bullying, have isolated them. Surveys can capture these sentiments before they reach a crisis point and allow you to actively work to raise student awareness and create an accepting environment for LGBTQIA+ students.

It is an ongoing process to ensure fidelity in implementation of the plan goals. Data collection is a continuous effort. New data will require additional analysis to measure progress toward the goals and to drive improvements. The coherent alignment of standards, curricula, and summative and formative assessments allows the team to monitor student growth and to revise and set new goals. The institutional professional learning activities, described in Chapter 3, can incorporate data analysis processes and work to meet the goals.

Once these steps take place, the school continues to evolve into an identity safe campus through an ongoing growth cycle as new data are gathered and analyzed and goals are updated, added, and implemented, and the monitoring cycle begins anew.

Closing the Gap Between Ideas and Action

In this chapter, we shared a structure and process for developing a collaborative process with diverse stakeholders to implement schoolwide identity safety. Here are steps for building a team approach and for developing, planning, implementing, and monitoring the transformation:

- Carry out a personal exploration and assessment of the school to design an inclusive process for engaging the full diversity of the community to shape and transform the vision into reality.

- Form a Leadership Team with a wide representation of administrators, teachers, counselors as well as other certificated and classified staff, parents/caregivers, and at the secondary level, students.

- Implement an *Identity Safe School Cycle of Inquiry and Implementation Process:*

  o **Step One:** Formulate and articulate a vision for identity safety and its values, beliefs, principles, and/or agreements.

  o **Step Two:** Carry out an equity-focused audit of all of the school's systems, practices, and policies using disaggregated data with an analysis of causes, forces, strengths, gaps, enablers, barriers, opportunities, and other dimensions of the current state.

  o **Step Three:** Identify five to seven Strategic Measurable Goals (linked to identity safety domains, components, and principles). Include specific metrics and growth targets. For each goal, specify action steps, activities, and persons responsible and include a timeline for all tasks.

  o **Step Four:** Assess progress on these goals and metrics. Monitor, adjust, and share findings. Set new goals in a continuous cycle of inquiry.

Launching schoolwide identity safety takes into equal consideration an inclusive process, with attention to relationships in order to achieve effective results. Through ongoing collaboration, the team can take steps to end the predictability of failure for Black and Latinx students and for any other student facing educational inequities. School change is a continuous and iterative process that requires a deep commitment to stay the course even when results are not as rapid as everyone would like.

Schools are a microcosm of the world. They are a mirror for the urgently needed efforts to create a world where no person feels othered, where every person feels a sense of belonging and agency, and where all identities contribute and are valued. Our schools can become places of interdependence and caring, fostering the agency, curiosity, and innovation needed to increase kindness, compassion, creative thinking, and academic achievement.

Check Yourself

- How have you audited all aspects of your school's climate, policies, and practices? Who participated? What identity safe strategies are already in place? What changes are needed?

- How does your existing school mission and vision align with identity safety? What changes, if any, might be needed?

- How does your change process provide for students and families, including their voices in school activities and decisions?

- What is your existing school plan? What aspects of equity and identity safety are addressed in the plan? How can it be enhanced or reworked to be an Identity Safe School Plan?

- How have you faced resistance from educators in different roles at the school? What steps have you taken to address it?

Using the Tools

Identity Safe School Planning Preparation Form

NOTE: Questions have been adapted from the Identity Safe and Inclusive School Program Guide (Cohn-Vargas, 2016).

Identity Safe School Vision

LIST YOUR SCHOOL'S VISION BELOW

Questions to Address During Data Analysis

Use these questions when developing surveys and analyzing data that have been collected:

School Climate and Culture

1. What are the main goals and concerns of students?

2. How do the different ethnic groups and other diverse student populations describe their sense of belonging and liking of school? What is being done for those who don't?

3. What actions has the school taken to promote diversity and intercultural understanding, awareness of gender identity and sexual orientation? What has been the impact of those activities?

4. What are the areas on campus, or on the way to and from school, where students feel safe? Where do students feel unsafe?

5. Do any students describe being subjected to physical or verbal bullying, cyberbullying, and teasing? If so, what have they described? Is any bullying or harassment based on race, ethnicity, language, religion, gender, or sexual orientation?

6. How do students describe the way school administrators and staff respond when they witness or experience teasing, bullying, or are subjected to violence?

7. Do the students feel adults care about them and will listen and help when they have problems? What supports are in place for student emotional well-being?

8. How do the adults feel at school? What are their major concerns?

Academic Program

1. What strategies, methodologies, and programs support student achievement and what is the impact of the efforts?

2. Do students believe they have the academic support they need? Do they feel their teachers express high expectations and motivate them to achieve their goals?

3. Do students find the curriculum challenging and motivating? Do they see themselves represented in the curriculum?

4. How are students placed in courses? Are large numbers of one racial group found in advanced or higher-level courses? If so, what is being done to diversify and increase access?

5. Are students advancing and progressing to meet grade-level standards, including those who are receiving remedial or tutoring services? What is offered to them?

6. Who is identified for special education? Is any one ethnic group overrepresented in special education courses? What services are offered? How is the special education program working to help students progress academically?

Behavior and Discipline

1. Do any students have attendance problems? Are there any patterns of absence among a particular ethnic group, income level, or language group? Can you discover why certain students do not come to school? What has been done to address attendance problems and what has worked?

2. Do discipline policies and procedures align with the school's vision and mission? Are the policies being implemented as intended? Are the policies and procedures effective in preventing and addressing all forms of violence and student conflict?

3. What are the policies and practices to address bullying, social exclusion, and intolerance? What has been the impact of these efforts?

4. How are behavioral norms, expectations, and school rules presented to students? How are they implemented?

5. How are students taught prosocial skills, character education, and empathy? What is the impact of these efforts?

Questions to Guide the Process of Setting Goals

Once you have analyzed data and determined areas of growth, select from the questions below—which are drawn from each of the identity safety principles—as you begin a process with your group for setting goals.

Principle One: *Colorblind teaching that ignores differences is a barrier to inclusion in the classroom.*

1. What alternatives to colorblind teaching will be incorporated that do not contribute to stereotyping students?

2. What will ensure that students of all backgrounds achieve at high levels while feeling that their identities are not invisible? How will you help students find their voice and deeply understand the content of your curriculum?

Principle Two: To feel a sense of belonging and acceptance requires creating positive relationships between teacher and students and among students with equal status for different social identities.

1. What will be done to enhance each student's sense of belonging?

2. What specific strategies will be used to ensure that teacher-student relationships are positive and nurturing?

3. How will positive student-student relationships and equal status be encouraged and monitored?

4. How will conflicts be addressed?

5. How will educators learn about and incorporate trauma-informed practices?

6. What behavior management strategies can ensure that student consequences and mistakes offer learning opportunities and ways to repair harm done? How can the growth mindset and learning from mistakes become part of the fabric of school life?

Principle Three: Cultivating diversity as a resource for learning and expressing high expectations for students promotes learning, competence, and achievement.

1. How will educators help students learn to value their own identities and create acceptance?

2. How will the growth mindset be taught and practiced?

3. How will you ensure educators are continually reflecting on and communicating high expectations?

4. How will educators work to develop challenging curriculum for students of all backgrounds and at all academic levels?

5. How will students and staff learn about implicit bias, microaggressions, and stereotype threat? How will everyone develop skills to respectfully call one another out when these situations occur and work to reduce the negative impacts? What new efforts can be incorporated?

6. How will staff become aware of and incorporate the power of counter-narratives?

Principle Four: *Educators need to examine their own social identities and feel a sense of identity safety to convey that feeling to students and create an identity safe environment for students.*

1. How will educators deepen their understanding of their own identities as well as their power and privilege?

2. How will you work to create identity safety for staff?

3. How will educators build trust with one another?

4. Are opportunities for equalizing status and honoring diverse voices of staff prevalent within the school community?

Principle Five: *Social/emotional safety is created by supporting students in defining their identities, refuting negative stereotypes, countering stereotype threat, giving them a voice in the classroom, and using SEL strategies.*

1. How can equity-focused SEL be promoted in ways that promote prosocial development of the students?

2. How can all students learn to work cooperatively and become self-motivated independent learners? How can a growth mindset culture be cultivated?

Principle Six: *Student learning is enhanced in diverse classrooms by teaching for understanding, opportunities for shared inquiry and dialogue, and offering a challenging, rigorous curriculum.*

1. What teaching practices can be added to enhance engagement in school?

2. Thinking of specific ethnic and racial subgroups, what goals do we have for improving our effectiveness and how will that manifest in student learning?

3. What are ways to ensure that all students find their voice and deeply understand the content?

4. What strategies will support student autonomy, agency, and confident academic identity?

Principle Seven: *Schoolwide equity flourishes for everyone in identity safe schools where the climate, the structures, practices, and attitudes prioritize equity, inclusion, and academic growth for students from all backgrounds. Leaders demonstrate emotional* *intelligence, attend to student needs, address racism, bias, and privilege, and serve as the architects of ongoing change.*

1. What operational infrastructure will sustain the positive changes?

2. What are the plans for professional development to build capacity of all adults on campus to create identity safe environments?

3. What barriers exist that hinder some students from becoming engaged or achieving? What steps will be taken to remove the barriers?

4. What existing resources support English learners, those with mental health needs, students with disabilities? How do you help those who bully or repeatedly harm others transform their behavior? What needs to be added?

5. What parent involvement and educational opportunities will enhance participation and increase their inclusion in the school?

online resources ➤ Available for download as a full-page form at
https://resources.corwin.com/BelongingandInclusionISS

Epilogue
Closing Thoughts

Things are not getting worse, they are getting uncovered. We must hold each other tight and continue to pull back the veil. . . . We must take the risk of leading. We must be willing to assert the solutions we believe in, to experiment with alternative ways of being human on this planet at this time. . . . Liberation is no small task—it is appropriately daunting for miraculous beings. It is a gift, to be given such undeniable purpose, such immense odds. Hold each other tight, and let's do this work.

— Adrienne Marie Brown

We thank you for joining us in this quest to transform our schools into identity safe spaces for students, staff, and families. In the spirit of the poet and activist Adrienne Marie Brown's words, we invite you to take the challenge and the risk to lead forward in spite of the immense odds that lie ahead. Now is the time to join thousands of educators, parents, students, and community leaders of all backgrounds who have stepped up to speak truth to power. These people have taken what they have learned from the global pandemic and from the courage of young people, standing up to racism during the protests after the brutal murder of George Floyd, to unearth, reverse, and redress systemic inequities.

Together, we can forge an education system that transforms biased attitudes, dismantles white supremacist structures, and works to end racist traditions that perpetuate them. We can keep the flame kindled that has awakened a long overdue moment of dialogue about race that will guide us toward a growing awareness of struggles to bridge the great chasms that have divided our nation by race since its inception. We can carry that awareness into bold action for change and social justice.

There will be moments when the burden of leadership will feel almost too strong to bear; the pressure of required internal changes, finding muscles of courage, overcoming resistance, and the dilemmas posed by the external world will make your task seem insurmountable. We have felt it too, but we believe that dedicating our lives to future generations is the most important thing we can do. While we cannot control everything happening in the world outside us, we can choose to be part of the solutions, joining communities seeking to heal from a pervasive sense of disconnection, isolation, and hopelessness.

We encourage our readers to stay strong, stay committed, and stay hopeful. We invite you as leaders to feel nothing short of awe as you step up to the challenge of creating an identity safe school during this period of the most rapid change in human history. What can be a more awesome task than working to prepare the next generation for the large-scale transformation needed to ensure a healthy future for our planet. It is our hope that identity safe schools can play a role in helping our students become valued members of society and that we all can contribute to the transformation. While it will always be a work in progress, in many ways this is our greatest challenge during this moment in history. A greater sense of identity safety, equity, and social justice in the world at large will humanize us all.

Appendix A

Equitable Data Inquiry Preparation Guide: Preparing for Equitable Data Dialogue, Analysis, and Reflection

Essential Questions:

- What knowledge, skills, and community agreements are central to holding equitable, data-driven, and responsive discussions about student learning?

- What does this process look like in practice?

TIME	ACTIVITY
10 min.	**Welcome & Opening Remarks**
10 min.	**Quickwrite and Pair Share**
15 min.	**Readings & Guiding Questions**
25 min.	**Small Group Discussion, Community Agreements** *(Examples & Non-Examples)*, **Intention Setting**
5 min.	**Closing**

QUICKWRITE:

- What have been your previous experiences in using student learning data in your teaching practice? How would you best describe these experiences?

- What knowledge, skills, and community agreements are central to holding equitable, data-driven, and responsive discussions about student learning?

READING MATERIAL

- Milner, H., IV. (2018, February). Confronting inequity/assessment for equity. *Educational Leadership*, 75(5), 88–89.

- Aguilar, E. (2019). *Onward: Cultivating emotional resilience in educators.* San Francisco, CA: Jossey-Bass. (See Chapter 9, pp. 223–247.)

- Gorski, P. (2017). *Equity literacy for educators: Definitions and abilities.* Equity Literacy Institute. http://www.edchange.org/handouts/Equity-Literacy-Introduction.pdf

EQUITY LITERACY FOR EDUCATORS	ONWARD - "BE A LEARNER," PP. 1-12, 33-41	CONFRONTING INEQUITY/ ASSESSMENT FOR EQUITY
Guiding Question: What are knowledge and skills to support our ability to attend to and disrupt inequity when identifying needs and responding to student learning and achievement?	What does it mean to be a learner? What mindsets, stances, or ways of being might help me engage in inquiry and reflection for my student learning data?	What is an essential purpose in using assessments in the classroom for student learning? How should assessments be used? What implications does the article have for how we analyze and respond to student data?
Reading Notes:		

Small Group Discussion (5 min.)

- In consideration of the guiding questions and our purpose today, what knowledge, skills, and community agreements are central to holding equitable, data-driven, and responsive discussions about student learning?

- What does this process look like in practice?

Community Agreements for Equitable Data Reflection & Planning

Purpose of Agreements: To ensure the focus of reviewing student learning data is to understand and explore ways to *instructionally* attend to student learning and academic achievement access barriers.

Community Agreements Activity Directions (15 min.): As a team, develop examples and non-examples for each Community Agreement. You may refer to the *Talking About Student Data* resource below to aid in this activity.

COMMUNITY AGREEMENT	EXAMPLE (LOOKS LIKE/SOUNDS LIKE)	NON-EXAMPLE (LOOKS LIKE/SOUNDS LIKE)
Hold a growth mindset for self and students		
Show curiosity when exploring student learning needs		
Respond with compassion to emotions that may arise		
Actively notice and challenge personal biases in the service of better understanding and dismantling instructional barriers to student learning		

Intention Setting

What is an intention or commitment you would like to make for today in the service of equitable data dialogue, analysis, and reflection?

Why Is Language Important?

- Our language powerfully impacts students' beliefs and stories about themselves and others. It is essential that our language reflects our belief in and excitement about their unlimited potential to grow. Asset-based language is particularly important to actively disrupt and interrupt stigmas fed by unjust societal discourses related to ethnicity, gender, immigration experience, and other demographic factors.

- Community relationships are built on respect, trust, and consistency. The students and families who we serve trust that we are respectful and consistent in our messages.

- We must know and name our students' strengths and abilities in order to help them internalize a growth mindset, construct a positive identity as a learner/scholar, and develop to their fullest potential.

As we enter into our collective work examining student data, we have the opportunity to commit to language that focuses on positive outcomes and personal strengths, rather than problems and barriers—and that denotes movement through developmental stages toward a goal rather than a fixed identity.

As evidenced in the table below, some language in common usage communicates *deficit* rather than *strength* and/or communicates *fixed identity* rather than *developmental stage*.

INSTEAD OF . . .	CONSIDER . . .	IDENTITY SAFE INQUIRY QUESTIONS
High kids/ high fliers	Students who/who have - met/exceeded _____ standard, - demonstrate(d) consistent level of proficiency, or - demonstrate(d) consistent fluency in _____ .	- What meaning am I making about where my students are and where I hope for them to be? - What assumptions might I be making in relation to why my students are able to master content and/or are in need of additional support?
Low kids/low fliers	Students who are - demonstrating emerging proficiency or - aspiring, emergent, developing, or novice.	

At risk, hard to reach, cluster class	• Students would benefit from/ is in need of _____. • I am curious about/need more support to learn _____. • I have noticed _____ when they _____ (identify cause and effect).	• How are my lessons scaffolded (or will be), so all students understand the content and move ahead? • What messages do I need to plan for in order to ensure my students can practice or maintain a growth mindset or learning orientation with respect to this assessment?
Advanced, Proficient, Basic, Below Basic, Far Below Basic	• My students have exceeded/ met/are developing/emerging in _____ standard/cluster/ topic as reflected by _____.	

 Available for download as a full-page form at
https://resources.corwin.com/BelongingandInclusionISS

Appendix B
Identity Safe Staff Self-Reflection Activity

CONSIDER YOUR PRACTICES	WHAT ADDITIONS/ CHANGES DO YOU WANT TO MAKE AS YOU INTRODUCE IDENTITY SAFETY?
PAY ATTENTION TO WHAT YOU SAY	
How do you encourage students, provide feedback, and respond to questions? Give an example of each.	
What words and positive presuppositions do you use to encourage and motivate students?	
What tone do you hear yourself using when you are annoyed, on a day when you do not feel great, or when your patience is being tried?	
CONSIDER RELATIONSHIPS	
What is your relationship with each of your students? Who stands out as in need of more TLC (tender loving care)?	

How do your students interact with each other? Who is excluded? Who shows dominance in their social groups?	

FOCUS ON YOUR CURRICULUM

Offer an example for how you scaffold instruction.	
Provide an example of a way you keep students challenged.	
Give one example of how you differentiate your curriculum.	

ASSESSING LEARNING

What formative assessment tools do you use?	
Share an example of how you give wise feedback.	
Do students use formative assessment to reflect on and guide their own learning in your class? Provide an example.	

An Additional Activity to Use With Mid-Career Educators

1. What aspects of identity safety have been a focus throughout your career? What data and evidence have you collected about the degree to which you are successful?

2. What challenges to meeting your goals for serving students have you overcome along the way? What challenges are foremost for you now?

3. What values guide the routines that you regularly use in your class-room?

4. How do you keep yourself excited and motivated to do this work of identity safe teaching? What are your personal ways to sustain your emotional resilience?

 online resources Available for download as a full-page form at
https://resources.corwin.com/BelongingandInclusionISS

Appendix C

Identity Safe Classroom Practices: Teacher Self-Assessment

PRINCIPLES

1: Colorblind teaching that ignores differences is a barrier to inclusion in the classroom.
2: To feel a sense of belonging and acceptance requires creating positive relationships between teacher and students and among students with equal status for different social identities.
3: Cultivating diversity as a resource for learning and expressing high expectations for students promotes learning, competence, and achievement.
4: Educators examine their own social identities to feel a sense of identity safety and convey that feeling to students, creating an identity safe environment for them.
5: Social and emotional safety is created by supporting students in defining their identities, refuting negative stereotypes, and countering stereotype threat, giving them a voice in the classroom while using social and emotional (SEL) strategies.
6: Student learning is enhanced in diverse classrooms by teaching for understanding, creating opportunities for shared inquiry and dialogue, and offering a challenging, rigorous curriculum.
7: Schoolwide equity flourishes for everyone in identity safe schools where the climate, the structures, the practices, and attitudes prioritize equity, inclusion, and academic growth for students from all backgrounds. Leaders demonstrate emotional intelligence; attend to student needs; address racism, bias, and privilege; and serve as the architects of ongoing change.

(Continued)

(Continued)

PRINCIPLE	TEACHER: INDICATE YOUR LEVEL OF MASTERY	BEGINNING	IN PROGRESS	PROFICIENT	COMMENTS
1	Affirming and celebrating differences to promote inclusion in the classroom				
1	Creating a culture of respect and belonging for all groups of students				
1	Addressing and intervening in incidents of stereotyping, stereotype threat, and bias in the classroom				
1	Noticing and repairing harm if something I've said or done has upset or felt harmful to a student				
2	Ensuring students of all social identities believe that you believe they can and will meet the high standards you hold				
2	Establishing belonging and trust with students of all social identities				
2	Providing opportunities for students to get to know each other				
2	Facilitating high levels of belonging and acceptance among students				
3	Helping students explore shared and different histories, languages, and perspectives				
3	Holding high standards for all students				
3	Integrating conversations about race and culture in lessons and class discussions				
3	Using cooperative learning to teach collaboration skills and also highlight each student's contributions and strengths				
4	(Appropriately) sharing my social identity with students as a model or example				
4	Raising and discussing stereotyping, stereotype threat, and bias with colleagues				
4	Bringing my full self into the classroom				
4	Enacting gender identity self-awareness				

4	Enacting racial identity self-awareness		
4	Sharing about social identity with colleagues		
5	Creating and sustaining connections with individual students		
5	Encouraging students to ask for help		
5	Ensuring that students have a voice in the classroom		
5	Having students do writing that connects to values and/or role models		
5	Modeling and teaching empathy, respect, hope, and other mindset qualities		
5	Noticing and praising effort		
5	Supporting students to define and develop their identities		
5	Using asset-based language with and about students		
6	Differentiating in response to student needs		
6	Preparing students in advance for changes in routines and activities		
6	Scaffolding to ensure access to and a pathway to mastery		
6	Teaching for understanding—prevalence of student "meaning-making" going on in the classroom		
6	Modeling and teaching growth mindset and learning from mistakes		
7. Note: Self-Assess in relation to equity across the school.	Contributing to the climate, the structures, the practices, and attitudes that prioritize equity, inclusion, and academic growth for students from all backgrounds.		

Appendix D

Identity Safe Classroom Observation Form

This form is designed for classroom observations.

Observation Tips:

Determine a focus of the observation in advance and highlight specific observations in comments.

Agree to protocols before the observation.

Inform students that the teacher is being observed.

Observers do not intervene in classroom activities.

Debriefing Tips:

Use positive feedback and highlight effective practices with specific feedback.

Avoid giving advice when debriefing.

Note: *T* stands for *Teacher* and *S* stands for *Student(s)*.

DOMAIN ONE: STUDENT-CENTERED TEACHING

	LISTENING FOR STUDENT VOICES	
	ACTION	**COMMENTS**
❑	S work displayed	
❑	Displays show all S work	
❑	T encourages expression of and reflection about feelings	
❑	T gives S role in classroom planning and decision-making	
❑	T evaluates S work or performance with S input	
❑	S has input in nonacademic discussion	
❑	S participates in decision-making	
❑	S comments freely, openly	
❑	S gives reasons for opinions	
❑	S elaborates on others' statements	
❑	S reads aloud, displays own work	

	TEACHING FOR UNDERSTANDING	
	ACTION	**COMMENTS**
❑	T leads reflection on past activity/uses anticipatory set	
❑	There is a full orientation to coming activity	
❑	There is a full reflection on completed activity	
❑	Emphasis on gaining understanding	
❑	T orients S to coming activity	
❑	Use of interest centers	
❑	Voluntary S selection of interest center(s)	
❑	Open-ended academic activities	
❑	T reads aloud to whole class or group	
❑	T engages S in extended discussion of individual experiences, backgrounds	
❑	T elaborates on S response	
❑	T asks S to elaborate on own/others' comments	

(Continued)

(Continued)

❑	T sustains questioning to elaborate ideas	
❑	Emphasis on relevance of material to broader issues	
❑	Emphasis on S imagination, creativity	
❑	T is responsive to S thoughts or viewpoints	
❑	T explains reason for rule, desired behavior, etc.	
❑	T encourages S comments (general)	
❑	T leads academic discussion	

FOCUS ON COOPERATION		
	ACTION	COMMENTS
❑	S helps other S	
❑	Spontaneous cooperation, collaboration	
❑	S shows concern for one another	
❑	Ss are helpful	
❑	S listens carefully to other S	
❑	Group activity is smooth	
❑	S in pairs/groups working on joint projects (with group goals)	
❑	S seats arranged in small groups	
❑	S in pairs/groups giving help	
❑	T encourages helping/cooperation	
❑	T takes steps to facilitate group interaction	

AUTONOMY FOR STUDENTS		
	ACTION	COMMENTS
❑	T gives choice of activities	
❑	T gives choice within activities	
❑	T mediates interpersonal problems	
❑	T has S solve own interpersonal problems	
❑	T provides for S autonomy and choice	
❑	S gets own materials, supplies	
❑	S moves around freely	
❑	S initiates nonacademic questions, comments, or conversation	
❑	T trusts in S	
❑	S asks T for academic help	

DOMAIN TWO: CULTIVATING DIVERSITY AS A RESOUCE

	USING DIVERSITY AS A RESOURCE FOR LEARNING	
	ACTION	COMMENTS
❑	Display(s)/prominent books regarding role models of minority background(s)	
❑	Display(s)/prominent books that include people of African American or African culture	
❑	Display(s)/prominent books representing Latinx culture	
❑	Display(s)/prominent books representing Asian/Pacific Islander culture	
❑	Display(s)/prominent books representing Indigenous cultures	
❑	Display(s)/prominent books representing other culture(s)	
❑	Display(s)/prominent books representing LGBTQIA+ people	
❑	Use of primary source materials and counter-narratives	
❑	S mixed by race/ethnic group	
❑	S mixed by gender	
❑	T uses foreign language	
❑	T mentions important contributions of individuals of color	
❑	T refers to relevant cultural capital and background, experience	
❑	Emphasis on cultural/ethnic diversity in classroom	

	HIGH EXPECTATIONS AND ACADEMIC RIGOR	
	ACTION	COMMENTS
❑	Focus on academic instruction/work	
❑	Class is highly task-oriented	
❑	There is a sense of academic press	
❑	T links S effort and learning	
❑	High expectations for learning expressed for students	

	CHALLENGING CURRICULUM	
	ACTION	COMMENTS
❑	T asks S for inference, hypothesis, deduction	
❑	T effectively stimulates S thinking	
❑	T asks advanced questions to S of all backgrounds	
❑	Class activities are exciting	

DOMAIN THREE: CLASSROOM RELATIONSHIPS

	TEACHER WARMTH AND AVAILABILITY TO SUPPORT LEARNING	
	ACTION	**COMMENTS**
❑	T is warm, personal	
❑	T shows sincere appreciation to S	
❑	T shows pleasure or delight	
❑	T is accepting of S	
❑	T is at ease, comfortable with S	
❑	T's apparent liking for, enjoyment of, interest in S	
❑	T relates personally to S	
❑	T is playful or humorous	
❑	T leads or helps small group	
❑	T gives S support, encouragement	
❑	T is available, accessible to S	
❑	T responsiveness to S needs or preferences	
❑	T is engaged	
❑	T encourages nonparticipants to participate	

	POSITIVE STUDENT RELATIONSHIP	
	ACTION	**COMMENTS**
❑	S smiles, laughs	
❑	S socializes, talks personally	
❑	S is friendly	
❑	S interacts with one another	
❑	S interacts with S of different ethnic groups	
❑	Friendly intergroup interaction	

DOMAIN FOUR: CARING CLASSROOMS

	TEACHER SKILL	
	ACTION	**COMMENTS**
❑	Smooth transitions	
❑	Clear behavioral directives	
❑	T seems confident	
❑	T is clear, understandable	
❑	Lessons are purposeful, planned	
❑	T uses tasks that engage S interest	
❑	Class is orderly	

❑	S on task, appropriate behavior	
❑	S engages in class activity	
❑	S is excited about class activities	
❑	S is engaged/involved	
❑	S is actively involved in learning experience	
❑	On-task behavior of S of all backgrounds	
❑	On-task behavior of Asian S	
❑	S participates	
❑	S engages in group activity	

EMOTIONAL AND PHYSICAL COMFORT		
	ACTION	**COMMENTS**
❑	Classroom harmoniousness	
❑	Class calm	
❑	Unrestricted verbal interaction	
❑	Community feeling in classroom	
❑	Observed tasks/activities	
❑	S at ease with T	
❑	There is a meeting area in the classroom	
❑	Spatial arrangements facilitate interaction	
❑	Materials are ample for S needs	
❑	Attention to S/T comfort	

ATTENTION TO PROSOCIAL DEVELOPMENT		
	ACTION	**COMMENTS**
❑	Display(s) of prosocial values	
❑	Display(s) of positive classroom behavior rules (dos)	
❑	Nonacademic discussion (including class meetings and/or advisory classes)	
❑	Focus on social/interpersonal skills	
❑	Focus on prosocial issues, interpersonal understanding	
❑	Emphasis on interpersonal/ intergroup understanding	

online resources ► Available for download as a full-page form at
https://resources.corwin.com/BelongingandInclusionISS

Appendix E
Inquiry Calendar Planner

PERSON, ROLE, OR TEAM:	DATE(S) COMPLETING CALENDAR:	SCHOOL YEAR OR TERM:

List Team members, if applicable:

Take 3–5 minutes to reflect and connect on the core purposes of this role or team. Jot down key phrases or words here:

What are your *impact* goals for this year/term? Which are your top one or two?

Impact goals for what will be gained in key areas such as sense of belonging, academic growth and mastery, satisfaction with school, community well-being, and so on.

What are your *process* goals for this year/term? Which are your top one to three? *Process* goals address our actions to achieve impact goals. Examples include participation and satisfaction with PD, number of positive phone calls home, number of formative assessment opportunities provided, number of staff gaining specific PD content, and the like.

Considering these goals, what data do we need?

Note any data access and availability questions/issues for follow-up:

Please take a few minutes to notice emotions or mindsets that come up related to working with these goals and data. What do you notice? What ideas, questions, or assumptions do you have about the mindsets and emotions others may bring?

INQUIRY CALENDAR PLANNER

TO TRACK AND INFORM PROGRESS ON THE IMPACT AND
PROCESS GOALS.

For each session, what **data** and which **guiding questions or hypotheses** will you
explore?

SESSION NAME/DATE(S)	IMPACT GOALS		PROCESS GOALS	
	DATA TO EXPLORE	GUIDING QUESTIONS	DATA TO EXPLORE	GUIDING QUESTIONS

What are any next steps to get access to these data, including results for race, gender, and subgroups of focus?

How and when will you hear the voices of those closest to the action and with the most at stake? (Using, for example, surveys or focus groups.)

Appendix F
We–Why Reflection Tool

Who Are We and What Shared Purpose Defines Us?

Please reflect on a shared purpose that brings you here today. In the inner circle below, please share key words or phrases about that shared purpose. Use the outer circles to represent the *we*—people, teams, groups, networks, communities, etc.—who are part of this shared purpose. *These can be from the past, present, and future.*

We are_____ who want/need
to _____ because _____.

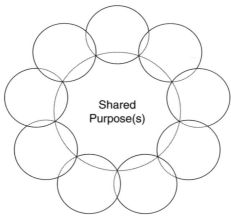

Shared Purpose(s)

Adapted from ideas and materials from the Office of Hawaiian Education HĀ project of the Hawaii Department of Education, http://www.hawaiipublicschools.org/TeachingAndLearning/StudentLearning/HawaiianEducation/Pages/HA.aspx.

 online resources Available for download as a full-page form at
https://resources.corwin.com/BelongingandInclusionISS

Appendix G

Identity Safe Formative Assessment Feedback Loop Reflection Questions & Planner

Planning Formative Assessment & Feedback Cycles

Learning Goal + Evidence Gathering Routine + Interpret / Response Plan = Formative Assessment

LEARNING GOAL	EVIDENCE ROUTINE	RESPONSE PLAN
Learning Goal(s) • Standards, learning targets, SWBAT . . . **Success Criteria** • Description and examples of what it looks like when done well	**Task/Assignment** • Assessment or Assignment **Learning Evidence** • What the Student will produce, e.g., essay or multiple choice responses **Feedback Planned** • Numeric scoring/rating and/or narrative feedback from teachers, peers and/or self	**Teacher Response Plan** • How the teacher will reflect, make meaning, and plan and carry out instructional next steps **Student Response Plan** • How the students will reflect, make meaning, and plan and take action to achieve learning goals

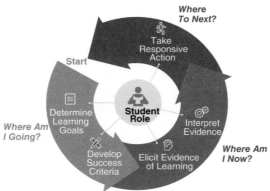

Source: Created by WestEd, wested.org. Reprinted with permission. Assessment for Learning. (n.d.). https://www.assessmentforlearningproject.org/

Editable Planning Template

LEARNING GOAL	EVIDENCE ROUTINE	RESPONSE PLAN
<u>Learning Goal(s)</u>	<u>Task/Assignment</u>	<u>Teacher Response Plan</u>
<u>Success Criteria</u>	<u>Learning Evidence Produced (Student Work)</u> <u>Feedback Planned</u>	<u>Student Response Plan</u>

Reflection Questions to Guide Action and Improvement

In Preparation and Throughout:

1. To what degree do you feel welcomed and valued as your full self at school? What do you think other educators and students would say to this question?

2. How does your cultural and social identity reflect or differ from that of educators/students? In what moments do you notice this, and what is the impact?

3. How do you learn about and connect with students' and families' home cultures? How are home cultural values and assets a centerpoint at school?

4. *Equity consciousness* is the knowledge, language, and skills that enable us to recognize, respond, and redress inequity in our spheres of influence (Gorski, 2014). What supports your equity consciousness, and what can get in the way? How will you continue to grow equity consciousness?

5. How do you build and sustain trust with and among students? With which students do you think this is easiest and hardest?

6. With students with whom trust is still emerging, what routines and practices do you use to express warmth and belief in their capacity to succeed?

7. Certain mindsets and habits (e.g., growth mindset, telling empowering stories, mindfulness, self-talk, journaling) are associated with stronger emotional regulation and capacity to connect and build trust. What mindsets and habits are you drawn to or find important to cultivate for yourself?

8. How do you embrace positive presuppositions that assume students have the best intentions and avoid critical language that undermines confidence?

9. How do you teach and model a growth mindset to ensure a Learning Zone in which mistakes are welcomed and well used to guide improvement?

10. What resources and support do you need?

Question Bank

Additional Reflection to Guide Action & Improvement

Use just a few at a time! Read and find one to three questions that draw you for reflection.

PHASE 1: WHERE AM I GOING?

1. How do you, students, and/or parents/caregivers participate in shaping learning goals and success criteria?

2. What do you appreciate about the learning goals and success criteria? What would you like to see changed or improved, and why?

3. What do students appreciate about the learning goals and success criteria? What would they like to see changed or improved, and why?

4. What do parents/caregivers and the community appreciate about the learning goals and success criteria? What would they like to see changed or improved, and why?

5. How do you activate and connect prior knowledge to the learning goals and success criteria?

6. How do you provide and gradually remove scaffolds? How do you explain how this works to students and parents?

7. How do you express high expectations *and* support, so the students trust your belief in and readiness to support their learning and success?

PHASE 2: WHERE AM I NOW?

1. How do tasks, evidence created, and feedback routines reflect and build from students' cultures, interests, and prior knowledge?

2. How well do the tasks and data/feedback align to the learning goals and success criteria?

3. How do the tasks and routines incorporate varied modalities (e.g., verbal, written, visual; peer, self-, and educator feedback; individual and group)?

4. Do the students view the tasks and feedback routines as relevant and engaging? What do they most/least appreciate about the tasks and routines?

5. Do students value the information they receive from the feedback routine? What do they most/least appreciate about the information provided?

6. In looking at data or student work, what messages do I need to plan for to support students' growth mindset and sense of hope as a learner?

7. What assumptions may you be making about why students did or did not master content? What assumptions may students be making?

8. What intentional messages do students receive (from tasks, routines, classroom language) about their competence and learner identity?

9. When peers are giving feedback to one another, how do you ensure trust is built for respectful support?

10. How do you gather and interpret evidence in ways that do not single out those who are academically behind, or create or reinforce hierarchies of academic status?

11. What works well in terms of the access you and students have to data and feedback? What could be improved?

12. How do you offer *Wise Feedback*—expressing to the students that you have high standards and that you know they can reach those standards; giving concrete, doable suggestions for what to do next to improve; identifying and providing needed support.

PHASE 3: WHERE TO NEXT?

1. What routines are in place for you and students to reflect, make meaning, set learning goals, and plan and take action to achieve learning goals?

2. How and when do you support students' learning plans (e.g., small groups in class, quick 1-on-1 check-ins during independent work time, office hours)?

3. What curricular resources are accessible for students to pursue study and practice targeted to their goals? What additional resources do you need?

4. How is grading growth-based to ensure that students who start low have the power to impact their grade (e.g., systems for retakes and redos, lowest possible score 50% rather than 0%, weighting or only counting the most recent score, dropping the lowest one or two scores)?

 Available for download as a full-page form at
https://resources.corwin.com/BelongingandInclusionISS

Appendix H

Developmentally Appropriate Conversations About Race and Gender With Children and Youth: Tips for Educators and Parents/Caregivers

Conversations with children and youth about topics of identity, race, and gender are important starting at a young age. At any age, do a lot of listening and let them know why you believe it is important to have the conversation. Ask open-ended questions, use age-appropriate language, and check for understanding. Pay attention to their reactions—notice if they are feeling anxious or frightened. If they come to you after being bullied, teased, or targeted for their race or gender, be ready to not only listen but to support them in standing up for themselves and when necessary, take action to resolve it. Ask them to generate solutions and help them manage their feelings. Offer ways to cope. Try to end every conversation with words of hope and remind them that you are always ready to listen to their questions and ideas and talk with them.

For children under 5 years of age:

- Expose them to people of many backgrounds. Let them see you interact positively.

- Point out how "we are all human and we are all unique and special."

- If they make a comment about differences, reply, "Yes, their skin color is not the same as yours and it's a really nice color, too."

- Get them skin tone crayons, available in 40 different colors.

- It is fine to bring up physical differences before your child does. "This doll has curly hair, that one doesn't; this one has brown eyes, that one doesn't." Treat differences as positive qualities.

- Expose them to people of all gender identities and racial groups and show them people from many backgrounds in a range of different professions.

- Foster empathy, acceptance, and kindness.

- Teach about the importance of treating everyone kindly and fairly. Explain how it is unfair to be mean to someone just because they are different from you.

- Read books and watch videos with diverse characters.

- Help them learn about people who have worked to make fairness and equality for all people.

- Teach them to say words in other languages. Talk about how people learn different languages and knowing more than one language will benefit them.

- Counter negative stereotypes/mean comments in simple language.

- Answer their questions openly.

For children 6–8 years old (all of the above and the following)

- Explain that skin color or the way someone looks or where they come from has nothing to do with being better than someone else.

- Teach them the word *racism* and what it means (e.g., racism is a word that describes treating groups of people badly because it is believed that having different skin color means they aren't as good as others).

- Let kids know that sometimes we make mistakes by saying hurtful things against someone who looks different from us, but it is important to learn from those mistakes and talk about how we can be different for next time.

- Help them develop pride in their own background and learn about their family history.

- Offer regular opportunities to learn about and appreciate other races, cultures, gender differences, religions, and so on.

- Talk about how all people have many things in common and other things that are different, and that makes the world a better place.

- Teach how bullying and mean comments, especially about differences, can be hurtful.

- Discuss how every person is a unique individual with a lot of potential.

- Break down racial and gender stereotypes with concrete examples (e.g., "Telling a girl she cannot run fast is not fair and not true").

- When they have said something racially insensitive (intentionally or not), discuss why it was hurtful. Help them understand we all make mistakes, can be accountable, and try not to make the same mistake again. Help them learn to apologize.

For children ages 9–11 years old (all of the above and the following)

- When they become aware of current events, let them take the lead and encourage questions. When you respond, tell the truth, responding in age-appropriate ways. This is also true when they come to learn about some racist or hate-filled events in history.

- Teach them the meaning of the word *stereotype* and explain how negative stereotyping can hurt others.

- Help them to notice when things in their immediate environment aren't representative of our diverse nation (e.g., schoolbooks, movies, and TV shows have a majority of White characters, history lessons on historical characters are mainly of White characters).

- As they study history (e.g., third graders study Native Americans, fifth graders study slavery/Civil War), hold discussions with them and listen to their questions. Expand beyond the textbooks. Offer counter-narratives with varying perspectives beyond the dominant narrative. Recognize that they may feel sad to learn about the ways people have hated and harmed each other.

- Listen to their feelings and fears. While telling the truth, pay attention to how they may become upset as they hear about bad things happening in the world (e.g., immigrant children separated from their parents and kept in cages). Help them learn about actions being taken to make change.

- As they become aware of current events (e.g., wars, immigration issues, incidents of racism), have discussions with them about the news, letting them take the lead.

- Begin teaching them to combat injustice and explain some of the unfair things that happened to people in different groups (Native American children sent to boarding schools) and ways that people organized to stop racism.

- Teach them to speak up if they see someone being harmed.

For children 12 years old and above (all of the above and the following)

- Give them opportunities to talk about their perceptions of their own identity and help them develop pride at a deeper level.

- Have in-depth conversations around issues of racism, homophobia, and prejudice. If there are questions you cannot answer, use the many resources that are available to help them think critically. (Note: Watch for any extremist views they might pick up from hate groups online.)

- Help them learn to read media reports critically and determine reliable news sources.

- Help them learn to discuss controversial topics and respectfully listen to perspectives that are different from their own.

- Use examples of stereotypes on television to point out bias and dispel myths.

- Point out leaders, efforts, and movements to address inequities and create social justice.

- Teach them how to be upstanders who speak up and stand up for themselves and others when people are mean or unfair.

- Get them involved in activism and community organizations. Find ways they can contribute to create social justice and an equitable society.

(Adapted from Corridan & Medina, *Parent's Magazine*, https://www.parents.com/parenting/better-parenting/teaching-tolerance/talking-about-race-with-kids/ and Dhalia Balmir of https://www.balmirinclusive.com/)

 Available for download as a full-page form at
https://resources.corwin.com/BelongingandInclusionISS

Appendix I

Grades 3–5 Student Identity Safe Classroom Survey

Name: (optional)_____

Grade:_____

Instructions: Please complete this survey. Add additional comments below.

STUDENT: LEVEL OF FREQUENCY RATING FOR EACH ELEMENT		DISAGREE	AGREE	STRONGLY AGREE
1	I feel culturally included and respected in this class.			
2	My teacher is interested and respectful of my culture.			
3	My teacher intervenes right away if stereotyping or bias occurs in the classroom.			
4	My teacher notices and takes responsibility if their words or actions felt harmful to a student.			
5	My teacher has faith in me and believes that I can achieve to high standards.			
6	My teacher seems to know if something is bothering me.			
7	In this class, students get to know each other in a real way.			
8	My teacher in this class makes me feel they really care about me.			

9	We learn how to see and respect different perspectives in this class.			
10	In this class, my teacher accepts nothing less than our full effort.			
11	We talk about race and culture in this class.			
12	Students collaborate well together in this class.			
13	I have opportunities to get to know my teacher as a person.			
14	In this class, students talk respectfully about race, gender, and other parts of identity.			
15	I can be my full self in this class.			
16	My teacher really tries to understand how students feel about things.			
17	Students in this class treat the teacher with respect.			
18	Students in this class treat each other with respect.			
19	My teacher wants us to share our thoughts.			
20	Students speak up and share their ideas about class work.			
21	My teacher respects my ideas and suggestions.			
22	This class helps me develop positive mindsets and habits.			
23	I get to explore aspects of my identity in this class.			
24	This class helps me build positive social and communication skills.			
25	This teacher does not tolerate racism or any kind of oppressive behavior in class.			
26	If you don't understand something, my teacher explains it another way.			
27	My teacher knows when the class understands and when we do not.			
28	My teacher doesn't let people give up when the work gets hard.			

(Continued)

(Continued)

STUDENT: LEVEL OF FREQUENCY RATING FOR EACH ELEMENT		DISAGREE	AGREE	STRONGLY AGREE
29	My teacher wants me to explain my answers—why I think what I think.			
30	In this class, we learn to correct our mistakes.			
31	My teacher takes the time to summarize what we learn each day.			
32	My teacher checks to make sure we understand what they are teaching us.			
33	We get helpful comments to let us know what we can improve on assignments.			
34	The comments that I get on my work in this class help me understand how to improve.			
35	My teacher takes the time to summarize what we learn each day.			

Make additional comments here:

online resources ⬉ Available for download as a full-page form at **https://resources.corwin.com/BelongingandInclusionISS**

Appendix J

Grades 6–12 Student Identity Safe Classroom Survey

Name: (optional)_____

Grade:_____

Instructions: Please complete this survey. Add additional comments below.

STUDENT: LEVEL OF FREQUENCY RATING FOR EACH ELEMENT		NEVER	RARELY	SOMETIMES	ALWAYS
1	I feel culturally included and respected in this class.				
2	My teacher is interested and respectful of my culture.				
3	My teacher intervenes right away if stereotyping or bias occurs in the classroom.				
4	My teacher notices and takes responsibility if their words or actions felt harmful to a student.				
5	My teacher has faith in me and believes that I can achieve to high standards.				
6	My teacher seems to know if something is bothering me.				

(Continued)

(Continued)

STUDENT: LEVEL OF FREQUENCY RATING FOR EACH ELEMENT		NEVER	RARELY	SOMETIMES	ALWAYS
7	In this class, students get to know each other in a real way.				
8	My teacher in this class makes me feel they really care about me.				
9	We learn how to see and respect different perspectives in this class.				
10	In this class, my teacher accepts nothing less than our full effort.				
11	We talk about race and culture in this class.				
12	Students collaborate well together in this class.				
13	I have opportunities to get to know my teacher as a person.				
14	In this class, students talk respectfully about race, gender, and other parts of identity.				
15	I can be my full self in this class.				
16	My teacher really tries to understand how students feel about things.				
17	Students in this class treat the teacher with respect.				
18	Students in this class treat each other with respect.				
19	My teacher wants us to share our thoughts.				
20	Students speak up and share their ideas about class work.				
21	My teacher respects my ideas and suggestions.				
22	This class helps me develop positive mindsets and habits.				
23	I get to explore aspects of my identity in this class.				
24	This class helps me build positive social and communication skills.				

25	This teacher does not tolerate racism or any kind of oppressive behavior in class.				
26	If you don't understand something, my teacher explains it another way.				
27	My teacher knows when the class understands and when we do not.				
28	My teacher doesn't let people give up when the work gets hard.				
29	My teacher wants me to explain my answers—why I think what I think.				
30	In this class, we learn to correct our mistakes.				
31	My teacher takes the time to summarize what we learn each day.				
32	My teacher checks to make sure we understand what they are teaching us.				
33	We get helpful comments to let us know what we can improve on assignments.				
34	The comments that I get on my work in this class help me understand how to improve.				
35	My teacher takes the time to summarize what we learn each day.				

Make additional comments here:

Appendix K

Identity Safe Signature Strategies Spreadsheet

The spreadsheet can be found on the Corwin Belonging and Inclusion in Identity Safe Schools resource page found at https://resources.corwin.com/Belongingand InclusionISS. Strategies are listed and described, explaining the connection with identity safe practices. Identity safe teaching is not a program, nor is it a checklist of strategies. These strategies are provided to offer ideas for implementation. There are many additional effective strategies that address these components.

References

Aaronson, A. E. (2020). Uncomfortable conversations with a black man [Video file]. Retrieved from https://uncomfortableconvos.com/

Aguilar, E. (2013). *The art of coaching*. San Francisco, CA: Jossey-Bass.

Aguilar, E. (2014, December 11). A powerful tool to help us learn. *Edutopia*, https://www.edutopia.org/blog/setting-intentions-powerful-tool-help-us-learn-elena-aguilar

Aguilar, E. (2018). *Onward: Cultivating emotional resilience in educators*. San Francisco, CA: Jossey-Bass.

Amels, J., Krüger, M., Suhre, C., & van Veen, K. (2019). Impact of inquiry-based working on the capacity to change in primary education. *Journal of Education Change, 20*, 351–374. https://link.springer.com/article/10.1007/s10833-019-09337-3

Assessment for Learning. (n.d.). https://www.assessmentforlearningproject.org/

Astor, M. (2020). Kamala Harris and the "double bind" of racism and sexism. *New York Times*, https://www.nytimes.com/2020/10/09/us/politics/kamala-harris-racism-sexism.html

Banks, J. (2005). *The history of multicultural education*. Diversity Lecture Series. Stanford, CA: Stanford University.

Baum, F., MacDougall, C., & Smith, D. (2006). Participatory action research. *Journal of Epidemiology and Community Health, 60*(10), 854–857. https://www.ncbi.nlm.nih.gov/pmc/articles/PMC2566051/

Baum, J., & Westheimer, K. (2015). Sex? Sexual orientation? Gender identity? Gender expression? *Teaching Tolerance Magazine, 50*.

Belanca, J., & Brandt, R. (2010). *21st century skills: Rethinking how students learn.* Bloomington, IN: Solution Tree Press.

Beloved Community. (n.d.). Our approach. https://www.wearebeloved.org/our-approach

Bergman, D. (2020). Does being a "legacy" increase your admission odds? *College Transitions,* https://www.collegetransitions.com/blog/college-legacy/

Berry, B., Daughtrey, A., & Wieder, A. (2009, December). Collaboration: Closing the effective teaching gap. *Center for Teaching Quality,* https://files.eric.ed.gov/fulltext/ED509717.pdf

Bivens, D. (2005). What is internalized racism? In M. Potapchuk & S. Leiderman, *Flipping the script: White privilege and community building* (pp. 43–52). https://www.racialequitytools.org/resourcefiles/potapchuk1.pdf

Blankstein, A. M. (2004). *Failure is not an option: Six principles that guide student achievement in high-performing schools.* Thousand Oaks, CA: Sage.

Blankstein, A. M., Noguera, P., & Kelly, L. (2015). *Excellence through equity: Five principles of courageous leadership to guide achievement for every student.* Alexandria, VA: ASCD.

Bogotch, I., & Shields, C. (2014). Introduction: Do promises of social justice trump paradigms of educational leadership? In I. Bogotch & C. Shields (Eds.), *International handbook of educational leadership and social (In)justice* (Vol. 1, pp. 1–12). Dordrecht, The Netherlands: Springer.

Briceño, E. (2017). *How to get better at the things you care about* [Video]. TED Conferences. https://www.ted.com/talks/eduardo_briceno_how_to_get_better_at_the_things_you_care_about

Briceño, E. (2018). *Personal interview.* Leadership Public Schools.

Brown, A. M. (2017). Living through the unveiling. http://adriennemareebrown.net/2017/02/03/living-through-the-unveiling/

Brown, R. T., Reynolds, C. R., & Whitaker, J. S. (1999). Bias in mental testing since Bias in Mental Testing. *School Psychology Quarterly, 14*(3), 208–238. https://doi.org/10.1037/h0089007

Brown, T., Tanner-Smith, E., & Lesane-Brown, C. (2007). Child, parent, and situational correlates of familial ethnic/race socialization. *Journal of Marriage and Family, 69*(1), 14–25. https://doi.org/10.1111/j.1741-3737.2006.00340.x

Butler, S. (2014). *Cracking the codes: The system of racial inequality* [Video]. New York, NY: World Trust Educational Services.

Camera, L. (2020). Black teachers improve outcomes for Black students. *US News & World Report*, https://www.usnews.com/news/education-news/articles/2018-11-23/black-teachers-improve-outcomes-for-black-students

Centers for Disease Control and Prevention (CDC). (n.d.). About the Kaiser Adverse Childhood Experiences (ACE) Study. https://www.cdc.gov/violenceprevention/aces/about.html? CDC_AA_refVal=https%3A%2F%2Fwww.cdc.gov%2Fviolenceprevention%2Facestudy%2Fabout.html

Choi, Y. W. (2020). How to address racial bias in standardized testing. *Reimagining Assessment.* https://www.nextgenlearning.org/articles/racial-bias-standardized-testing

Clark, D., & Williamson, S. (2018, May 15). 3 ways our district avoids data overload. https://www.eschoolnews.com/2018/05/15/3-ways-our-district-avoids-data-overload/

Cohn-Vargas, B. (2016). *NIOS identity safe and inclusive school program.* Oakland, CA: Not In Our Town, a Project of the Working Group.

Cohn-Vargas, B. (2017). Teaching from the bulls-eye. *Teaching Tolerance, 57.* https://www.tolerance.org/magazine/fall-2017/teaching-from-the-bullseye

Cohn-Vargas, B., & Gross, K. (1998, May). A partnership for literacy. *Engaging Parents and the Community in Schools, 55*(8), 45–48.

Cohn-Vargas, B., Kahn, A. C., & Epstein, A. (2020). *Identity safe classrooms grades 6–12: Pathways to belonging and learning.* Thousand Oaks, CA: Corwin.

Cohn-Vargas, B., & Zacarian, D. (2020, May 20). Strengthening the spirits of community partnership. *Share My Lesson,* https://sharemylesson.com/blog/community-partnership

Comer, J. P. (2005). Childhood and adolescent development: The critical missing focus in school reform. *Phi Delta Kappan.* https://doi.org/10.1177/003172170508601008

Cushman, K. (1999). The cycle of inquiry and action: Essential learning communities. *Horace, 15*(4). http://essentialschools.org/horace-issues/the-cycle-of-inquiry-and-action-essential-learning-communities/

Darling-Hammond, L. (1997). *The right to learn: A blueprint for creating schools that work.* San Fancisco, CA: Jossey-Bass.

Darling-Hammond, L., & Cook-Harvey, C. (2018). *Educating the whole child: Improving school climate to support student success.* Leadership Policy Institute. Retrieved from https://learningpolicyinstitute.org/product/educating-whole-child-brief

Darling-Hammond, L., & George, J. (2020). *How will each of us contribute to racial justice and educational equity now?* Palo Alto, CA: Learning Policy Institute. https://learningpolicyinstitute.org/blog/racial-justice-educational-equity

Delgado Bernal, D. (2002). Critical race theory, Latino critical theory, and critical raced-gendered epistemologies: Recognizing students of color as holders and creators of knowledge. *Qualitative Inquiry,* https://doi.org/10.1177/107780040200800107

Delpit, L. (1995). *Other people's children.* New York, NY: The New Press.

Deutsch, M. (1992). *The effects of training in conflict resolution and cooperative learning in an alternative high school: Summary report.* New York, NY: International Center for Cooperation and Conflict Resolution.

DiAngelo, R. (2018). *White fragility: Why it's so hard for white people to talk about racism.* Boston, MA: Beacon Press.

Dudley-Marling, C., & Dudley-Marling, A. (2015). Inclusive leadership and poverty. In G. Theoharis & M. K. Scanlan (Eds.), *Leadership for increasingly diverse schools.* New York, NY: Routledge.

Dusek, J. B., & Joseph, G. (1983). The bases of teacher expectancies: A meta-analysis. *Journal of Educational Psychology, 75,* 327. http://doi.org/10.1037/0022-0663.75.3.327

Dweck, C. (2006). *Mindset: The new psychology of success.* New York, NY: Random House.

Emdin, C. (2016, May 2). Christopher Emdin's thoughts on transformative pedagogy for National Teacher Appreciation Week. https://www.beaconbroadside.com/broadside/2016/05/christopher-emdins-thoughts-on-transformative-pedagogy-for-national-teacher-appreciation-week.html

Epstein, J. L., Simon, B. S., & Salinas, K. C. (1997). Involving parents/caregivers in homework in the middle grades. *Research Bulletin,* No. 18, Phi Delta Kappan/Center for Evaluation, Development and Research.

Equity Literacy Institute. (n.d.). About equity literacy. https://www.equityliteracy.org/equity-literacy

Esensten, A. (2020, July 9). Black Jewish educator advocates for more inclusive classrooms. Retrieved from https://www.myjewishlearning.com/jewish-and/black-jewish-educator-advocates-for-more-inclusive-classrooms/?fbclid=IwAR0u4KM6cwRJflIqownFWx3LRXA14kYZyfiYWrHOdND6t-8GIAEz8sf9cQiE

Everyday Democracy. (2008). A guide for training public dialogue facilitators. Retrieved from http://www.everyday-democracy.org/en/Resource.106.aspx

Feldman, J. (2018). *Grading for equity: What it is, why it matters, and how it can transform schools and classrooms.* Thousand Oaks, CA: Corwin.

Flores-González, N. (1999). Puerto Rican high achievers: An example of ethnic and academic identity compatibility. *Anthropology & Education Quarterly, 30,* 343–362. http://doi.org/10.1525/aeq.1999.30.3.343

Freire, P. (1972). *Pedagogy of the oppressed.* New York, NY: Penguin Books.

Fronius, T., Darling-Hammond, S., Persson, H., Guckenburg, S., Hurley, N., & Petrosino, A. (2019). Restorative justice in US schools: An updated research review. *West Ed Justice and Review Center.* https://www.wested.org/wp-content/uploads/2019/04/resource-restorative-justice-in-u-s-schools-an-updated-research-review.pdf

Fryberg, S. (2016). Creating identity safe spaces: Seattle jobs initiative 2016 conference [Video]. https://www.youtube.com/watch? v=65LT8pwD8xk

Fullan, M. (2001). *Leading in a culture of change.* San Francisco, CA: Jossey-Bass.

Gaertner, S. L., & Dovidio, J. F. (2000). *Reducing intergroup bias: The common in-group identity model.* New York: Routledge.

Gannon, M. (2016). Race is a social construct, scientists argue. *Scientific American,* https://www.scientificamerican.com/article/race-is-a-social-construct-scientists-argue/

Gates, E. (2019). Beyond blackface. *Virginia,* Summer 2019. *https://uvamagazine.org/articles/beyond_blackface*

Gierl, M. J., & Khaliq, S. N. (2001). Identifying sources of differential item and bundle functioning on translated achievement tests: A confirmatory analysis. *Journal of Educational Measurement, 38*(2), 164–187.

Gonzalez, J. (2017, March 12). Four ways teachers can support students of color: An interview of Dena Simmons. *Cult of Pedagogy,* https://www.cultofpedagogy.com/students-of-color/

Good, T. L. (1981). Teacher expectations and student perceptions: A decade of work. Alexandria, VA: ASCD.

Google. (n.d.-a). Blackface on college campuses. https://www.google.com/search?safe=active&sxsrf=ALeKk0101zcVU7MnI3h6TYoTtijVqeD2Hw%3A1606847502500&ei=DozGX5-GHpX9-gT50aT4CQ&q=blackface+on+college+campus&oq=blackface+on+college+campus&gs_lcp=CgZwc3ktYWIQDDoECCMQJ1DnE1jbPWCnTGgAcAB4AIABgQOIAdsQkgEIMTEuMi4zLjGYAQCgAQGqAQdnd3Mtd2l6wAEB&sclient=psy-ab&ved=0ahUKEwifxeC0ta3tAhWVvp4KHfkoCZ8Q4dUDCA0

Google. (n.d.-b). Blackface on high school campuses. https://www.google.com/search?safe=active&sxsrf=ALeKk03igxTgoRczvGhem-McIOCkcFfQPA%3A1606847687292&ei=x4zGX-yrEdLj-gSeyY74AQ&q=blackface+at+high+school&oq=blackface+at+high+school&gs_lcp=CgZwc3ktYWIQARgAMgQIIxAnMgYIABAWEB4yBggAEBYQHjIGCAAQFhAeMgYIABAWEB4yBggAEBYQHjIGCAAQFhAeMgYIABAWEB4yBggAEBYQHjIGCAAQFhAeOgIIADoJCAAQyQMQFhAeUOS9Dlilzg5gl-wOaABwAHgAgAGQAYgBqwmSAQQxMC4zmAEAoAEBqgEHZ3d3LXdpesABAQ&sclient=psy-ab

Gordon, M. F., & Louis, K. S. (2009). Linking parent/caregiver and community involvement with student achievement: Comparing principal and teacher perceptions of stakeholder influence. *American Journal of Education, 116*(1), 1–31. https://doi.org/10.1086/605098

Greater Good Science Center. (n.d.). Compassion: Defined. https://greatergood.berkeley.edu/topic/compassion/definition

Grindal, T., Schifter, L., Schwartz, G., & Hehir, T. (2019). Racial differences in special education identification and placement: Evidence across three states. *Harvard Education Review, 89*(4), 525–553.

Grolnick, W. S. (2015). Mothers' motivation for involvement in their children's schooling: Mechanisms and outcomes. *Motivation and Emotion, 39*(1), 63–73. https://doi.org/10.1007/s11031-014-9423-4

Gutierrez, K., & Rogoff, B. (2003). Cultural ways of learning: Individual traits or repertoires of practice. *Educational Researcher, 34*(5), 19–25.

Hagerman, M. A. (2018, September 4). Why white parents need to do more than talk to their kids about racism. *Time,* https://time.com/5362786/talking-racism-with-white-kids-not-enough/

Hamoudi, A., Murray, D., Sorensen, L., & Fontaine, A. (2015). Self-regulation and toxic stress: A review of ecological, biological, and developmental studies of self-regulation and stress. Center for Child and Family Policy, Duke University. Retrieved from https://www.acf.hhs.gov/opre/resource/self-regulation-and-toxic-stress-a-review-of-ecological-biological-and-developmental-studies-of-self-regulation-and-stress

Harry, B., & Anderson, M. G. (1994). The disproportionate placement of African American males in special education programs. A critique of the process. *Journal of Negro Education*, *63*(4), 602–620.

Harvard Center on the Developing Child. (n.d.). Learning communities. https://devhcdc.wpengine.com/collective-change/key-concepts/learning-communities

Hattie, J. (2017, November). Visible Learning 250+ influences on student achievement. https://visible-learning.org/wp-content/uploads/2018/03/VLPLUS-252-Influences-Hattie-ranking-DEC-2017.pdf

Hawaii Department of Education. (n.d.). Nā Hopena Aʻo (HĀ). https://tinyurl.com/HAHawaii

Hébert, T. P., & Reis, S. M. (1999). Culturally diverse high-achieving students in an urban high school. *Urban Education*, *34*, 428–457. https://doi.org/10.1177/0042085999344002

Heitlin Loewus, L. (2015, November). Should formative assessment be graded? *Ed Week*, https://www.edweek.org/teaching-learning/should-formative-assessments-be-graded/2015/11

Helms, J. E. (1992). *A race is a nice thing to have: A guide to being a white person or understanding the white persons in your life*. Topeka, KS: Content Communications.

Henderson, A. T., & Mapp, K. L. (2002). *A new wave of evidence: The impact of school, family, and community connections on student achievement*. Austin, TX: Southwest Educational Development Laboratory. Retrieved from https://eric.ed.gov/?id=ED474521

Hilliard, A. (2003). No mystery: Closing the achievement gap between Africans and excellence. In T. Perry, C. Steele, & A. Hilliard (Eds.), *Young, gifted, and Black: Promoting high achievement among African–American students* (pp. 131–166). Boston, MA: Beacon Press.

Hofstede, G. (1980). *Culture's consequences: International differences in work-related values*. Beverly Hills, CA: Sage.

Hofstede, G. (1991). *Cultures and organizations: Software of the mind*. London, UK: McGraw-Hill.

Horng, E., Klasik, D., & Loeb, S. (2009). Principal time-use and school effectiveness. In Institute for Research on Education Policy & Practice (Ed.), *School leadership research report* (Vol. 09-3). Stanford, CA: Stanford University.

Humanitas. (n.d.). Our vision and mission. http://www.sjhumanitas.org/about-us/our-vision-and-mission/

Identity Safe Classrooms. (n.d.). http://www.identitysafeclassrooms.com/

Interaction Associates. (2019). Facilitative leadership: Balancing the dimensions of success. *Interaction Associates*. Retrieved from http://interactionassociates.com/insights/blog/facilitative-leadership-balancing-dimensions-success#.XMiWqpNKhTY

Interfaith Community Services. (2020). *On the front lines: 2020 annual report*. Retrieved from https://www.interfaithservices.org/2020-annual-report/

Johnson, D. W., Johnson, R., Dudley, B., & Acikgoz, K. (1994). Effects of conflict resolution training on elementary school students. *The Journal of Social Psychology, 134*(6), 803–817.

Jones, S. (2020). If you're serious about equity, prove it by including leaders of color at your school. *Education Post*. https://educationpost.org/if-youre-serious-about-equity-prove-it-by-including-leaders-of-color-at-your-school/

Juvonen, J., Kogachi, K., & Graham, K. (2017). When and how do students benefit from ethnic diversity in middle school? *Child Development*. https://doi.org/10.1111/cdev.12834

Kahn, A. C., & Epstein, A. (2019). Equitable data inquiry participants guide. https://tinyurl.com/EquitData

Katz, P. A., & Kofkin, J. A. (1997). Race, gender, and young children. In S. S. Luthar & J. A. Burack (Eds.), *Developmental psychopathology: Perspectives on adjustment, risk, and disorder* (pp. 51–74). New York, NY: Cambridge University Press.

Kendi, I. X. (2019). *How to be an anti-racist*. New York, NY: Random House.

King, J. (2020). Restarting and reinventing school for equitable and empowering learning. Learning Policy Institute Webinar. Retrieved from https://learning-policyinstitute.org/event/webinar-restarting-reinventing-school-equitable-empowering-learning

Knips, A. (2019). Six steps to equitable data analysis. *Edutopia*, https://www.edutopia.org/article/6-steps-equitable-data-analysis

Knowles, M. (1973). *The adult learner: A neglected species.* Houston, TX: Gulf Publishing Company.

Kouzes, J. M., & Posner, B. Z. (2002). *Leadership, the challenge* (3rd ed.). San Francisco, CA: Jossey-Bass.

Kozol, J. (2005). *Shame of a nation: Apartheid schooling in America.* New York, NY: Crown Publishers.

Kruse, A. J. (2016). Cultural bias in testing: A review of literature and implications for music education. *Update: Applications of Research in Music Education*, *35*(1), 23–31.

Ladson-Billings, G. (1994). *Dreamkeepers: Successful teachers of African-American children*. San Francisco, CA: Jossey-Bass.

Ladson-Billings, G. (1999). Just what is critical race theory, and what's it doing in a nice field like education? In L. Parker, D. Deyhle, & S. Villenas (Eds.), *Race is . . . race isn't: Critical race theory and qualitative studies in education.* Boulder, CO: Westview Press.

Leadership Challenge. (n.d.). The five practices of Exemplary Leadership model. Leadership Challenge.com, https://www.leadershipchallenge.com/research/five-practices.aspx

Lee, V. E., Winfield, L. F., & Wilson, T. C. (1991). Academic behaviors among high achieving African-American students. *Education and Urban Society*, *24*, 65–86. https://doi.org10.1177/0013124591024001006

Leithwood, K., Seashore Louis, K., Anderson, S., & Wahlstrom, K. (2004). A review of research: How leadership influences student learning. *Learning from Leadership Project*. Wallace Foundation, https://www.wallacefoundation.org/knowledge-center/pages/how-leadership-influences-student-learning.aspx

Lewis, A. E. (2003). *Race in the schoolyard: Negotiating the color line in classrooms and communities*. New Brunswick, NJ: Rutgers University Press.

Lieberman, A., Saxl, E. R, & Miles, M. B. (2000). Teacher leadership: Ideology and practice. In *The Jossey-Bass reader on educational leadership* (pp. 348–365). San Francisco, CA: Jossey-Bass.

Lightfoot, S. L. (1978). *Worlds apart: Relationships between families and schools.* New York, NY: Basic Books.

Lindsey, R., Robbins, K. N., & Terrell, R. D. (1999). *Cultural proficiency: A manual for school leaders.* Thousand Oaks, CA: Sage.

Love, B. (2019). *We want to do more than survive: Abolitionist teaching and the pursuit of educational freedom.* Boston, MA: Beacon Press.

Love, B., & Mohammed, G. (2017). Critical community conversations: Cultivating the elusive dialogue about racism with parents, community members, and teachers. *Phi Delta Kappan.* https://bettinalove.com/wp-content/uploads/2018/09/Critical-Community-Conversations-Cultivating-the-Elusive-Dialogue-About-Racism-With-Parents-Community-Members-and-Teachers-.pdf

LPS Student Interviews. (2018). *LPS student interviews.* Leadership Public Schools.

Marzano, R. J. (2008). *Classroom assessment & grading that work.* Alexandria, VA: ASCD.

McIntyre, R. B., Paulson, R. M., & Lord, C. G. (2003). Alleviating women's mathematics stereotype threat through salience of group achievements. *Journal of Experimental Social Psychology, 39,* 83–90.

Menakem, R. (2017). *My grandmother's hands: Racialized trauma and the pathway to mending our hearts and bodies.* Las Vegas, NV: Central Recovery Press.

Merriam-Webster. (n.d.). They. In *Merriam-Webster.com dictionary.* Retrieved from https://www.merriam-webster.com/dictionary/they

Milner, H. R. (2017, September). Confronting inequity/building community knowledge. *Educational Leadership, 75*(1), 88–89. http://www.ascd.org/publications/educational-leadership/sept17/vol75/num01/Building-Community-Knowledge.aspx

Modan, N. (2020). Survey: Superintendents still overwhelmingly white, male. American Association of School Superintendents, https://www.k12dive.com/news/survey-superintendents-still-overwhelmingly-white-male/572008/

Mohammed, A., & Sharroky, H. (2011). *The will to lead, the skill to teach.* Bloomington, IN: The Solution Tree.

Monroe, L. (1997). *Nothing's impossible: Leadership lessons from inside and outside the classroom*. New York, NY: Public Affairs, a member of the Perseus Group.

Murphy, J. T. (2000). The unheroic side of leadership. In *The Jossey-Bass reader on educational leadership*. San Francisco, CA: Jossey-Bass.

Murray, D. W., Rosanbalm, K., & Christopoulos, C. (2016). Self-regulation and toxic stress: Implications for programs and practice. Center for Child and Family Policy, Duke University. Retrieved from https://fpg.unc.edu/sites/fpg.unc.edu/files/resources/reports-and-policy-briefs/SelfRegulationReport4.pdf

Nakashima D. J., & Roué, M. (2002). Indigenous knowledge, peoples and sustainable practice. In P. Timmerman (Ed.), *Encyclopedia of global environmental change* (Vol. 5, pp. 314–324). Chichester, UK: John Wiley & Sons.

National Center on Educational Outcomes (NCEO). (2016). Universal design of assessments: Overview. https://nceo.info/Assessments/universal_design/overview

Neff, K. (2020). 5 myths of self compassion. *Greater Good Science Center*, https://centerformsc.org/5-myths-of-self-compassion/

Nieto, S. (1998). *Affirmation, solidarity and critique: Moving beyond tolerance in education*. Washington, DC: Network of Educators on the Americas.

Noguera, P. (2003). *City schools and the American dream*. New York, NY: Teachers College Press.

Noguera, P. (2017). *Taking deeper learning to scale*. Palo Alto, CA: Learning Policy Institute. https://learningpolicyinstitute.org/sites/default/files/product-files/Taking_Deeper_Learning_Scale_REPORT.pdf

Not In Our Town. (2014). *Leaving a positive footprint*. Video. https://www.niot.org/nios-video/leaving-positive-footprint

Oakland Unified School District. (n.d.-a). Yemen: Global, Local, Household: Additional resources for learning about Yemen & Yemeni-Americans. https://www.ousd.org/cms/lib/CA01001176/Centricity/Domain/4900/Yemen%20Resources.pdf

Oakland Unified School District. (n.d.-b). African American male achievement. https://www.ousd.org/Page/12804

Ondracek, N., & Flook, L. (2018). How to help all students feel safe to be themselves. *Greater Good Science Center*, https://greatergood.berkeley.edu/article/item/how_to_help_all_students_feel_safe_to_be_themselves

Ondrasek, N., & Flook, L. (2020). How to help all students feel safe to be themselves. *Greater Good Science Center*, https://greatergood.berkeley.edu/article/item/how_to_help_all_students_feel_safe_to_be_themselves

O'Neil, J. (1996). *Leadership aikido: 6 business practices to turn around your life*. New York, NY: Harmony Books.

Orange, T. (2018). *There there: A novel*. New York, NY: Alfred A. Knopf.

Osta, K. (2020). Targeted universalism: Our path forward. *Medium*, https://medium.com/national-equity-project/targeted-universalism-our-path-forward-3dffc921d198

Othering and Belonging Institute. (n.d.). https://belonging.berkeley.edu/targeteduniversalism

Paddington Teaching and Learning. (2013). What works best? John Hattie, effect size "visible learning." https://paddingtonteachingandlearning.files.wordpress.com/2013/02/what-works-best-summary.pdf

Paley, V. G. (1979). *White teacher*. Cambridge, MA: Harvard University Press.

Park, S., Hironaka, S., Carver, P., & Nordstrum, L. (2013). Continuous improvement in education. *Carnegie Foundation for the Advancement of Teaching*. https://www.carnegiefoundation.org/wp-content/uploads/2014/09/carnegie-foundation_continuous-improvement_2013.05.pdf

Peck, R. (2016). *I am not your negro*. Magnolia Pictures.

Peters, W. (Director). (1985, March 26). *A class divided* [TV series episode]. *Frontline Films*. *Frontline* Season 3, Episode 9. Available at https://www.pbs.org/video/frontline-class-divided/

powell, j., & Menendian, S. (2016). The problem of othering: Towards inclusiveness and belonging othering and belonging. *Othering & Belonging*, *1*(Summer 2016), 14–39. Retrieved from https://otheringandbelonging.org/wp-content/uploads/2016/07/OtheringAndBelonging_Issue1.pdf

Project Implicit. (n.d.). Preliminary information. https://implicit.harvard.edu/implicit/takeatest.html

Purdie-Vaughns, V., Steele, C. M., Davies, P. G., Ditlmann, R., & Crosby, J. R. (2008). Social identity contingencies: How diversity cues signal threat or safety for African Americans in mainstream institutions. *Journal of Personality and Social Psychology*, *94*, 615–630.

Quillian, L., Pager, D., Midtbøen, A. H., & Hexel, O. (2017, October 11). Hiring discrimination against black Americans hasn't declined in 25 years. *Harvard Business Review*, https://hbr.org/2017/10/hiring-discrimination-against-black-americans-hasnt-declined-in-25-years? utm_medium=email&utm_source=newsletter_weekly&utm_campaign=insider&referral=03551&spMailingID=18281110&spUserID=ODQ5NzQ5OTM3NgS2&spJobID=1120833791&spReportId=MTEyMDgzMzc5MQS2

Rodriguez, L. J. (2005). *Always running: La vida loca: Gang days in L. A.* New York, NY: Touchstone.

Rong, X. L. (1996). Effects of race and gender on teachers' perception of the social behavior of elementary students. *Urban Education*, *31*, 261–290. https://doi.org/10.1177/0042085996031003003

Russell, T. (2020, June 3). How black and white families talk about race. *Washington Post*, https://www.washingtonpost.com/lifestyle/2020/06/03/how-do-families-talk-about-racism-with-their-kids/

Sackstein, S. (2018, December). Earning good grades versus learning. *EdWeek*.

Saphier, J. & King, M. (1985). Good seeds grow in strong cultures. *ASCK*, http://www.ascd.org/ASCD/pdf/journals/ed_lead/el_198503_saphier.pdf

Schmoker, M. J. (2011). *Focus: Elevating the essentials to radically improve student learning*. Alexandria, VA: ASCD.

Senge, P. M. (2000). Give me a lever long enough . . . and single-handed I can move the world. In J. Bass (Ed.), *The Jossey-Bass reader on educational leadership* (pp. 13–25). San Francisco, CA: John Wiley & Sons.

Shakman, K., Bailey, J., & Breslow, N. (2017). A primer for continuous improvement in schools and districts. *Education Development Center*, https://www.edcorg/sites/default/files/uploads/primer_for_continuous_improvement.pdf

Society for Research in Child Development. (2013, September 24). Cross-ethnic friendships in urban middle schools make youths feel less vulnerable, safer. https://www.eurekalert.org/pub_releases/2013-09/sfri-cfi091713.php

Sparks, S. (2020). Training bias out of teachers: Research shows little promise so far. *Education Week*, https://www.edweek.org/leadership/training-bias-out-of-teachers-research-shows-little-promise-so-far/2020/11

Steele, C. M. (1999). Thin ice: "Stereotype threat" and black college students. *The Atlantic Monthly, 284*(2), 44–47, 50–54. Retrieved from https://www.theatlantic.com/magazine/archive/1999/08/thin-ice-stereotype-threat-and-black-college-students/304663/

Steele, C. M. (2011). *Whistling Vivaldi: How stereotypes affect us and what we can do.* New York, NY: W. W. Norton & Company.

Steele, D. M. (2012). Creating identity safe classrooms. In J. A. Banks (Ed.), *Encyclopedia of diversity in education* (Vol. 1, pp. 1125–1128). Thousand Oaks, CA: Sage.

Steele, D. M., & Cohn-Vargas, B. (2013). *Identity safe classrooms grades K–5: Places to belong and learn.* Thousand Oaks, CA: Corwin.

Steele, D. M., & Cohn-Vargas, B. (2016). Creating identity safe classroom environments. *Illinois Reading Council Journal, 44*(3).

Test bias (2015)The glossary of education reform, Great Schools Partnership https://tinyurl.com/edtestbias

Theory of Change. (n.d.). Center for Theory of Change, https://www.theoryofchange.org/

Townsend, B. (2000). The disproportionate discipline of African American learners: Reducing school suspensions and expulsion. *Exceptional Children, 66,* 381–392. https://journals.sagepub.com/doi/abs/10.1177/001440290006600308

Ubben, G. C., Hughes, L. W., & Norris, C. J. (2011). *The principal: Creative leadership for excellence in schools* (7th ed., p. 302). Upper Saddle River, NJ: Pearson Education.

Uiterwijk-Luijk, L., Krüger, M., Zijlstra, B., & Volman, M. (2017). The relationship between psychological factors and inquiry-based working by primary school teachers. *Educational Studies, 43,* 147–164.

University of California (2016). *Smart goals: A how-to guide.* https://tinyurl.com/GetSMARTGoals

Villenas, C., & Zelinski, S. (2018). *Creating school communities of courage: Lesson from the field.* New York, NY: NSCC. Retrieved from https://www.schoolclimate.org/themes/schoolclimate/assets/pdf/NSCC%20Lessons%20from%20the%20Field.pdf

Walsh, M. B., Hancock, M., Bowser, M., Breed, L, Durkan, J. Lightfoot, . . . & Sweet, P. (2020). 27 US mayors want to address systemic racism? Start with housing. *Washington Post*, https://www.washingtonpost.com/opinions/2020/07/24/27-us-mayors-want-address-systemic-racism-start-with-housing/

Wasserman, D. L., Sabater, A., & Hill, F. (2017). Strengthening families: The Journey Project model for engaging low-income black families in children's education. *Black Child Journal, Education and the Black Child*, (Summer). Retrieved from http://nropi.org/books/

Wasserman, D. L., & Sabater, A. (2018). Toward authentic family engagement with counter-narrative and self-determination. *Journal of Underrepresented and Minority Progress*, 2(1), 32–43. https://doi.org/10.5281/zenodo.1322158

Waters, A., & Asbill, L. (2013, August). Reflections on cultural humility. American Psychological Association, *CYF News*, https://www.apa.org/pi/families/resources/newsletter/2013/08/cultural-humility

W. Edwards Deming Institute. (n.d.). The PDSA cycle. https://deming.org/explore/pdsa/

Wells, A., Fox, L., & Cordova-Cobo, D. (2016). *How racially diverse schools and classrooms can benefit all students*. The Century Foundation Report. Retrieved from https://tcf.org/content/report/how-racially-diverse-schools-and-classrooms-can-benefit-all-students/?agreed=1

Werner, E. (1995, June). Resilience in development. *Current Directions in Psychological Science*, 4(3). https://doi.org/10.1111/1467-8721.ep10772327

Whaley, A. L., & Smyer, D. A. (1998). Self-evaluation process of African American youth in high school completion program. *Journal of Psychology: Interdisciplinary & Applied*, 132(3), 317–327.

Wheatley, M. (n.d.). Leadership and the new science. Retrieved from https://margaretwheatley.com/books-products/books/leadership-new-science/

Wheatley, M. (2000). Goodbye command and control. In Jossey-Bass (Ed.), *The Jossey-Bass reader on educational leadership*. San Francisco, CA: Jossey-Bass.

Williams, D. (2016). Everyday Racism Scale. https://scholar.harvard.edu/files/davidrwilliams/files/measuring_discrimination_resource_june_2016.pdf

Williams, J. M., & Bryan, J. (2013). Overcoming adversity: High-achieving African American youth's perspectives on educational resilience. *Journal of Counseling and Development*, 91, 291–300.

Winkler, E. (2009). Children are not colorblind: How young children learn race. *PACE, 3*(3). https://inclusions.org/wp-content/uploads/2017/11/Children-are-Not-Colorblind.pdf

X, M., Haley, A., Handler, M. S., & Davis, O. (2015). *The autobiography of Malcolm X.* New York, NY: Ballantine Books.

Yeager, D. S., Purdie-Vaughns, V., Garcia, J., Apfel, N. P., Master, A, . . . Cohen, G. L. (2013). Breaking the cycle of mistrust: Wise interventions to provide critical feedback across the racial divide. *Journal of Experimental Psychology: General, 143,* 804–824.

Yosso, T. J. (2005, March). Whose culture has capital? A critical race theory discussion of community cultural wealth. *Race, Ethnicity and Education, 8*(1), 69–91. https://drive.google.com/file/d/0B39QOsm78N4pcFUtQjhTX3NVZXM/edit

Young, K. (2020). A black mother reflects on giving her 3 sons "the talk" . . . again and again. National Public Radio. https://wbhm.org/npr_story_post/2020/a-black-mother-reflects-on-giving-her-3-sons-the-talk-again-and-again/

Zakaria, F. (2020). Interview with David Williams. *CNN,* https://www.cnn.com/videos/tv/2020/06/07/exp-gps-0607-williams-on-black-americans-and-covid.cnn

Zacarian, D. (2011). *Transforming schools for English learners.* Thousand Oaks, CA: Corwin.

Zambo, R., & Zambo, D. (2008). *The impact of professional development in mathematics on teachers' individual and collective efficacy: The stigma of underperforming.* https://files.eric.ed.gov/fulltext/EJ810663.pdf

Index

CORWIN

A SAGE Publishing Company

Helping educators make the greatest impact

CORWIN HAS ONE MISSION: to enhance education through intentional professional learning.

We build long-term relationships with our authors, educators, clients, and associations who partner with us to develop and continuously improve the best evidence-based practices that establish and support lifelong learning.